Dr. Justice AR. Lakshmanan
on

Criminal Law

Including
Contempt of Court

The daring publisher, Universal Law Publishing Company, among the foremost in the law publishing field and progressive in venturing to bring out rare legal literature of avant garde *character has rightly enriched the* corpus juris *of India*

Justice V R Krishna Iyer
Random Reflections, page 14

Criminal Law

Including
Contempt of Court

Dr. Justice AR. Lakshmanan
Former Chairman, Law Commission of India
Former Judge, Supreme Court of India

Universal
Law Publishing Co. Pvt. Ltd.

2014 Edition

ISBN: 978-93-5035-386-8

Published by

Universal
Law Publishing Co. Pvt. Ltd.
NEW DELHI - INDIA

A-58, G.T. Karnal Road Industrial Area,
(Near Azadpur Metro Station), Delhi-110033
Tel. : 011-47082254, 27458529, 27215334 Fax : 011-27458529
e-mail: unilaw@vsnl.com

- Showroom : C-27, Connaught Place, New Delhi-110001
  e-mail: sales@unilawbooks.com
- Editorial : edit@unilawbooks.com
- Website : **www.unilawbooks.com**

Join us on Facebook
www.facebook.com/unilawbooks

Recommended citation: Dr. Justice AR. Lakshmanan on *Criminal Law* (New Delhi: Universal Law Publishing Co. Pvt. Ltd., 2014).

Computer Typeset at Aesthetic and *Printed* at Deepak Printers, Delhi.

CONTENTS

TABLE OF CASES

T

U

V

Y

Ravi

v.

State Rep. By Inspector of Police

Appeal (Crl.) 1150-1151 of 2003

Decided on 12-8-2004

Coram: **K.G. Balakrishnan, J.**
Dr. AR. Lakshmanan, J.

FACTS:

The appellant along with four others committed murder of one Shanmugam. After trial the Sessions Judge convicted the appellant under sections 148, 364, 448 and 302, and was sentenced to undergo imprisonment for life. On appeal, the Madras High Court upheld the conviction. Aggrieved thereby, the appellant preferred an appeal before the Supreme Court.

ISSUE:

Whether the prosecution has proved its charge against the appellant?

HELD:

The evidence of P.W. 2, the mother of Shanmugam, is cogent and convincing. In her evidence she has in categorical terms stated that on the fateful day at around 12.30 p.m. Shanmugam was lying in a room of her house. At that time Ravi came along with 6 persons, entered her house and attacked Shanmugam who was lying inside a room. He assaulted Shanmugam with knife and another person beat Shanmugam with a stick. She clearly identified the accused Ravi as the person who was having the knife and assaulted the deceased. She also identified the accused at the identification parade. The prosecution thus, has clearly established the guilt of the accused-appellant beyond any reasonable doubt and that the appeals filed by the accused-appellant failed and was dismissed.

JUDGMENT

Dr. AR. Lakshmanan, J.—The above appeals were filed against the judgment dated 14-2-2003 passed by the High Court of Judicature at Madras in Criminal Appeal Nos. 315 and 539 of 1999 filed by A-1 Ravi and A-2 Pakkaraji. The appellant herein was the appellant in Criminal Appeal No. 315 before the High Court and was A-1 before the Court of Additional Sessions Judge, Pondicherry. The learned Sessions Judge acquitted A-2 of the offence under section 302 I.P.C. The State also has not filed any appeal against the said acquittal of A-2 of the offence of murder.

2. The following charges were made against the accused:

> The Inspector of Police, Villianur Circle, Pondicherry has laid a charge-sheet against the accused alleging that on 6-3-1996 at about 12.30 hrs. the

accused A-1 (Ravi), A-2 (Raja @ Pukkaraji) and four others alleging that they formed themselves into an unlawful assembly, armed with deadly weapons with a common object of such assembly, *viz.*, to cause the death of one Shanmugam due to previous enmity and in furtherance of common object of such assembly, trespassed into the house of Adhikesavan, the brother of the deceased Shanmugam and caused bleeding injuries to Shanmugam by assaulting him with deadly weapons, all the accused chased him and forcibly took him in an autorickshaw to maidan near Pavanar Nagar, Reddiarpalayam, Pondicherry beat him with deadly weapons' left him with bleeding injuries and the deceased Shanmugam subsequently died in the General Hospital, Pondicherry and thus the accused had committed the offence of murder of Shanmugam and thus committed offences punishable under sections 148, 149, 448/149, 364/149 & 302/149.

3. On behalf of the prosecution, PW-1 to PW-11 were examined and Exs. P1 to 22 and MOs.1 to 3 were marked.

4. The case of the prosecution, in brief, is as follows:—

The brother of the deceased Shanmugam, along with other brothers Krishnamurthy, deceased Shanmugam Siva and sister Gangabhavani were staying in Pudhusaram and Krishnamurthy after marriage went to his father-in-law's house. About 8 years prior to the incident, the deceased Shanmugam developed intimacy with one Sarasu and was living separately with her. About six months prior to the incident he came and started living five or six houses away from his house. About two or three days prior to the death of Shanmugam *i.e.,* on 4-3-1996 Shanmugam's wife Sarasu committed suicide by self immolation by pouring kerosene and setting fire to herself and died. Shanmugam came and told P.W. 1 that the brothers of Sarasu thought that he was responsible for suicide and they were threatening him and he also told that while he tried to save Sarasu, he sustained burn injuries on his hand and wanted to take treatment and so he wanted to stay in their house and his father also consented for the same and started staying with them and on 6-3-1996 A1-Ravi s/o Munuswamy came along with five persons armed with knife and sticks and entered the house and asked whether Shanmugam was there and they got into the room where Shanmugam was lying and beat him there and Shanmugam ran out and the crowd chased him and she asked P.W. 1 to find out what had happened to Shanmugam. P.W. 1 along with his brother Krishnamoorthy went in search of him and he saw Shanmugam with bleeding injuries lying down on a maidan behind the house of A1 Ravi slightly breathing and without speech. They took Shanmugam in an autorickshaw to General Hospital, Pondicherry. He returned home at 4.30 p.m. and informed his mother about the same. He then lodged a complaint before police. Ex. P.1 is the complaint given by him. Shanmugam died on 7-3-96 due to the injuries sustained by him on 6-3-96.

5. The Sessions Judge, Pondicherry, on consideration of the evidence on record, came to the conclusion that the evidences of P.Ws. 2, 3 and 6 showed that A-1 and A-2 were accompanied by five other persons and that A-1 and A-2 assaulted the deceased Shanmugham and that A-3 to A-7 were not identified by any witnesses. The Sessions Judge further held that the first accused committed the offence under sections 148, 364, 448 and 302 and for the main offence, he was sentenced to undergo imprisonment for life. For other offences, sentence of imprisonment ranging from 1 to 7 years were imposed. The second accused was found guilty of offence punishable under sections 148, 448 and 324.

6. Aggrieved by the same, appeals were filed before the High Court by A-1 and A-2. The High Court, on consideration of the evidence on record came to the conclusion that the conviction of the accused for the offences is supported by legal materials and there is no illegality in the judgment under challenge. The High Court was also of the opinion that the delay in lodging the complaint has been reasonably and satisfactorily explained and that there was no suspicious circumstances at all in the oral evidence of PW-1. The High Court has also held that the evidence of PW-2, who is an eye witness to the occurrence is convincing and that the infirmities which are referred to in Ex. P-1 or Ex. P-18 would not affect the oral evidence of PW-2 regarding the occurrence. The High Court felt that the omissions pointed out in Ex. P-1 and in Ex. P-18 were too trivial in the fact, and the evidence of PW-2 established beyond doubt the involvement of A-1 and A-2 in attacking the deceased.

7. Dissatisfied with the above judgment, the appellant, A-1, preferred these appeals by way of special leave petitions before this Court. We heard Ms. Prashanthi Prasad, learned counsel appearing for the appellant and Mr. V.G. Pragasam, learned counsel appearing for the State. We have been taken through the evidence on record and the judgment rendered by the Sessions Court and also of the High Court.

8. Learned counsel appearing for the appellant raised the following submissions:

(1) the reasons advanced by the prosecution witnesses were not sufficient to explain the enormous delay in filing the FIR and that the High Court has erred in coming to the conclusion that the delay has been explained properly.

(2) The complaint lodged by the complainant PW-1 at the Reddiarpalayam is well outside the jurisdiction of the alleged place of occurrence and that the High Court has failed to appreciate that there seems to be no reason or explanation as to why PW-1 has not given the complaint at the D. Nagar Police Station which is the nearest one and the one to which the jurisdiction pertains to.

(3) The prosecution has failed to establish beyond reasonable doubt the guilt of the accused, appellant herein.

(4) The non-examination of the material witnesses more so of the eye witnesses is fatal to the prosecution and hence the impugned judgment of the High Court ought to be set aside.

9. *Per contra,* learned counsel appearing for the State submitted that the High Court, on a careful consideration of the evidence on record and under the circumstances, has rightly found A-1 guilty for the offence under section 302,

I.P.C. and is not wrong in relying on the evidence tendered by the witnesses who were relatives.

10. In the background facts of this case, the point for determination is whether the prosecution has proved its charge against the appellant A-1 who was convicted and sentenced to undergo the various sentences imposed on him by various sections of the Code.

11. We have gone through the evidence on record and the judgments rendered by the Sessions Court and also of the High Court. The contention of the learned counsel for the appellant, in our opinion, has no force since the prosecution sought to prove its case based on the eye witnesses to the incident P.W. 2, P.W. 3 and P.W. 6 which clearly implicate the accused and that A-1 and A-3 had grudged against the deceased consequent to the death of their sister Sarasu. A-1 and A-2 also gave confession statements independently and on the basis of the statements of A1, the knife MO-2 and the shirt MO-2 were recovered under the mahazar Ext P 6 and on the basis of the statement of A-2 the wooden reaper MO-1 was recovered under Ext P5. MOs 1 to 3 contained blood stains and the blood on the shirt was identified as human blood.

12. Learned counsel for the appellant contended that the evidences of P.W. 1 and P.W. 2 should not be relied upon since they are related and are interested witnesses and there was no confession and the recovery alleged to have been effected by the prosecution. We are unable to appreciate this contention. It is settled by catena of cases by this Court that the evidence of eye witnesses cannot be rejected merely because they are related. In such a situation, the evidence of P.W. 2 in the present case, there is no strong motive or ill-will on the part of P.W. 2 to exonerate the real person who caused the injuries to her son and to implicate the accused.

13. Learned counsel for the appellant contended that there is inordinate delay in lodging the complaint. This contention, in our opinion, has no leg to stand.

14. On the fateful day, all the six accused were appeared armed with knife and stick and by entering the room where Shanmugam was sleeping. A-1 attacked him with a knife followed by another person with a dark complexion hitting him with a stick. Out of fear, Shanmugam started running out of the house for safety chased by all the accused, which was watched by P.W. 2 and others at home. P.W. 2 tried to reach them but she could not and she came to know that her son was taken in an autorickshaw by the assailants. At 1.30 p.m., on that day her other son, namely, P.W. 1 came home, to whom she informed as to what happened and requested him to find out as to what happened to Shanmugam, since deceased. He came home around 4.30 p.m. and informed her that Shanmugam his brother that he is lying in an open ground near Bhoomiyanpet and that he had admitted him in the hospital. She had identified the person having dark complexion, in the test identification parade held, as A-2 P.W. 1 is admittedly not an eye witness to the occurrence but had stated as to what his mother told him about the occurrence on reaching the house at 1.30 p.m. On hearing about the same from his mother, he went in search of his brother and he found his brother lying in an open ground struggling for life. Accordingly, after admitting him in the hospital, he came home at 4.30 p.m. informed his mother/P.W. 2 and then went to the police station to lodge the complaint, Ex. P.1. The above facts would clearly go to show that there is no delay in lodging the complaint.

15. P.W. 8 Thiru P. Nallathambi Judicial First Class Magistrate has stated that on 25-3-96 he received a requisition to conduct identification parade as per Ex. P. 10. Consequently, he conducted identification parade on 28-3-96 at 3.00 p.m. in the Central Jail premises. Three chances were given to the witnesses P.W. 2 and Gangabhavani to identify A-2 Raja @ Pukkaraj who correctly identified him in all the three chances. Ex. P. 11 is the record of the test identification parade containing 3 sheets.

16. The contention of the learned counsel for the appellant that the complaint has not been registered within the Police Station which has a jurisdiction. This contention also has no force. This point of jurisdiction was not urged before the Sessions Court and also before the High Court. This was raised by the learned counsel for the appellant at the time of addressing the arguments before us. Hence, we decline to entertain this plea at this belated stage.

17. We have carefully gone through the annexures, the evidence of P.W. 2 who is an eye-witness. Her evidence is cogent and convincing. In her evidence she stated that the deceased Shanmugam has been living with one Sarasu for about 8 years prior to his death, and six months prior to his death they came and were living in a house nearby their house. About a week prior to that he was staying in their own house. About a week prior to the death of Shanmugam, Sarasu committed self immolation by pouring kerosene on herself and died after four or five days. A1-Ravi, the brother of Sarasu and her mother, and brothers thought that Shanmugam was responsible for the death of Sarasu and beat him. Deceased Shanmugam told them that he fears danger to his life and wanted to stay in their house for safety purpose. They also consented for that. On 6-3-96 at 12.30 p.m. Shanmugam was lying in the room of her house while PW-2, her husband Adimoolam and daughter Gangabhavani were having food and at that time, A1-Ravi along with six persons armed with knife and sticks entered into their house and went inside the room where Shanmugam was lying and attacked him. A1 Ravi assaulted Shanmugam with knife and a person with black complexion beat Shanmugam with a stick. Unable to bear the beatings Shanmugam climbed down the staircase and started running and the seven persons chased him. When she came out she found that all the seven persons forcibly took Shanmugam in an autorickshaw. She told this fact to P.W. 1 at 1.30 p.m. when he came to her house. P.W. 1 and her other son Krishnamurthy went in search of Shanmugam and at 4.30 p.m. P.W. 1 came to her and informed her that Shanmugam had sustained injuries and was lying near Boomiyanpet and that they admitted him in Hospital. Subsequently, her son Shanmugam died. She has stated that she identified the second accused before Magistrate in the jail as the person with black complexion who beat her son apart from A1.

18. P.W. 7 Dr. R. Balaraman who conducted the post-mortem examination on the dead body and on external examination found seven injuries and on internal examination, there was sub-dural haemorrage over left cerebral hemisphere. Brain was odomatous. Extensive contusion was seen over the left side of neck at the level of hyoid bone. Viscera was sent for chemical analysis and it was free from poison. He gave his final opinion on 30-12-1996 that the deceased Shanmugam died of injuries on head and neck. Ex. P7 is the post mortem examination report and Ex. P8 is the chemical examiner's report. Ex. P9 is the final opinion. All the injuries in Ex. P7 were ante-mortem in nature. Injuries 1 and 2 with the corresponding internal injuries are fatal in nature, sufficient to cause death in the ordinary course of nature. He has opined that injuries 1, 3 to 6 are possible with No. 1 while injury No. 2 is possible with No. 2 Injury No. 7 can be a burn injury or may be due to some other reason.

19. P.W. 10, Vijayasundaram, the Inspector of Police has stated that he recovered the weapon under a cover of the mahazar Ex. P5 and then proceeded to the house of A1 who identified and produced the Koduval Kathi (Knife) M.O. 2 and a full hand shirt M.O. 3 which were recovered under cover of mahazar Ex. P6. M.O. 1 to 3 contained blood stains. P.W. 11, the Inspector of Police who took further investigation from P.W. 10 obtained the opinion from P.W.7 Dr. Balaraman and examined him and also obtained a copy of the F.I.R. of D. Nagar Police Station pertaining to the death of Sarasu, wife of deceased Shanmugam who had succumbed to burn injuries, despite treatment given to her in the Government Hospital, Pondicherry. He further stated that he completed the investigation and laid the charge-sheet against all the accused under various sections.

20. For the foregoing reasons, we are of the opinion that the prosecution has established its case that A-1 has caused the death of the deceased and the evidence of P.W. 2, P.W. 3 and P.W. 6 which are important which clearly implicate the accused which caused the injury to the deceased. It is an admitted fact that the accused A-1 had been living with the deceased as his wife P.W. 2 the mother of the deceased Shanmugam knows A-1 Ravi. She has in categorical terms stated that on the date of the incident A-1 came along with 6 persons and entered her house and attacked Shanmugam who was lying inside a room. She clearly identified A-1 as the person who was having the knife and assaulted the deceased. She does not know A2. She has also identified the accused at the identification parade.

21. For the reasons aforesaid, we hold that the prosecution has clearly established the guilt of the accused-appellant beyond any reasonable doubt and that the appeals filed by A-1, therefore, fail and are dismissed.

Arun Garg

v.

State of Punjab

Appeal (Crl.) 289-290 of 2004

Decided on 29-9-2004

Coram: **K.G. Balakrishnan, J.**
Dr. AR. Lakshmanan, J.

FACTS:

The appellant was alleged to have committed dowry death by administering aluminium phosphide to his wife, who is daughter of the respondent. The trial court convicted the appellant under section 304B, I.P.C. and sentenced him to undergo rigorous imprisonment for a period of ten years and to pay a fine of Rs. 2000. On appeal the High Court upheld the conviction and enhanced the amount of fine to Rs. 2 lakhs. Aggrieved thereby, the appellant approached the Supreme Court by way of special leave petition.

ISSUE:

Dowry death. Imposition of fine under section 304B of I.P.C.

HELD:

The Sessions Judge, who imposed a fine of Rs. 2,000 to the appellant did not take notice that for the offence under section 304B, the Court is not empowered to impose fine as a punishment. The direction of the High Court to pay a sum of Rs. 2 lakhs as fine was not warranted by law. The appeals are partly allowed confirming the sentence of imprisonment for a period of 10 years. The direction to pay a fine of Rs. 2 lakhs was set aside.

JUDGMENT

Dr. AR. Lakshmanan, J.—These appeals are directed against the impugned judgment and order dated 30-5-2003 passed by the High Court of Punjab & Haryana at Chandigarh in Criminal Appeal No. 161-SB of 2001. The High Court dismissed the said appeal of the appellant and confirmed the sentence of ten years rigorous imprisonment awarded by the Sessions Judge, Ludhiana but enhanced the fine from Rs. 2000 to Rs. 2,00,000 in Criminal Revision No. 1251 of 2001 filed by the complainant against the appellant.

Briefly stated, the case of the prosecution is as follows:

> The marriage between Seema, daughter of Ramesh Chander Bansal, PW-1 and the appellant-accused, Arun Garg took place on 25-2-1996. According to the prosecution, she died under very tragic circumstances on 30-3-1999, that is, within three years of her marriage with the appellant. The appellant was alleged to have administered aluminium phosphide causing unnatural death of the daughter of the respondent and thus the appellant

was liable for the offence under section 304B of the Indian Penal Code. At the time of marriage, household articles, clothes, gold etc., and cash amount of Rs. 2,00,000 was also given in dowry. However, few days after the marriage, Seema started complaining that her husband, Arun Garg, father-in-law, Sham Lal Garg and mother-in-law, Shimla Garg were not satisfied with the dowry given to her at the time of her marriage and all of them often used to taunt her on the ground that she had not brought sufficient dowry at the time of her marriage. It was further submitted that on 10-4-1996, Seema telephoned the respondent herein that her father-in-law and mother-in-law were making a demand for Rs. 40,000 and thereupon the respondent accompanied by Parkash Chand and Sohan Lal who had arranged the marriage of Seema with Arun Garg went to the house of Arun Garg. Thereupon, on the insistence of Parkash Chand and Sohan Lal, the respondent purchased household articles worth Rs. 20,000 and supplied the same to the family of Arun Garg. It is the case of the prosecution that since February 1997, the appellant and his parents did not allow Seema to see her parents and had not allowed her to visit their house. When the parents went to see Seema at the house of her in-laws on the eve of Teej festival, Seema told them that her husband, father-in-law, mother-in-law and sister-in-law Neena used to ill-treat her and often made a demand for more cash. There are other instances on 22-2-1999 and on 26-3-1999 of demanding dowry. On 26-3-1999, Seema telephoned the respondent herein that her husband, father-in-law, mother-in-law and sister-in-law were planning to kill her. The respondent, who is a government servant, could not, however, obtain leave from the office and go to see Seema at the house of her in-laws.

On 28-3-1999, at about 6.00 p.m., the respondent received information that her daughter Seema had been administered some poisonous substance by her husband and in-laws and sister-in-law Neena and that she had been admitted in the Dayanand Medical College, Ludhiana. The respondent accompanied by his wife immediately rushed to the hospital and found that Seema was unconscious and her condition was found to be serious. The respondent thereafter went to the police station and lodged an FIR on the same day which was registered as FIR No. 139 of 1999 under section 307 read with section 34 of the Indian Penal Code, against Arun Garg, his father, Sham Lal Garg, mother Shimla Garg and sister Neena. On the same day, *i.e.*, 28-3-1999, police made an application for recording the statement of Seema, which was declined as she was declared medically unfit to make the statement. Police again made an application for recording the statement of Seema on 29-3-1999 which was also declined as Seema was not medically fit to make the statement. Unfortunately, Seema died in the hospital on 30-03-1999. On the death of Seema, the case was converted into one under section 304B of the Indian Penal Code and all the three accused, namely, Arun Garg, Sham Lal Garg and Shimla Garg were arrested in the case on 31-3-1999. After the death of Seema, the dead body was sent for post-mortem examination. The findings of the Medical Board are as under:

"Eyes and mouth were closed. Post Mortem staining was present on the left, lateral side of body. Cyanosis of nails, lips and tongue was present.

Face was congested. Multiple needle prick marks were present on the body. Larynx, trachea and both lungs were congested. The right side of the heart contained blood and blood sample was sealed in jar No. 4. Both the ends of the stomach were ligated and were sent to the Chemical Examiner in Jar No. 1. Small and large intestines were congested and a portion of each was sent to the Chemical Examiner in Jar No. 2. Liver, Spleen and Kidney were congested and portion of each was sent to the Chemical Examiner in Jar No.3. Urinary bladder was healthy and empty. The genitalia was healthy and uterus contained Copper T."

On receipt of the report of the Chemical Examiner, the pesticide aluminium phosphide was detected in the stomach and large and small intestines. While phosphide, a constituent of aluminium phosphate was detected in liver, spleen, kidney and blood. Thereafter, the doctors opined that death of Seema had caused due to intake of aluminium phosphide poisoning which was sufficient to cause death in the ordinary course of nature. The challan was presented by the police in the Court of Sessions Judge, Ludhiana against the appellant, his father and mother. The Sessions Judge, by his judgment dated 22-1-2001, acquitted Sham Lal Garg and Shimla Garg giving them benefit of doubt and convicted the appellant, Arun Garg, under section 304B, I.P.C. in connection with the death of his wife Seema Garg and sentenced him to undergo rigorous imprisonment for a period of ten years and to pay a fine of Rs. 2000 or in default of payment of fine to undergo further rigorous imprisonment for a period of two months.

Aggrieved by the said judgment, the appellant filed Criminal Appeal No. 161-SB of 2001 before the High Court along with the application for bail. The State of Punjab also filed Criminal Appeal No. 489-DBA of 2001. The respondent herein filed two separate revision petitions being Revision Petition No. 1245 of 2001 challenging the acquittal of Sham Lal Garg and Shimla Garg and Revision Petition No. 1251 of 2001 seeking enhancement of the sentence imposed upon the appellant.

The High Court, by its order dated 14-2-2001, admitted the appeal filed by the appellant and stayed the recovery of fine, however, declined the prayer for bail.

The High Court, by a common order dated 30-5-2003, while upholding the conviction made by the trial Court, dismissed Criminal Appeal No. 161-SB filed by the appellant herein and partly allowed the Revision Petition No. 1251 of 2001 filed by the respondent herein. The High Court, by the impugned judgment, enhanced the fine from Rs. 2,000 to Rs. 2,00000. By the said order, the High Court also dismissed Criminal Appeal No. 489-DBA of 2001 filed by the State of Punjab and Criminal Revision No. 1245 of 2001 filed by the respondent herein.

Against the said order, the appellant has approached this Court by way of special leave petition. Leave was granted by this Court on 23-2-2004.

We heard Mr. K.G. Bhagat, learned counsel appearing for the appellant and Mr. Arun K. Sinha, learned counsel appearing for the contesting respondent and Mr. Sudhir Walia, learned counsel appearing for the State of Punjab.

Learned counsel appearing for the appellant took us through the judgments of both the Courts and documents filed in the Court. He made the following submissions:

(1) that in the FIR dated 28-3-1999, there was no imputation by the complainant that 'soon before death' the deceased was subjected to cruelty or harassment by her husband or any relative of her husband for, and in connection with any demand of dowry. In this regard, he invited our attention to the relevant portions of the FIR.

(2) That no independent witness came in the witness box to corroborate the interested version of PW-3 and PW-4, the parents of the deceased. Elaborating the submission, learned counsel for the appellant submitted that the complainant had emphatically alleged that he had gone to the house of the appellant along with middleman Parkash Chand and Sohan Lal but they were never associated during the investigation nor were they produced in the Court, which fact itself is sufficient to disbelieve the witness of the complainant.

(3) The ingredients of demand of dowry soon before the death of the deceased and the harassment thereon under section 304B has not been proved beyond reasonable doubt.

(4) The complainant has nowhere proved the payment of Rs. 2,00,000 to the appellant at the time of marriage or proved spending Rs. 20,000 worth of items given to the appellant. No withdrawal from any Bank is shown, no loan is taken, no receipt of any sort is produced.

(5) The appellant has proved withdrawal of large sums of monies from their different bank accounts to prove that they had advanced Rs. 2,00,000 to the complainant to help him to settle his son and when the same was demanded back by the appellant, the complainant felt offended and had that grudge in his mind.

(6) Had the appellant been responsible of administering aluminium phosphide to the deceased, he would not have taken the deceased to a most reputed hospital of Dayanand Medical College of Ludhiana to save her.

(7) The demand of dowry or harassment of the deceased is not proved by any independent evidence except the bald statement of parents of the deceased as PW-1 and PW-3, and though the appellant had led sufficient independent evidence especially of the neighbours and others as DW-1 to DW-11 especially DW-4, DW- 10 and DW-11 who sufficiently elaborated that nothing happened at the house of the appellant and in fact, everybody including Seema was happy and on 27-3-1999, she attended Jagrata in the neighbourhood and attended Kanjak ceremony in the morning on 28-3-1999 at the same house along with her daughter and thereafter she went to the house of her mother.

(8) There is hardly any evidence to prove the offence under section 304B and 498A, I.P.C. against the accused. Even from the evidence on record, no offence is made out under section 304B of I.P.C. There is no material on record to support the conclusion of cruelty or harassment.

(9) The enhancement of fine from Rs. 2000 to Rs. 2,00,000 in revisional jurisdiction is all the more uncalled for and unwarranted and not permissible under law.

Learned counsel appearing for the State of Punjab submitted that the investigation revealed that the accused was responsible for causing the death of the deceased, Seema and also subjected her to cruelty for and in connection with the demand of dowry articles. He would further submit that due to harassment, as proved in the evidence, which was caused by the appellant to his wife apparently due to demand of more dowry, a precious human life was lost. Such type of social crime should be viewed seriously and suitable punishment is called for so as to serve as deterrent to others and that the appellant is guilty of forcibly administering poison to his wife, Seema, and is responsible for causing her unnatural death within seven years of her marriage and thus such person cannot be allowed to remain at liberty in the society.

Concluding his submission, it was submitted that keeping in view the facts and circumstances of the case and the gravity of the offence committed by the appellant, the present appeals deserve to be dismissed.

Learned counsel appearing for the contesting respondent (father of the deceased) submitted that the contents of various grounds are not correct. It was submitted by the appellant that it is nowhere proved that payment of Rs. 2,00,000 was made to the appellant and that no withdrawal from any Bank is shown, no loan is taken and no receipt of any sort is produced. In regard to this, it was submitted by the learned counsel for the respondent that the respondent had withdrawn Rs. 1,23,000 from his GPF account and his wife Pushpa Rani, who is also a government servant had withdrawn Rs. 94,000 from her GPF account. It was further submitted that no documentary evidence has been put forth by the appellant regarding advancement of any money by the parents of the appellant to the respondent herein.

Before considering the rival contentions, it will be appropriate to note the relevant provisions of section 304B of the Indian Penal Code. section 304B reads thus:—

> "*304B. Dowry death.*—(1) Where the death of a woman is caused by any burns or bodily injury or occurs otherwise than under normal circumstances within seven years of her marriage and it is shown that soon before her death she was subject to cruelty or harassment by her husband or any relative of her husband for, or in connection with, any demand for dowry, such death shall be called "dowry death", and such husband or relative shall be deemed to have caused her death.
>
> *Explanation* For the purpose of this sub-section, "dowry" shall have the same meaning as in section 2 of the Dowry Prohibition Act, 1961 (28 of 1961).
>
> (2) Whoever commits dowry death shall be punished with imprisonment for a term which shall not be less than seven years but which may extend to imprisonment for life." (emphasis supplied)

The ingredients necessary for the application of section 304B I.P.C. are:

(i) that the death of a woman is caused by any burns or bodily injury or occurs otherwise than under normal circumstances;

(ii) within seven years of her marriage;

(iii) it must be shown that before the death she was subject to cruelty or harassment by her husband or any relative of the husband or in connection with the demand of dowry.

In the light of these ingredients, the evidence of the prosecution is to be scanned.

The appellant was married with the deceased in the year 1996. The deceased died on 30-3-1999. So she died within seven years of the marriage. It is also not disputed that the deceased had not died a natural death. The only controversy between the parties is with regard to the third ingredient as to whether soon before the death the deceased was harassed and was subjected to cruelty on account of demand of dowry.

In the instant case, the prosecution had examined the complainant, PW-1, Ramesh Chander Bansal, Dr. Dhiraj Bhatia, PW-2, Pushpa Bansal, PW-3, Dr. U.S. Sooch, PW-4, Harminder Singh, PW-5, Inspector Gurinderjit Singh, PW-6, HC Kuldip Singh, PW-7, ASI Amrik Singh, PW-8, Constable Prithi Pal Singh, PW-9, Dr. N. Siridhar Rao, PW-10, Constable Gursharanvir Singh, PW-11 and constable Kamaljit Singh, PW-12. Since Parkash Chand and Pt. Sohan Lal died on 19-6-1999 and 9-5-2000 respectively, they could not be examined.

The Courts below have carefully gone through the facts of the case and the evidence on record and have found that the appellant is liable for the offence under section 304B, I.P.C. The courts below, after appreciation of the facts and evidence recorded have reached the conclusion that Seema Garg died an unnatural death at the house of her in laws within a period of seven years of her marriage with the appellant due to intake of poisonous substance.

It was argued on behalf of the appellant that there are contradictions in the statements of PW-6, Gurinderjit Singh and the complainant, respondent herein. In fact, two site plans of the place of occurrence were prepared one being Ex. PL prepared on 29-3-1999 by the Investigating Officer, PW-6, and the other being Ex. PG prepared on 22-6-1999 by Harminder Singh, Draftsman, PW-5. This site plan was prepared at the instance of the respondent herein.

It was argued on behalf of the appellant that in the FIR, there was no imputation by the complainant that 'soon before death' the deceased was subjected to cruelty or harassment by her husband or any relative of her husband for and in connection with, any demand of dowry. We have perused the FIR in this connection. PW-1 deposed that on 26-3-1999 Seema informed him on telephone that her father-in-law, mother-in-law, sister-in-law and her husband had been conspiring to kill her and this fact had mentioned in his first information statement. The High Court had dealt with this in detail and reached the conclusion that the most vital circumstances of an offence under section 304B, I.P.C. that the demand for dowry had been made soon before the death had been proved beyond doubt. According to PW-1, the appellant had been demanding more dowry after the marriage and that he had accepted further dowry of Rs. 20,000 on 10-4-1996 when they, in fact, had demanded Rs. 40,000. PW-1 further deposed that in July, 1998, at the time of Teej, they had demanded more dowry but they were made to understand not to harm Seema. This demand of more dowry remain unfulfilled because of which the appellant and his family members continued to harass Seema and ultimately they killed Seema by administering poison on 28-3-1999.

In reply to the argument advanced by the counsel for the appellant, it was submitted that Seema made a telephone call on 10-4-1996 to the respondent herein saying that the appellant had demanded more dowry. Thereafter, the respondent along with Parkash Chand and Sohan Lal went to the house of the appellant on 21-4-1996 and gave them articles wroth Rs. 20,000 to the appellant. It is pertinent to mention here that the trial Court had rightly observed that even if the accused be away, there is no reason why the telephonic call could not be made from outside.

It was further reiterated by the respondent that the deceased made a telephone call to the respondent herein on 26-3-1999 alleging that her husband and parents-in-law were conspiring to kill her. It has come in cross-examination of the respondent herein/complainant that as Vidhan Sabha Sessions was going on, therefore, leave could not be granted to him for 27-3-1999, although it was a Saturday but he was put on duty due to Session of Vidhan Sabha. As already stated, Parkash Chand died on 19-6-1999 and Sohan Lal died on 9-5-2000. It is pertinent to note here that examination for PW-1, the respondent herein, was made on 22-5-2000. As both the above said persons died before the said date, they could not be examined as witnesses.

There is no substance in the argument of the learned counsel appearing the appellant that the interested evidence of the parents of the deceased has not been supported by independent evidence or witness of the locality while the stand of the defence has been that the deceased Seema was never harassed or tortured by the appellant or by any of his family members for demand of dowry. Likewise, there is no substance in the submission of the learned counsel appearing for the appellant that there is no demand of dowry by the appellant or by any of his family members soon before the death of Seema. The evidence discussed, as in paragraphs supra, would clearly go to show that this submission has no force.

Section 304B was inserted by the Dowry Prohibition (Amendment) Act, 1986 with a view to combating the increasing menace of dowry death. By the same Amendment Act, section 113B has been added in the Evidence Act, 1872 for raising a presumption. It reads thus:

> "Presumption as to dowry death.—When the question is whether a person has committed the dowry death of a woman and it is shown that soon before her death such woman had been subjected by such person to cruelty or harassment for, or in connection with, any demand for dowry, the Court shall presume that such person had caused the dowry death.

Explanation.—For the purpose of this section "dowry death" shall have the same meaning as in section 304B of the Indian Penal Code."

Once the three essentials under section 304B as referred to in paragraphs supra are satisfied the presumption under section 113B would follow. This rule of evidence is added in the Statute by amendment to obviate the difficulty of the prosecution to prove as to who caused the death of the victim. Of course, this is a rebuttable presumption and the accused by satisfactory evidence can rebut the presumption. In the instant case, the appellant could not rebut the presumption, and the prosecution, even without the aid of this presumption under section 113B proved that the appellant was responsible for the death of the deceased Seema. Hence, the conviction of the appellant for the offence under section 304B, I.P.C. is only to be confirmed.

Our attention was also drawn to section 498A. In our view, sections 304B and 498A are not mutually exclusive. They deal with different and distinct offences. In both the sections, 'cruelty' is a common element. Under section 498A, however, cruelty by itself amounts to an offence and is punishable. Under section 304B, it is the dowry death that is punishable and such death must have occurred within seven years of the marriage. No such period is mentioned in section 498A. Moreover, a person charged and acquitted under section 304B can be convicted under section 498A without a specific charge being there, if such a case is made out.

In the instant case, the Trial Court convicted the appellant for the offence punishable under section 304B and sentenced him to undergo imprisonment for a period of 10 years and to pay a fine of Rs. 2,000 or in default to undergo further rigorous imprisonment for a period of three months. But unfortunately, the Sessions Judge who imposed a fine of Rs. 2,000 to the appellant did not take notice that for the offence under section 304B, the Court is not empowered to impose fine as a punishment. The punitive clause of section 304B Dowry Death has already been extracted in paragraph supra.

Section 304B is one of the few sections in the Indian Penal Code where imposition of fine is not prescribed as a punishment. The Division Bench of the High Court which confirmed the conviction of the appellant under section 304B instead of setting aside the fine, which is not warranted by law, enhanced a sum to Rs. 2 lakhs and also directed that the fine, if recovered, shall be paid to the complainant. The appellant could have been sentenced only to a punishment which is prescribed under the law. As no fine could be imposed as punishment for offence under section 304B, the direction to the appellant to pay a fine of Rs. 2 lakhs was wholly illegal.

The learned Counsel for the respondent contended that no fine could be imposed as part of the punishment, the direction to pay a fine of Rs. 2 lakhs is in accordance with the section 357(c) of the Cr. P.C., section 357 is an enabling provision by which the Court can give direction to the effect that when passing judgment, sentence imposed for payment of fine can be recovered and applied either for defraying the expenses properly incurred in the prosecution or in payment to any person as compensation for any loss or injury caused by the offence, when compensation can be recoverable by such person in a Civil Court. Section 357(1) is applicable in cases where fine forms the part of the sentence whereas under section 357(3), the Court can direct the convicted person to pay compensation even in cases where the fine does not form part of the sentence. Section 357(3) reads as follows:—

> "When a Court imposes a sentence, of which fine does not form a part, the Court may, when passing judgment order the accused person to pay, by way of compensation such amount as may be specified in the order to the person who has suffered any loss or injury by reason of the act for which the accused person has been so sentenced."

The learned Counsel for the respondent contended that even if the Court is not competent to impose fine as a punishment, the Court can still order compensation under section 357(3) of the Cr. P.C. and the direction of the High Court to pay Rs. 2 lakhs to the complainant is to be treated as the direction given under section 357(3). The contention of the respondent's learned Counsel cannot be accepted. Hear the Trial Court had imposed a sentence of fine of Rs. 2,000 as fine and the High Court enhanced the quantum of fine without there being any further discussion on the matter. Therefore, the direction to the appellant to pay a fine of Rs. 2 lakhs could only be treated as enhancement of fine already imposed by the Sessions Judge. Moreover, section 357(3) contemplates a situation where the complainant has suffered any loss or injury and for which the accused person has been found *prima facie* responsible. There is no such finding or observation by the High Court. Of course, the daughter of the complainant passed away but the direction of the High Court to pay Rs. 2 lakhs was on the assumption that the complainant had paid Rs. 2 lakhs as part of the dowry to the appellant. There is no evidence to show that such an amount was given to the appellant. On the other hand, the appellant's learned Counsel contended that it was a love marriage between the appellant and the deceased and no dowry passed between the parties. It is also pertinent to note that section 357(5) of the Cr. P.C. says that at the time of awarding compensation in any subsequent civil suit relating to the same matter, the Court shall take into account any sum paid or recovered as compensation under this section. The direction to pay compensation under section 357(3) is on the assumption of basic civil liability on the part of person who committed the offence to redress the victim or his dependents by payment of compensation. The complainant could not have filed a civil suit for recovery of the dowry amount, if any, as the payment itself was illegal and prohibited under law. In any view of the matter, the direction of the High Court to pay a sum of Rs. 2 lakhs as fine was not warranted by law and we set aside the same and also further direction that the appellant to undergo default sentence.

In the result, the appeals are partly allowed confirming the sentence of imprisonment for a period of 10 years. The direction to pay a fine of Rs. 2 lakhs is set aside.

Hira Lal Hari Lal Bhagwati

v.

C.B.I., New Delhi

Criminal Appeals Nos. 676 with 677 of 2003 [arising out of S.L.P. (Cri.) No. 1356 with 1363 of 2002]

AIR 2003 SC 2545: 2003 AIR SCW 2735

Decided on: 2-5-2003

Coram: **Brijesh Kumar, J.**
Dr. AR. Lakshmanan, J.

FACTS:

It was alleged that the appellants along with some others entered into a conspiracy and cheated the Government of India by evading customs duty and by violating the provisions of 'actual user' condition as per Import Export Policy during the year 1987-88 despite acknowledging the fact that the customs duty has been paid by the appellants to the Customs Department and settled under the Kar Vivad Samadhan Scheme, 1998. A charge-sheet was prepared for commission of offence under section 120B read with section 420 of the Indian Penal Code. In the meantime, the appellants preferred Special Criminal Applications before the High Court of Gujarat at Ahmedabad seeking quashing of the FIR. However, the same was disposed of as withdrawn on the ground of jurisdiction with a liberty to file a fresh petition before an appropriate Court. Thereupon the appellants filed Criminal Miscellaneous (Main) Petitions under section 482 of the Code of Criminal Procedure read with article 227 of the Constitution of India in the High Court of Delhi seeking an appropriate order/directions to the respondent quashing the FIR concerned. The learned single Judge of the High Court of Delhi, by his final order, dismissed the said petitions. Hence these two appeals by way of Special Leave Petitions.

ISSUE:

Criminal proceeding for an offence which was compromised and settled under civil proceeding amounts to double jeopardy.

HELD:

As per the Kar Vivad Samadhan Scheme, 1998 whoever is granted the benefit under the said Scheme is granted immunity from prosecution from any offence under the Customs Act, 1962 including the offence of evasion of duty. In the circumstances, the complaint filed against the appellants is unsustainable. As the customs duty has already been paid, the Central Government has not suffered any financial loss. In the present case, the alleged criminal liability stands compounded on a settlement with respect to the civil issues and, therefore, the first information report was erroneously issued and was totally unwarranted. It is also a settled law that once a civil case has been compromised and the alleged offence has been compounded, to continue the criminal proceedings thereafter would be an abuse of the judicial process.

Judgment

Brijesh Kumar, J.—I have the benefit of going through the detailed and elaborate judgment prepared by brother Lakshmanan, J. I am in respectful agreement with the same. I would, however, like to emphasise yet another aspect of the matter by reason of which also it does not lie for the respondent, to initiate or continue the criminal proceedings against the appellants.

2. Since the facts have been set out in detail, in the judgment of brother Lakshmanan, J., it is not necessary to dwelve upon the factual position anymore. It is true, so far the scheme and the terms under which determination of liability is made thereunder, provides for immunity from initiation of criminal proceedings under the Customs Act, in respect of the matters covered under the declaration under section 88 of the Scheme but more important in that regard for this case is section 95 of the Kar Vivad Samadhan Scheme, Chapter IV of Finance (No. 2) Act, 1998, which is quoted below:

"95. The provisions of this Scheme shall not apply—

(i) xx xx xx

(ii) in respect of tax arrear under any indirect tax enactment,—

(a) in a case where prosecution for any offence punishable under any provisions of any indirect tax enactment has been instituted on or before the date of filing of the declaration under section 88, in respect of any tax arrear in respect of such case under such indirect tax enactment;

(b) xx xx xx

(c) xx xx xx

(iii) to any person in respect of whom prosecution for any offence punishable under Chapter IX or Chapter XVII of the Indian Penal Code (45 of 1860), the Foreign Exchange Regulation Act, 1973 (46 of 1973), the Narcotic Drugs and Psychotropic Substances Act, 1985 (61 of 1985), the Terrorist and Disruptive Activities (Prevention) Act, 1987 (28 of 1987), the Prevention of Corruption Act, 1988 (49 of 1988), or for the purpose of enforcement of any civil liability has been instituted on or before the filing of the declaration or such person has been convicted of any such offence punishable under any such enactment;

xx xx xx"

According to the above provision, a person will not be eligible or entitled to take benefit of the Scheme against whom a prosecution for punishment of an offence under Chapter IX or XVII of the I.P.C. is pending on or before the date of the declaration or such person has been convicted for any of such offences indicated above. There is no dispute on the fact that on the date the appellants submitted their declaration under section 88 no prosecution was pending nor they stood convicted for an offence falling in Chapter IX or XVII of the IPC. Section 420, I.P.C. falls in Chapter XVII of the IPC. The other condition of eligibility so as to be entitled to take the benefit of the Scheme is that where any proceeding is pending in the High Court or the Supreme Court against any order in respect of tax arrear, the declarant is obliged to withdraw such appeal or proceeding and is further liable to furnish the proof of such withdrawal as provided under section 90 of the Scheme of 1998. The case of the petitioner was settled, the tax liability was determined on 10-2-1999 by the Designated Authority, and the certificate of full and final settlement was issued on 19-7-1999. The appeal pending in this Court against the order of the CEGAT was withdrawn by the appellants on 16-3-1999. It is thus obvious that certificate of full and final settlement was issued in view of the fact that the conditions enumerated above were fulfilled.

3. It appears that despite the statement of settlement having been filed under section 88 of the Act of 1998, an FIR was lodged and a case was registered on 6-1-1999 on the basis of which, later on a charge-sheet was also submitted. On the one hand final settlement was made after determining the tax liability on the premises that the appellants were neither convicted nor criminal proceedings were pending, relating to any offence under Chapter IX or XVII of the I.P.C., yet the criminal proceedings are being prosecuted which is apparently against the very spirit of the Scheme promulgated under the Finance (2) Act of 1998. If a person against whom criminal proceedings were pending, relating to offence under Chapter IX or XVII of the I.P.C. or who stood convicted under any of the provisions of those chapters, he would not have been eligible to seek benefit under the Scheme and after accepting that position and the due settlement, there was no occasion to initiate and continue the criminal proceedings, which could bring about the conviction of the same persons, in case prosecution ended successfully in favour of the State and against the appellants. If such a condition is provided that on a particular date a criminal proceeding should not be pending against a person nor he should have been convicted of an offence, as a condition precedent for a settlement, and on that basis a settlement is brought about, it does not mean that later on, one could turn around and get the declarant convicted for a criminal offence too, after settlement of the liability. Moreso, when in view of section 90, clause (iv) of the Scheme the declarant is obliged to withdraw an appeal or proceedings regarding tax liability pending before the High Court or the Supreme Court, which had also been done in the case in hand. That is to say on one hand declarant is not permitted to pursue the remedy, regarding tax liability, which is already pending before the Courts of law, as they are either deemed to be withdrawn by operation of law or they have to be withdrawn by a positive act of the party and yet prosecute such persons for their conviction as well. The declarant could not be dragged and chased in criminal proceedings after closing the other opening making it a dead end. It is highly unreasonable and arbitrary to do so and initiation and continuance of such proceedings lack *bona fides*.

4. In the background given above, there is every reason to legally infer that the position as it stood, in regard to the criminal prosecution and conviction on the date the declaration was filed, as conditions precedent to settlement under the Scheme, would also stand finalized on full and final settlement of the matter under the Scheme. That is to say the position that no criminal prosecution was pending against the declarant on the date of filing of the declaration nor he stood convicted for such an offence in relation to the matter covered under the declaration, it would stand finalized with acceptance of the declaration and settlement of the matter fully and finally. Later on, the declarant could not be or continued to be subjected to criminal prosecution to alter the position as it stood on the relevant date of the submission of declaration and get him convicted for such offences in respect of which, if he stood convicted earlier while filing statement he would not have been entitled to seek the benefit under the Scheme. The appellants virtually foreclosed their right to further pursue the proceedings before the authorities or Courts of law challenging the legality, validity or the tax liability in terms of the Scheme. Undoubtedly, if the appellants's appeal which was pending in this Court against the order of CEGAT relating to the tax liability, had been allowed it might have affected the criminal proceeding too on merits. In certain circumstances, it could be put up as a defence by the declarant, in the criminal case but in terms of the scheme he was bound to withdraw his appeal. The criminal prosecution could not be allowed to proceed by putting an end to a possible defence, before hand. It certainly amounts to abuse of process of law. The appeals thus deserve to be allowed.

5. In the result, we allow the appeals and the order of the High Court is set aside and the FIR No. R.C.1 (E)/99/EOW-1/DL1 and the proceedings initiated in pursuance thereto against the appellants in the Court of Chief Metropolitan Magistrate, Delhi under section 420 read with 120B of the Indian Penal Code are quashed.

6. DR. AR. LAKSHMANAN, J.—Leave granted.

7. These two appeals arise out of the final judgment and order passed by the High Court of Delhi at New Delhi in Criminal Miscellaneous (M) Nos. 360/2002 and 447/2002 filed under section 482 of the Criminal Procedure Code read with article 227 of the Constitution of India by the appellants herein seeking the invocation of the inherent powers of the High Court for quashing the F.I.Rs. and the proceedings initiated in pursuance thereto, as also the process issued by the Chief Metropolitan Magistrate, Delhi. The learned single Judge of the Delhi High Court, by the impugned final orders, held against the appellants that obtaining from the Ministry of Health Customs Duty Exemption Certificate, that was meant for 'actual user' on false assertion makes out the offence under section 120B read with section 420 of the Indian Penal Code.

8. The respondent herein (Central Bureau of Investigation, New Delhi) initiated criminal proceedings under section 120B read with section 420 of the Indian Penal Code against the appellants on the ground that the appellants in conspiracy with the Director of Gujarat Cancer and Research Institute, Mr. T.B. Patel (deceased), Secretary of the Gujarat Cancer Society, Mr. N.L. Patel and Dr. Viral C. Shah with each other have cheated the Government of India in terms of evasion of Customs Duty and by concealment of facts obtained Customs Duty Exemption Certificate in respect of MRI and Lithotripsy machines and by violating the provisions of 'actual user' condition as per Import Export Policy and Customs Notification No. 279/83 dated 30-9-1983 and Customs Notification No. 64/88 dated 1-3-1988 during the year 1987-90, despite acknowledging the fact that the Customs Duty has been paid by the appellants to the Customs Department and settled under the Kar Vivad Samadhan Scheme, 1998. In the instant case, two machines were imported into India by the Gujarat Cancer Society (hereinafter referred to as "the GCS") who availed of the duty exemption on the basis of the exemption certificate issued in the name of the Gujarat Cancer and Research Institute (hereinafter referred to as "the GCRI") on a *bona fide* premise that since all the activities of the GCRI were funded by the GCS and all the operations of GCS were carried out through the GCRI and that they are akin to holding any subsidiary company, the same could be done. The Customs Authority raided the premises of the GCRI and seized the machines and necessary paper work on the ground that the exemption certificate was issued in the name of the GCRI and not in the name of the GCS and thus the GCS was not entitled to exemption and was, therefore, liable to pay Customs Duty. The machines were immediately released on giving a usual undertaking. On 11-10-1991, show cause notice was issued to the GCS which was replied to by them. The Collector of Customs, Bombay by an order dated 10-4-1993 held that the GCS was liable to pay the Customs Duty, thus denying the concessional duty benefit under Customs Notification Nos. 279/1983 and 64/1988 and demanded a duty of Rs. 2,16,80,444 under section 28 of the Customs Act, 1962 read with the proviso to the said section. The said duty was to be paid by the importer – GCS and Canbank Financial Services as well as ICICI being joint holder of the said imported machines. However, considering the charitable and philanthropic activities of the GCS, no prosecution was recommended and only a token redemption fine of Re. 1 was imposed. No penalty was imposed on the above said financial organisations, namely, Canbank Financial Services and ICICI as they were acting as a lessor, who had extended financial extension to the above charitable organisation for import of sophisticated machines. A personal penalty was imposed on M/s. Shah Diagnostic Institute Pvt. Ltd., Ahmedabad and its Director, Dr. Viral C. Shah jointly under section 112A, the Customs Act, 1962.

9. Against the order of the Collector of Customs, the appellants preferred appeals before the Customs, Excise and Gold (Appellate) Tribunal, West Regional Branch, Bombay which confirmed the findings of the Collector of Customs.

10. Against the order of the Customs, Excise and Gold (Appellate) Tribunal, the GCS came up in appeal before this Court in Civil Appeal No. 31/1999. Whilst the matter was pending before this Court, the Government of India launched the Kar Vivad Samadhan Scheme, 1998, whereby whoever takes the benefit under the said Scheme is granted immunity from prosecution from any offence under the Customs Act including the offence of evasion of duty. In accordance with the Kar Vivad Samadhan Scheme, 1998, the GCS had agreed to deposit the stipulated amount of over Rs. 98 lakhs which had already been deposited earlier and withdrew the Civil appeal pending before this Court. On 19-7-1999, a certificate for full and final settlement of tax arrears in respect of the Kar Vivad Samadhan Scheme, 1998 was issued to the GCS. The said Certificate, *inter alia*, certified, the receipt of payment from the GCS towards full and final settlement of tax arrears determined in the order dated 10-2-1999 of the Designated Authority and further granting immunity to the GCS from any proceedings for prosecution from any offence under the Customs Act, 1962 or from the imposition of penalty under the said enactment, in respect of the matters covered in the declaration made by the GCS.

11. However, a case was registered against the appellants on 6-1-1999 by the respondent alleging that the appellants in conspiracy with the Director of the GCRI, Mr. T.B. Patel (deceased), Secretary of the GCS, Mr. N.L. Patel and Dr. Viral C. Shah had cheated the Government of India in terms of evasion of Customs Duty and by violating the provisions of 'actual user' condition as per Import Export Policy during the year 1987-88. A charge-sheet was prepared for commission of offence under section 120B read with section 420 of the Indian Penal Code. On presentation of the said charge-sheet, the trial Court by its order took cognizance and summoned the appellants. The appellants were furnished copies of the charge-sheet. In the meantime, the appellants preferred Special Criminal Applications before the High Court of Gujarat at Ahmedabad seeking quashing of the FIR. However, the same was disposed of as withdrawn on the ground of jurisdiction with a liberty to file a fresh petition before an appropriate Court. Thereupon the appellants filed Criminal Miscellaneous (Main) Petitions under section 482 of the Code of Criminal Procedure read with article 227 of the Constitution of India in the High Court of Delhi at New Delhi seeking an appropriate order/directions to the respondent quashing the FIR concerned. The learned single Judge of the High Court of Delhi, by his final order, dismissed the said petitions. Hence these two appeals by way of special leave petitions.

12. We have heard Shri P. Chidambaram, learned senior counsel, appearing for the appellants in both the appeals and Shri K.K. Sood, learned Additional Solicitor General, appearing for the respondent.

13. Before considering the rival submissions of the respective counsel appearing on either side, it is useful to reproduce the short order passed by the learned single Judge of the High Court of Delhi on 4-3-2002 which reads as under:

> "This petition has been filed with a prayer to quash FIR No. R.C. 1(E)/99/EOW-1/DLI under section 120B read with section 420, I.P.C. and the proceedings initiated in pursuance thereto.

It is the case of the petitioner that petitioner has compounded the offence by taking recourse to Kar Vivad Samadhan Scheme, 1998 and that no prosecution for offence after compounding of offence can be instituted. He draws my attention to a judgment of the Supreme Court in *Smt. Sushila Rani* v. *Commissioner of Income-tax,* AIR 2002 SC 823: 2002 AIR SCW 485: 2002 Tax LR 211, para 10 2002 Vol. II AD Apex Decisions, where the Supreme Court has held that:

> "The appellant in the course of the declarations filed specifically stated that any adjustment of refunds towards tax arrears of the appellant by the Department in the earlier years without following the mandatory procedure of section 245 of the Act would still remain as tax arrears for the purpose of the KVSS and it is on that basis the declarations were accepted by the department. Having accepted the claim of the appellant on that basis, it will not be permissible for the respondents now to turn around and take a different stand."

The case of the prosecution is that this is not a question of mere evasion of custom duties but it is a question of obtaining custom duty exemption certificate from the Ministry of Health by making a false assertion that the machines imported are for actual user. The compounding of offence subsequent thereto only indicates that a certificate was falsely induced from the Ministry of Health.

Having heard learned counsel for parties and having gone through the judgment relied upon by learned counsel for the petitioner, I am of the view that obtaining a certificate, that was meant for actual user, on false assertion, makes out the offence. Crl. M. (M) 360/2002 is dismissed."

14. Learned senior counsel appearing for the appellants submitted that to the show cause notice, the appellants had sent a proper reply and after hearing the case of the GCS, the Collector of Customs, Bombay held that the GCS was liable to pay the Customs Duty but in view of the activities of the Society and the *bona fides* of the Society, and considering charitable and philanthropic activities of the Society, no prosecution was recommended and moreover, only a token redemption fine of Re. 1 was imposed. Thus, he submitted that the concerned authorities were satisfied that there was no intention to evade the Customs Duty as stated by the authorities. It was further submitted that the GCS was immuned from any criminal proceedings pursuant to the Certificates issued under the Kar Vivad Samadhan Scheme, 1998 and the present appellants are being prosecuted in their capacity as office bearers of the GCS. As the Customs Duty has already been paid, the Central Government has not suffered any financial loss. Moreover, as per the Kar Vivad Samadhan Scheme, 1998, whoever is granted the benefit under the Kar Vivad Samadhan Scheme, 1998 is granted immunity from prosecution from any offence under the Customs Act, 1962, including the offence of evasion of duty. In the circumstances, the complaint filed against the appellants is unsustainable and that the appellants are reputed persons who had never even contemplated committing any violation of law or thought of taking undue advantage of the exemption Notifications under the Customs Act and that when the Society availed of the exemption Notification in respect of the two machines, it acted *bona fide* in the belief, that since the machines were being imported, purely for the benefit of the cancer patients of the GCRI, by such importation, cancer patients would be benefited, as they would get diagnosis and treatment in the GCRI itself and would not have to go to Bombay and other places. He further contended that the impugned order passed by the High Court of Delhi is bad in law and fact inasmuch as the learned single Judge has erred in passing the impugned order, dismissing the petitions filed under section 482 of the Criminal Procedure Code on the basis of an erroneous reading and a total misinterpretation of the judgment and despite the well-settled principle of law cited by the petitioners. In this context, he cited the judgment of this Court in the case of *Suhila Rani (Smt.)* v. *Commissioner of Income-tax,* (2002) 2 SCC 697. He also cited the judgment of this Court in the case of *Central Bureau of Investigation, SPE, SIU (X), New Delhi* v. *Duncans Agro Industries Ltd., Calcutta,* (1996) 5 SCC 591. Placing reliance on the above judgments, he urged that the alleged criminal liability stands compounded on a settlement with respect to the civil issues and, therefore, the FIR was erroneously issued and was totally unwarranted. He further submitted that under the penal law, there is no concept of vicarious liability unless the said statute covers the same within its ambit. In the instant case, the said law which prevails in the field *i.e.*, the Customs Act, the appellants have been therein under wholly discharged and the GCS granted immunity from prosecution. He also contended that the learned single Judge failed to appreciate that the GCS had taken the benefit of the Amnesty Scheme of Kar Vivad Samadhan Scheme, 1998 and, therefore, implicating the appellants being office bearers of the Society under section 120B read with section 420 of the Indian Penal Code is against the purpose and object of the said Scheme, and, therefore, there is no *prima facie* case against the appellants in respect of the alleged offence. He further submitted that evasion of Customs Duty, in the present case, was predominantly a civil case and that the ingredients of criminal offence were missing/wanting and which liability, in any case, stood settled and that, therefore, in such a scenario, the appellants to undergo an agony of a long criminal trial would be an abuse of process of Court and against the interest of justice.

15. He invited our attention to the pleadings, in particular, the F.I.R., the Annexures of the S.L.Ps., the provisions of the Kar Vivad Samadhan Scheme, 1998, the relevant provisions of the Indian Penal Code, the Customs Act, 1962 and the rulings relied on by him.

16. Shri K.K. Sood, learned Additional Solicitor General, appearing for the respondent, submitted that the material gathered in the investigation clearly show and establish commission of offences by the accused persons indicating the appellants herein under sections 420 and 120B of the Indian Penal Code and that there is no infirmity in the order of the Chief Metropolitan Magistrate taking cognizance or in the order of the High Court declining to quash criminal proceedings at the interlocutory stage. He further submitted that the criminal proceedings in respect of which cognizance has been taken by the Court can be interfered with or quashed only if the allegations even if taken on their face value do not satisfy or make out the ingredients of offences alleged and no offence is at all made out or there is legal or statutory impediment in prosecuting the accused person. He submitted that none of these grounds exist in the present case. According to him, in the present case, material on record clearly show and establish commission of offences under the Indian Penal Code by the appellants and since the charges are supported by documentary evidence which establish the same, there is no warrant or justification or basis for seeking the relief of quashing the criminal proceedings. He further submitted that the High Court has rightly declined to quash the criminal proceedings and, therefore, the same does not call for any interference by this Court. In regard to the judgments cited by Shri P. Chidambaram, learned senior counsel appearing for the appellants, he submitted that the reliance placed upon those judgments is also without any merit and in the present case, material on record clearly show and establish the criminal conspiracy to cheat the Government and actually cheating the Government of India pursuant to the same and that it is not a civil dispute as has been sought to be made out and that the conduct of the accused persons is criminal in nature and material on record clearly establish commission of criminal offences by them. Thus, he would submit that the judgment in the case of *Duncans Agro Industries Ltd., Calcutta* (supra) has no application to the present case. Referring to the plea that the duty payable has been subsequently paid, he submitted, that such payment is not a ground for quashing criminal proceedings or absolving the accused persons of their criminal liability. According to him, the judgment in the case of *Sushila Rani* (supra) dealt with proceedings; AIR 1996 SC 2452: 1996 AIR SCW 3019: 1996 Cr LJ 3501; AIR 2002 SC 823: 2002 AIR SCW 485: 2002 Tax LR 211 under the Income-tax Act and held that once the matter is settled under the Kar Vivad Samadhan Scheme, 1998, such settlement cannot be reopened except under specified grounds and that the stated grounds do not exist in the said case and that there is nothing in the said judgment warranting the plea of the appellants, in the present case, that criminal proceedings under the Indian Penal Code are prohibited merely because disputes concerning tax have been settled under the Kar Vivad Samadhan Scheme, 1998. According to him, such settlement only protects the individual from prosecution under the taxing Statute which is a limited protection and limited to the proceedings under the taxing Statute only. Coming to the certificate issued by the authorities under the Kar Vivad Samadhan Scheme, 1998, he submitted that the certificate issued by the authorities under the said Scheme cannot be the ground and basis for quashing the criminal proceedings. According to him, a perusal of the certificate would show that the settlement under the Kar Vivad Samadhan Scheme, 1998 gives immunity only from prosecution under relevant taxing Statute and not under the Indian Penal Code. Concluding his arguments, he submitted that the criminal proceedings cannot be quashed merely on account of the fact that Customs Duty payment has been settled.

17. Before proceeding to consider the rival submissions, it is beneficial to refer to certain annexures filed along with the special leave petitions. The true copy of the agreement dated 28-4-1988 between the GCS and Dr. Viral C. Shah has been filed. This agreement was made at Ahmedabad on 28-4-1988 as an addendum to the original agreement dated 24-2-1987 entered into between the GCS on the one part and Dr. Viral C. Shah as the second part. The relevant clauses of the agreement are extracted below:

"(1) The Gujarat Cancer Society shall acquire ESWL and MRI machines in its own name and for this Dr. Viral Shah shall make necessary arrangements for the construction of the buildings for housing the said two equipments by way of arranging donations to the Society of an amount equivalent to the total cost of construction of premises required for the instalment of said machines. The Society shall construct the required premises in a portion of the land in the hospital complex and on completion the said building, the ownership of the said premises so constructed shall vest with the Society.

(2) The overall control in regard to appointment of all categories of staff and running and maintenance of these two equipments will be with the Gujarat Cancer and Research Institute, Ahmedabad as per the tripartite agreement with the Govt. of Gujarat, the Gujarat Cancer Society, and the Gujarat Cancer and Research Institute.

(3) Raising of loan, Dr. Shah will arrange for the Society procuring finance from financial institutions including leasing company or companies for meeting the cost for the matching out the purchase of procuring such finance the said machines may be mortgaged or leased to leasing company or financial institution which in turn will be leased out to the Society.

(4) In consideration of the Society having entrusted the running and maintaining the said machine to the said Dr. Shah as herein provided the said Dr. Shah shall pay to the Society rental which shall be equivalent to the amount of monthly instalment and interest and/or hire charges payable by the Society to the financial institutions and/or to the leasing company from whom the finances shall have procured for the said machines.

. . . .

(6) The institute agrees that Dr. Shah through the Gujarat Cancer Society shall be entitled to work, run, and maintain the said two machines for a maximum period of ten years and Dr. Shah or his nominees shall be responsible for the repairs and replacements of parts thereof, during the said period."

18. The First Information Report filed as Annexure P-2 along with the S.L.P. is as under:

"RC. 1(E)/99-EOW.I.DLI 6-1-1999 at 16.00 hrs.

Place of occurrence with State Date and time of ocurance Delhi, Mumbai and Ahmedabad during the year 1987-90

Name of complainant and Informant with address Joint Secretary, Ministry of Health and Family Welfare, Government of India, New Delhi.

Offence 120-B read with 420, I.P.C.

Name and address of accused

1. Sh. N.L. Patel, Director Gujarat Cancer Research Institute, Ahmedabad.
2. Dr. Viral C. Shah, Director, M/s. Shah Diagnosis Institute (P) Ltd., Mumbai and Ahmedabad.
3. Sh. D.D. Patel, Secretary Gujarat Cancer Society, Ahmedabad and others unknown. Action taken RC is registered and investigation taken up, Investigating Officer Shri Rajveer Singh, DY. SP. CBI/EOW-I/ NEW DELHI

INFORMATION

The Joint Secretary, Ministry of Health and Family Welfare, Government of India, New Delhi *vide* his D.O. No. C-18011/5/96-VIG(PT) dated 22/24-12-98 has sent a copy of the report dated D.O.F. No. IMP/CDE/1/1/97-RC (Guj-4), dated 17-8-1998 submitted by Sh. P. Rosha, Chairman of Speical Committee appointed by Hon'ble High Court, Delhi to inquire into the import of equipments against Customs Duty exemption certificate for use in Charitable Hospitals. The Hon'ble

High Court, Delhi has approved the suggestion to refer the matter to CBI for registration of case and investigation. Accordingly, the Joint Ministry of Health and Family Welfare, Government of India, New Delhi has requested CBI to investigate the matter."

19. Our attention was drawn to the Rosha Committee Report dated 17-8-1998 and application dated 15-10-1987 for import licence for import of LITHO ESWL Equipment by 'actual users' (Non-Industrial). There is another application for import of another machine. The agreement copy was also enclosed for ready reference to the Joint Chief Controller, Import and Export Trade Organisations, Ahmedabad. Along with the application, the agreement between the GCS, the GCRI and the State Government of Gujarat was also enclosed as Annexure No. 4.

20. Our attention was also drawn to the Text of the Kar Vivad Samadhan Scheme, 1998, under Chapter IV of Finance (No. 2) Act, 1998. Our attention was also drawn to sections 86 to 98 of the said Scheme which are relevant for the present purpose. Our attention was further drawn to the Memorandum to Finance (No. 2) Bill, 1998 explaining the provisions of the Kar Vivad Samadhan Scheme, 1998. The said Scheme seeks to provide a quick and voluntary settlement of tax dues outstanding as on 31-3-1998, both in various direct tax enactments as well as indirect taxes enactments by offering waiver of a part of the arrear taxes and interest and providing immunity against institution of prosecution and imposition of penalty. The assessee on his part shall seek to withdraw appeals pending before various appellate Authorities and Courts. The Kar Vivad Samadhan Scheme, 1998 comes into force on the first day of September, 1998 and ends on 31st day of December, 1998. The Kar Vivad Samadhan Scheme, 1998 is applicable to tax arrears outstanding as on 31-3-1998 under various direct tax enactments and indirect tax enactments. Clauses 3 and 4 of the Memorandum to Finance (No. 2) Bill, 1998 read as under:

> "3. A person desiring to avail the Scheme is required to file a declaration in the prescribed form before the designated authority notified for this purpose. The designated authority shall pass an order within sixty days of the declaration determining the amount payable in accordance with the provisions of the Scheme and grant a certificate indicating the particulars of tax arrears and the sum payable and intimate the same to the declarant. The declarant will pay the sum payable as determined by designated authority within thirty days of the passing of such order. The order passed by the designated authority shall be conclusive and shall not be reopened in any other proceedings or under any law for the time being in force. Where the declarant has filed an appeal or reference before any Authority, Tribunal or Court, notwithstanding anything contained in any other provision of law for the time being in force, such appeal, reference or reply shall be deemed to have been withdrawn. Where writ petitions have been filed before the High Court or Supreme Court the declarant shall move an application for withdrawing such petitions and furnish the proof of the same along with the intimation. Any amount paid in pursuance of declaration made under the Scheme shall not be refundable under any circumstances.

4. The designated authority shall subject to the conditions provided in the Scheme grant immunity from prosecution or penalty under the relevant Acts in respect of matters covered in the declaration".

21. Section 87(h) of the Kar Vivad Samadhan Scheme, 1998 defines "direct tax enactment" which reads thus:

> "direct tax enactment" means the Wealth-tax Act, 1957 (27 of 1957) or the Gift-tax Act, 1958 (18 of 1958) or the Income-tax Act, 1961 (43 of 1961) or the Interest-tax Act, 1974 (45 of 1974) or the Expenditure-tax Act, 1987 (35 of 1987)."

22. Sub-clause (j) of section 87 defines "indirect tax enactment" which reads thus:

> "indirect tax enactment" means Customs Act, 1962 (52 of 1962) or the Central Excise Act, 1944 (1 of 1944) or the Customs Tariff Act, 1975 (51 of 1975) or the Central Excise Tariff Act, 1985 (5 of 1986) or the relevant Act and includes the rules or regulations made under such enactment."

23. The present case comes under the tax arrears payable under the indirect tax enactment. Section 89 of the Kar Vivad Samadhan Scheme, 1998 deals with particulars to be furnished in declaration and section 90 of the Scheme deals with time and manner of payment of tax arrears. Clause (2) of section 90 provides that the declarant shall pay, the sum determined by the Designated Authority within thirty days of the passing of an order by the Designated Authority and intimate the fact of such payment to the Designated Authority along with proof thereof and the Designated Authority shall thereupon issue the certificate to the declarant. Clause (3) of section 90 of the said Scheme provides that every order passed under sub-section (1), determining the sum payable under this Scheme shall be conclusive as to the matters stated therein and no matter covered by such order shall be reopened in any other proceeding under the direct tax enactment or indirect tax enactment or under any other law for the time being in force. Sub-clause (4) of section 90 of the said Scheme provides that where the declarant has filed an appeal or reference or a reply to the show-cause notice against any order or notice giving rise to the tax arrear before any authority or Tribunal or Court, then, notwithstanding anything contained in any other provisions of any law for the time being in force, such appeal or reference or reply shall be deemed to have been withdrawn on the day on which the order referred to in sub-section (2) is passed.

24. It is pertinent to notice that the First Information Report was filed on 6-1-1999 and the Certificate under the Kar Vivad Samadhan Scheme, 1998 was issued to the appellants on 19-7-1999 by the Commissioner of Customs (Adjudication) and Designated Authority (KVSS-98). It is also to be noticed that section 95 of the Kar Vivad Samadhan Scheme, 1998 provides that the provisions of this Scheme shall not apply in certain cases. Under section 95(ii)(a) of the said Scheme, in a case where prosecution for any offence punishable under any provisions of any indirect tax enactment has been instituted on or before the date of filing of the declaration under section 88, in respect of any tax arrear in respect of such case under such indirect tax enactment, this Scheme shall not apply. Clauses (ii) and (iii) of section 95 of the Kar Vivad Samadhan Scheme, 1998, which are relevant for our purpose are reproduced hereunder:

"(ii) in respect of tax arrear under any indirect tax enactment,—

(a) in a case where prosecution for any offence punishable under any provisions of any indirect tax enactment has been instituted on or before the date of filing of the declaration under section 88, in respect of any tax arrear in respect of such case under such indirect tax enactment;

(b) in a case where show cause notice or a notice of demand under any indirect tax enactment has not been issued;

(c) in a case where no appeal or reference or writ petition is admitted and pending before any appellate authority or High Court or the Supreme Court or no application for revision is pending before the Central Government on the date of declaration made under section 88;

(iii) to any person in respect of whom prosecution for any offence punishable under Chapter IX or Chapter XVII of the Indian Penal Code (45 of 1860), the Foreign Exchange Regulation Act, 1973 (46 of 1973), the Narcotic Drugs and Psychotropic Substances Act, 1985 (61 of 1985), the Terrorist and Disruptive Activities (Prevention) Act, 1987 (28 of 1987), the Prevention of Corruption Act, 1988 (49 of 1988), or for the purpose of enforcement of any civil liability has been instituted on or before the filing of the declaration or such person has been convicted of any such offence punishable under any such enactment;"

25. Sections 166 to 177 of Chapter IX of the Indian Penal Code deal with offences relating to public servants. Likewise, sections 378 to 462 of Chapter XVII of the Indian Penal Code deal with offences against property. Thus immunity is granted to the persons in respect of whom the offence is punishable under Chapter IX or Chapter XVII of the Indian Penal Code.

26. Annexure P-1 is the Certificate issued to the GCS under the Kar Vivad Samadhan Scheme, 1998, Form-4 (Rule 5(b)). This certificate has been issued for full and final settlement of tax arrears under section 90(2) read with section 91 of the Finance (No. 2) Act, 1998 in respect of Kar Vivad Samadhan Scheme, 1998. Before issuing the certificate, the Commissioner of Customs (Adjudication) and Designated Authority (KVSS-98) takes into consideration the following facts:

(a) that the Gujarat Cancer Society, Ahmedabad had made declaration under section 88 of the Finance (No. 2) Act, 1998;

(b) that the designated authority by order dated 10-2-1999 determined the amount of Rs. 98,40,222 payable by the declarant in accordance with the provisions of the Kar Vivad Samadhan, 1998;

(c) that the certificate is granted towards full and final settlement of tax arrears as per the details given in the certificate;

(d) that the Civil Appeal No. 31/1999 filed by the GCS, Ahmedabad in this Court under section 130E of the Customs Act, 1962 against the judgment and order Nos. 758 to 761/98-b2 passed by the Customs, Excise and Gold (Control) Tribunal, New Delhi was withdrawn. The order was passed by this Court on 16-3-1999 and a copy of the said order was produced before the authorities as proof of such withdrawal in accordance with the provisions contained in the proviso to sub-section (4) of section 90.

(e) The declarant has paid Rs. 98,40,222 being the sum determined by the Designated Authority.

27. In exercise of the powers conferred by sub-section (2) of section 90 read with section 91 of the Finance (No. 2) Act, 1998, the Designated Authority issued the certificate to the declarant in the following terms:

(a) Certifying the receipt of the payment from the declarant towards full and final settlement of tax arrears determined in the order dated 10-2-1999 on the declaration made by the aforesaid declarant;

(b) Granting immunity, subject to the provisions contained in the Kar Vivad Samadhan Scheme, 1998, from instituting any proceeding for prosecution for any offence under the Customs Act, 1962, or from the imposition of penalty under said enactment, in respect of matters covered in the aforesaid declaration made by the declarant;

28. It is thus crystal clear that the Commissioner of Customs (Adjudication) and Designated Authority (KVSS-98) granted immunity from instituting any proceeding for prosecution for any offence under the Customs Act, 1962, or from the imposition of penalty under the said enactment, in respect of matters covered in the aforesaid declaration made by the declarant. After hearing the case of the GCS, as already noticed, the Collector of Customs, Bombay held that the GCS was liable to pay the Customs Duty but in view of the activities of the Society and the *bona fides* of the Society, and considering charitable and philanthropic activities of the Society, no prosecution was recommended. Moreover, only a token redemption fine of Re. 1 was imposed. Thus it is seen that the Customs Authorities were satisfied that there was no intention to evade the Customs Duty. However, the Collector denied the GCS the concessional duty benefit under Customs Notification Nos. 279/1983 and 64/1988 and demanded the duty of Rs. 2,16,80,444 under section 28 of the Customs Act, 1962 read with the proviso of the said section. The said duty was to be paid by the GCS (Importer) and Canbank Financial Services as well as ICICI being the joint holder of the said imported machines. A personal penalty of Rs. 10 lakh was imposed on Dr. Viral C. Shah and M/s. Shah Diagnosis Institute Pvt. Ltd., Ahmedabad and Bombay jointly under section 112(a) of the Customs Act, 1962.

29. We have carefully gone through the Kar Vivad Samadhan Scheme, 1998 and the certificate issued by the Customs Authorities. In our opinion, the GCS is immuned from any criminal proceedings pursuant to the certificates issued under the said Scheme and the appellants are being prosecuted in their capacity as office bearers of the GCS. As the Customs duty has already been paid, the Central Government has not suffered any financial loss. Moreover, as per the Kar Vivad Samadhan Scheme, 1998 whoever is granted the benefit under the said Scheme is granted immunity from prosecution from any offence under the Customs Act, 1962 including the offence of evasion of duty. In the circumstances, the complaint filed against the appellants is unsustainable.

30. We shall now analyse the judgment in the case of *Sushila Rani* (supra). That case also refers to the Kar Vivad Samadhan Scheme, 1998. The appellant before this Court in that case is the widow of the original assessee under the Income-tax Act, 1961 for the Assessment Year 1988-89, the appeal was pending before the Commissioner of Income-tax (Appeals) while for Assessment Years 1989-90 and 1991-92, appeals were pending before the Income-tax Appellate Tribunal. The appellant requested the Department to indicate or compute the tax arrears as per the Kar Vivad Samadhan Scheme, 1998 so that all disputes in relation to these three assessment years can be resolved. As there was no response from the Department, the appellant submitted three separate declarations under sections 88 and 89 of the Kar Vivad Samadhan Scheme, 1998 and also pointed out the mandatory nature of section 245 of the Act. Respondent 1, on receipt of the declarations for the three assessment years evaluated and verified the same in accordance with the provisions of the Kar Vivad Samadhan Scheme, 1998 and on being satisfied with the correctness of the declaration in every respect, issued on 26-2-1999 a statutory certificate prescribed in Form 2-A and rule 4(a) under the provisions of section 90(1) of the Kar Vivad Samadhan Scheme, 1998. On receipt of the said certificate under section 90(1) of the Kar Vivad Samadhan Scheme, 1998, the appellant deposited the sum determined and demanded the issue of certificate under section 90(2) of the Scheme for the deemed withdrawal of the appeal filed by the appellant for these years which were pending adjudication. Respondent No. 1 issued a certificate in Form 3 as required in favour of the appellant certifying the receipt of payments from the appellant towards full and final settlement of the tax arrears determined in the order dated 26-2-1999 and granting immunity from instituting any proceeding for prosecution of any offence under the Act or from imposing any penalty under the said Act. Thereafter on 11-8-1999 certificate was issued by the Department to the effect that no arrears or demand of any kind is outstanding against the appellant as per the records of the respondents. On 26-10-1999, the appellant submitted a representation requesting the respondents to refund all the amounts along with interest as per the provisions of the Act upon the finalisation of the declarations made by the appellant under the provisions of the Kar Vivad Samadhan Scheme. This claim resulted in the issue of a notice on 23-6-2000 under section 90(1) of the Kar Vivad Samadhan Scheme calling upon the appellant to explain as to why, the certificate issued under section 90(1) of the Scheme earlier be not amended, on the ground that the determination made by the Department for the three assessment years in question was on the Department's wrong understanding of the judgment of the Allahabad High Court. The appellant, thereupon, filed a writ petition challenging the issuance of the notice on the ground that the same is without jurisdiction. The High Court took the view that what is under challenge in the writ petition is only a show cause notice and it would be open to the appellant to highlight the question relating to lack of jurisdiction before the Commissioner when the matter is taken up for further consideration. The High Court did not express any opinion on the facts of the case and disposed of the writ petition. Hence, the appeal by special leave. In paragraphs 6 and 8 of the judgment, this Court held:

"An examination of the scheme of sections 89, 90 and 91 KVSS would reveal that every person entitled to make a declaration under the said Scheme was obliged to submit the declaration on or before 31-1-1999; that a period of 60 days has been stipulated under section 90(1) for the designated authority under the Scheme to determine the amount payable by the declarant and the certificate to this effect under section 90(1) has to be granted by the designated authority after determination towards full and final settlement of the tax arrears within a period of sixty days. Thereafter, except on ground of false declaration made by the declarant, every order passed under sub-section (1) of section 90 determining the sum payable under the scheme, is absolutely conclusive as to the matters stated thereunder and no matter covered by such order can be reopened in any other proceeding under any law for the time being in force. After this determination under section 90(1) KVSS, another certificate is issued under section 91 KVSS on the basis of which immunity is granted to the declarant from instituting any proceeding for prosecution for any offence under any direct tax enactment or indirect tax enactment.

We may notice that a certificate issued under section 90(1) KVSS making a determination as to the sum payable under KVSS, is conclusive as to the matter stated therein and cannot be reopened in any proceedings under any law for the time being in force, except on the ground of false declaration by any declarant. Therefore, before issue of a notice, there should be satisfaction that the declarant has made a false declaration. There is no such allegation in the course of the notice issued. All that is stated is that adjustments already made should have been taken into account when calculating the tax arrears. As such there is a mistake in calculation, which needs rectification". The whole basis of the notice is only that adjustments already made had not been taken note of. If this is the basis of the issuance of the notice and not the false declaration and that information was available with the Department even at the time of the finalisation of the proceedings under section 90 KVSS, we fail to understand as to how the matter could be reopened at this stage. That information was already available with them and there is no false declaration in that regard. In that view of the matter, the notice issued is without jurisdiction."

31. In that view of the matter, this Court allowed the appeal, set aside the order made by the High Court by allowing the writ petition filed by the appellant and quash the notice issued by the Department calling upon the appellant to explain as to why the order issued earlier under section 90(1) KVSS be not amended.

32. On a reading of the judgment in the case of *Sushila Rani* (supra), it is clear to us that if an assessee takes the option under this Scheme, he obtains immediate immunity under any proceeding under any and all laws in force. As such the present proceedings initiated under section 120B read with section 420 of the Indian Penal Code are bad and ought to have been quashed with immediate effect. AIR 2002 SC 823: 2002 AIR SCW 485: 2002 Tax LR 211.

33. We shall now consider the judgment cited by learned senior counsel for the appellants in the case of *Duncans Agro Industries Ltd., Calcutta,* AIR 1996 SC 2452: 1996 AIR SCW 3019: 1996 Cr LJ 3501, which, *inter alia,* held that:

> "In the facts of the case, it appears to us, that there is enough justification for the High Court to hold that the case was basically a matter of civil dispute. The Banks had already filed suits for recovery of the dues of the Banks on account of credit facility and the said suits have been compromised on receiving the payments from the companies concerned. Even if an offence of cheating is *prima facie* constituted, such offence is a compoundable offence and compromise decrees passed in the suits instituted by the Banks, for all intents and purposes, amounts to compounding of the offence of cheating."

It was further held that,

> "Considering the fact that the claims of Banks have been satisfied and suits instituted by the Banks have been compromised on receiving payments, we do not think that the said complaints should be pursued any further. In our view, proceeding further with the complaints will not be expedient."

34. In our view, in the present case, the alleged criminal liability stands compounded on a settlement with respect to the civil issues and, therefore, the First Information Report was erroneously issued and was totally unwarranted. From the aforesaid judgment, the proposition that follows in the instant case is that the Kar Vivad Samadhan Scheme, 1998 issued by the Government of India was a voluntary Scheme whereby if the disputed demand is settled by the Authority and pending proceedings are withdrawn by an importer, the balance demand against an importer shall be dropped and the importer shall be immuned from penal proceedings under any law in force. We are, therefore, of the opinion that this judgment squarely comes in the face of any argument sought to be propounded by the respondent that the Kar Vivad Samadhan Scheme, 1998 does not absolves the appellants from criminal liability under the Indian Penal Code. The learned single Judge of the High Court of Delhi, in our opinion, has not appreciated the fact that the continuance of the proceedings in the instant case would only tantamount to driving the present appellants to double jeopardy when they had been honourably exonerated by the Collector of Customs by their adjudication and further the GCS of which one of the appellants is the General Secretary in which capacity he is accused in the present case was granted amnesty under the Kar Vivad Samadhan Scheme, 1998. In our opinion, the present case does not warrant subjecting a citizen especially senior citizens of the age of 92 and 70 years to fresh investigation and prosecution on an incident or fact situation giving rise to offence under both the Customs Act and the Indian Penal Code when the matter has already been settled. Likewise, the respondent herein has initiated criminal proceedings against Accused No. 2 and Accused No. 1, *inter alia,* on the ground alleging that the appellants in conspiracy with the co-accused named therein with each other have cheated the Government of India in terms of evasion of Customs Duty and by concealment of facts obtained CDEC in respect of MRI and Lithotripsy machines and by violating the provisions of 'actual user' condition as per Import Export Policy and Customs Notification No. 279/83, dated 30-9-1983 and Customs Notification No. 64/88, dated 1-3-1988 during the year 1987-90, despite acknowledging the fact that Customs Duty has been paid by the appellants to the Customs Department and settled and that commission of offences under section 120B read with section 420 of the Indian Penal Code are made out.

35. In our view, under the penal law, there is no concept of vicarious liability unless the said statute covers the same within its ambit. In the instant case, the said law which prevails in the field *i.e.*, the Customs Act, 1962 the appellants have been therein under wholly discharged and the GCS granted immunity from prosecution. It is well-established principle of law that the matter which has been adjudicated and settled need not to be dragged into the Criminal Courts unless and until the act of the appellants could have been described as culpable. The true fact and import of the Kar Vivad Samadhan Scheme, 1998, in our view, is that once the said Scheme is availed of and all the formalities complied with including the payment of the duty, the immunity granted under the provisions of the Customs Act, 1962 also extends to such offences that may *prima facie* be made out on identical allegations *i.e.*, of evasion of customs duty and violation of any Notification issued under the said Act.

36. In our view, there is no *prima facie* case made out in respect of the alleged offence under section 120B read with section 420 of the Indian Penal Code and, therefore, the charge-sheet and the process issued thereunder has to be quashed.

37. To bring home the charge of conspiracy within the ambit of section 120B of Indian Penal Code. It is necessary to establish that there was an agreement between the parties for doing an unlawful law. It is difficult to establish conspiracy by direct evidence.

38. Likewise the ingredients of section 420 of the Indian Penal Code are also not made out. There is no reason as to why the appellants must be made to undergo the agony of a criminal trial as has been held by this Court in the case of *G. Sagar Suri* v. *State of Uttar Pradesh,* (2000) 2 SCC 636: AIR 2000 SC 754: 2000 AIR SCW 296: 2000 Cr LJ 824: 2000 All LJ 496, paras 8 and 7. In this case, this Court held that:

> "Jurisdiction under section 482 of the Code has to be exercised with great care. In exercise of its jurisdiction the High Court is not to examine the matter superficially. It is to be seen if a matter, which is essentially of a civil nature, has been given a cloak of criminal offence. Criminal proceedings are not a short cut of other remedies available in law. Before issuing process a Criminal Court has to exercise a great deal of caution. For the accused, it is a serious matter. The Supreme Court has laid certain principles on the basis of which the High Court is to exercise its jurisdiction under section 482 of the Code. Jurisdiction under this section has to be exercised to prevent abuse of the process of any Court or otherwise to secure the ends of justice. Merely because the accused persons had already filed an application in the Court of Additional Judicial Magistrate for

their discharge, it cannot be urged that the High Court cannot exercise its jurisdiction under section 482 of the Code. Though the Magistrate trying a case has jurisdiction to discharge the accused at any stage of the trial if he considers the charge to be groundless but that does not mean that the accused cannot approach the High Court under section 482 of the Code or article 227 of the Constitution to have the proceeding quashed against them when no offence has been out against them and still why must they undergo the agony of a criminal trial."

39. Section 415 of the Indian Penal Code deals with cheating. To hold a person guilty of cheating as defined under section 415 of the Indian Penal Code, it is necessary to show that he has fraudulent or dishonest intention at the time of making the promise with an intention to retain the property. In other words, section 415 of the Indian Penal Code which defines cheating, requires deception of any person (a) including that person to: (i) to deliver any property to any person, or (ii) to consent that any person shall retain any property or (b) intentionally inducing that person to do or omit to do anything which he would not do or omit if he were not so deceived and which act or omission causes or is likely to cause damage or harm to that person, anybody's mind, reputation or property. In view of the aforesaid provisions, the appellants state that person may be induced fraudulently or dishonestly to deliver any property to any person. The second class of acts set forth in the section is the doing or omitting to do anything which the person deceived would not do or omit to do if he were not so deceived. In the first class of cases, the inducing must be fraudulent or dishonest. In the second class of acts, the inducing must be intentional but not fraudulent or dishonest.

40. In view of the aforesaid provisions of law, as the customs duty has been paid by the GCS, there is no fraudulent or dishonest intention on the part of the GCS or its office-bearers to retain the property. Moreover, there is no inducing on the part of the GCS or its office-bearers intentionally to retain the property in view of the fact that the customs duty has been paid by the GCS and, therefore, the ingredients of the offence of cheating are missing for issuing the process against the appellants and, therefore, the same, in our view, is liable to be quashed and set aside.

41. Section 111 of the Customs Act, 1962 which provides for confiscation of improperly imported goods, etc. insofar as it is relevant reads thus:

"Section 111. Confiscation of improperly imported goods, etc.—The following goods brought from a place outside India shall be liable to confiscation—

. . . .

(o) any goods exempted, subject to any condition, from duty or any prohibition in respect of the import thereof under this Act or any other law for the time being in force, in respect of which the condition is not observed unless the non-observance of the condition was sanctioned by the proper officer."

42. The question is whether the import of the machines in question was contrary to law in any manner and whether the machines are liable to be confiscated under the Customs Act, 1962, the only provision relied upon by the learned counsel for the appellants is clause (o) in section 111 of the Customs Act, 1962 which we have set out herein above. In our opinion, clause (o) of section 111 of the Customs Act, 1962 is not attracted in the present case. The subsequent proceedings initiated for confiscation of the goods is of no relevance nor does it retrospectively render the import illegal.

43. This Court in *Union of India* v. *Sampat Raj Dugar,* AIR 1992 SC 1417: 1992 AIR SCW 1420, has, while considering the scope and ambit of clause (o) of section 111, observed as under:

> "Clause (o) contemplates confiscation of goods which are exempted from duty subject to a condition, which condition is not observed by the importer. Occasion for taking action under this clause arises only when the condition is not observed within the period prescribed, if any, or where the period is not so prescribed, within a reasonable period. It, therefore, cannot be said that the said goods were liable to be confiscated on the date of their import under clause (o).

44. In other words, clause (o) is a new provision under which any goods exempted from duty or from import prohibition subject to certain conditions will become liable to confiscation if those conditions are not observed without the prior permission of the appropriate officer. The penal clause is being introduced to check misuse of exemptions granted in respect of the goods imported.

45. It is settled law, by catena of decisions, that for establishing the offence of cheating, the complainant is required to show that the accused had fraudulent or dishonest intention at the time of making promise or representation. From his making failure to keep up promise subsequently, such a culpable intention right at the beginning that is at the time when the promise was made cannot be presumed. It is seen from the records that the exemption certificate contained necessary conditions which were required to be complied with after importation of the machine. Since the GCS could not comply with it and, therefore, it rightly paid the necessary duties without taking advantage of the exemption certificate. The conduct of the GCS clearly indicates that there was no fraudulent or dishonest intention of either the GCS or the appellants in their capacities as office-bearers right at the time of making application for exemption. As there was absence of dishonest and fraudulent intention, the question of committing offence under section 420 of the Indian Penal Code does not arise. We have read the charge-sheet as a whole. There is no allegation in the First Information Report or the charge-sheet indicating expressly or impliedly any intentional deception or fraudulent/dishonest intention on the part of the appellants right from the time of making the promise or misrepresentation. Nothing has been said on what those misrepresentations were and how the Ministry of Health was duped and what where the roles played by the appellants in the alleged offence. The appellants, in our view, could not be attributed any *mens rea* of evasion of customs duty or cheating the Government of India as the cancer society is a non-profit organization and, therefore, the allegations against the appellants levelled by the prosecution are unsustainable. Kar Vivad Samadhan Scheme Certificate along with the *Duncan's* and *Sushila Rani's* judgments clearly absolve the appellants herein from all charges and allegations under any other law once the duty so demanded has been paid and the alleged offence has been compounded. It is also settled law that once a civil case has been compromised and the alleged offence has been compounded, to continue the criminal proceedings thereafter would be an abuse of the judicial process.

46. In the result, both the appeals stand allowed. The orders of the High Court which are impugned in these appeals are set aside.

Appeals allowed.

Bathusingh

v.

State of M.P.

Criminal Appeal Nos. 1295-1296 of 2004
AIR 2004 SC 4279: 2004 AIR SCW 4746
Decided on: 25-8-2004

Coram: **K.G. Balakrishnan, J.**
Dr. AR. Lakshmanan, J.

FACTS

The appellants committed murder of two persons. The trial court sentenced the appellants to life imprisonment. On appeal, the M.P. High Court acquitted some of the accused persons but upheld the conviction of the appellant. Aggrieved thereby, the appellant preferred an appeal before the Supreme Court by way of a Special Leave Petition. The appellant contended that they acted in self defence and therefore entitled to acquittal.

ISSUE

Scope of the right of private defence under I.P.C..

HELD

The right of private defence given by the Penal Code is essentially one of defence or self protection and not a right of reprisal or punishment. It is subject to the restrictions indicated in section 88 which are so important as the right itself. In the instant case, the assault on both the deceased was exceedingly vindictive and maliciously excessive. Under these circumstances, the appellants were not entitled for right of private defence and two persons were done to death by the appellants without there being any imminent danger to their property or lives. There is no evidence on record much less to establish the defence version of acting in self-defence, which is a defence which was set up at a very late stage. The appeals have no merits and were, accordingly, dismissed.

Judgment

Dr. AR. Lakshmanan, J.—These appeals are directed against the judgment and order dated 19-4-2002 passed by the High Court of Madhya Pradesh, Bench at Indore in Criminal Appeal Nos. 697 and 831 of 1995 whereby the High Court has partly allowed Criminal Appeal No. 697 of 1995 by acquitting appellant No. 1, Balu Singh, appellant No. 4, Richhu, appellant No. 6, Bhangdibai and appellant No. 7, Nanbai of the offence they were charged and the appeal of appellant No. 2 Bathusingh, appellant No. 3, Nar Singh and appellant No. 4, Bhal Singh was dismissed.

2. The case of the prosecution, in brief, is as follows:—

> The appellants and the deceased persons as well as PW-1, Sardar Singh, PW-2, Jagat Singh and PW-3, Humabai are related to each other. On the fateful day, the deceased Dhan Singh @ Dhania was digging a well in his field and was storing stones on the embankment of the field for which the accused persons were having objection. At that time, all the appellants reached the place in question having arrow and bow, Denga (lathi) and stones and started assaulting the deceased Dhania. The deceased Bhuru also reached over there and he too was assaulted by the appellants. Jhillibai, sister of PW-1, Sardar Singh, was also assaulted when she was going to serve water to him. The incident was witnessed by PW-1, Sardar Singh, PW-2, Jagat Singh, PW-3, Humabai and other witnesses named Bhagat Singh, Buddhibai, Jalam Singh, Pratap Singh and Bhim Singh.

3. PW-1, Sardar Singh, informed this incident to village Chaukidar and thereafter lodged a report Ex. P-1 at the police station at 2.00 p.m. Both Dhania and Bhure died on the spot. Their bodies were sent for post mortem examination and injured persons Hirabai and Jhillibai were sent for medical examination. They were examined by PW-4, Dr. Fateh Singh. The deceased Dhania sustained two stab wounds at his stomach caused by pointed sharp edged weapon and a fracture on left temporal bone caused by hard and blunt object. His post-mortem report is Ex. P-2.

4. Dr. Fateh Singh, PW-4, on performing the autopsy on the dead body of Bhure, found one stab wound at the left chest caused by a sharp pointed object and a fracture of temporal bone. His post-mortem report is Ex. P-3. The police after completing the investigation filed the challan in the Court. The appellants denied the allegations of the prosecution and pleaded self-defence as appellant, Baley Singh appeared and examined as DW-5, and stated that his wheat, Bajara and Urad crops in threshing field near his house were set on fire and thereafter they started throwing stones at his house. On coming out from the house, Bhagat Singh and Jagat Singh shot arrows from bow and in defence, the appellants also shot arrows and in that process one Bathu Singh sustained injury by arrow. The appellants examined five defence witnesses in their defence. Prosecution examined eight prosecution witnesses during trial. The trial Court held guilty of offences under section 302/148 I.P.C. against Balu Singh, Bathu Singh, Nar Singh and Bhal Singh and sentenced them to life imprisonment and fine of Rs. 1000, in default, rigorous imprisonment for one year and six months, and Richhu, Bhangdibai and Nanbai were convicted under sections 302 read with 149 and 148 I.P.C. and sentenced them to undergo imprisonment for life and rigorous imprisonment for one year. Both the sentences were directed to run concurrently.

5. The appellant, being dissatisfied by the judgment and order dated 31-8-1995, filed an appeal before the High Court of Madhya Pradesh against their conviction and sentence passed by the trial Court.

6. The High Court partly allowed Criminal Appeal No. 697 of 1995 by acquitting appellant No. 1, Balu Singh appellant No. 4, Richhu, appellant No. 6, Bhangdibai and appellant No. 7, Nanbai of the offence they were charged and the appeal of the appellants Bathu Singh (appellant No. 1 herein), Nar Singh (appellant No. 2 herein) and Bhal Singh (appellant No. 3) was dismissed.

7. Being aggrieved by the said judgment, the appellants preferred these appeals by way of special leave.

8. We heard Mr. Vidya Dhar Gaur, learned counsel appearing for the appellants and Ms. Vibha Datta Makhija, learned counsel appearing for the respondent.

9. Learned counsel appearing for the appellants submitted that the incident occurred all of a sudden and the appellants had to resort in self-defence as their crops in the thrashing field were set on fire and their house was stoned. When the appellants acted in self-defence, they sustained injuries on their persons, so they immediately went to the police station to seek their assistance. In the meantime, complainant party also reached in the police station and the appellants were detained and put behind the bar. It was further submitted that the investigation made by the prosecution is a tainted one because the police has shown arrest of the appellants after three days of the incident and kept them in illegal detention since the day of the incident, the police has not medically examined the appellants for the injuries they sustained during the incident in spite of their requests. It was also submitted that the prosecution has examined all interested and partisan witnesses and has withheld independent witnesses, though shown to be present on the spot and were injured. The injured witnesses have also not been examined in the Court. Concluding his arguments, learned counsel submitted that the witnesses examined by the prosecution in the Court are not trustworthy, and, therefore, reliance cannot be placed on them and that the prosecution has failed to prove their case beyond any reasonable doubt, therefore, the appellants are entitled for acquittal.

10. Learned counsel appearing for the respondent, *per contra*, submitted that the evidence on record clearly establishes that the appellants, after forming an unlawful assembly, committed murder of both Dhania and Bhuru and also caused injuries to two other persons and they were also armed with deadly weapons and none of the appellants had received any injury during the course of the incident. When the material on record is clearly establishing that the appellants were not acting in self-defence, they are not entitled for acquittal.

11. We have gone through the entire record and judgments rendered by both the Courts. As already noted, the prosecution has examined PW-1, Sardar Singh, PW-2, Jagat Singh and PW-3, Humbai as eye-witnesses of the incident. According to them, when the deceased Dhania reached at his field for digging the well and thereafter the deceased Bhuru for watching the mango crop, Balu Singh (appellant No. 1 in the High Court) gave a lathi blow on the head resulting into fall of deceased Dhania on the ground. Thereafter, Nar Singh shot an arrow piercing in his stomach. Bathu Singh (appellant No. 2 before the High Court) shot an arrow piercing at the chest of the deceased Bhuru and Bhal Singh (appellant No. 4 before the High Court) gave a lathi blow (Denga) on his head whereas Richhu Nanbai and Bhangdibai used the stones in the incident. These three eye-witnesses have also stated that when they and other villagers tried to intervene in the incident, the appellants chased them away. Thereafter PW-1 and PW-2 came to the village and gave information to village Chaukidar and thereafter reached the spot and found Dhania and Bhuru lying dead there.

12. PW-4, Dr. Fateh Singh, had performed the autopsy on the dead bodies of Dhania and Bhuru. The doctor witnessed two stab wounds on the stomach and two fractures of parietal bone of Dhania and one stab injury and fracture of occipital bone on the person of Bhuru. According to him, both the deceased died because of shock and excessive bleeding. PW-4 has also examined Jhillibai who too was assaulted by the accused persons during the course of the incident. He found two diffused swelling on her person. Thus it is seen that the evidence of PW-4, Dr. Fateh Singh, is clearly corroborating the statements of eye-witnesses so far as participation of Bathu Singh (appellant No. 1 herein), Nar Singh (appellant No. 2 herein) and Bhal Singh (appellant No. 3 herein) is concerned. It is significant to note that Dr. Fateh Singh found, in all, four injuries on the person of deceased Dhania *i.e.* two stab wounds, one fracture of left temporal bone and on dissection, he noted one fracture of temporal and parietal bone.

13. So far as the appellants herein are concerned, there is overwhelming ocular evidence on record duly corroborated by the medical evidence and the statement of PW-1, Sardar Singh.

14. Learned counsel appearing for the appellants has also taken us through the statements of PW-1 (Thumlibai), DW-2 (Sukliya), DW-3 (Hirasingh), DW-4 (SDOP Rajendrasingh Kushwah) and DW-5 (Balusingh) examined as defence witnesses. The statements of these DWs are also not helpful to the appellants Bathu Singh, Nar Singh and Bhal Singh because DW-1 has not named any of the deceased or the prosecution witness. DW-2, who is a village chowkidar has not levelled any allegation against the witnesses and the deceased persons about setting fire to their crop. On the contrary, this witness has contradicted the case of the appellants about setting fire to the wheat crop. Likewise, there is absolutely nothing in the statement of DW-3 which could support the defence version. We cannot also draw any inference from the statement of DW-4 who made a vague statement and that no inference can be drawn by this Court that the deceased and the witnesses had set fire on the crop. The statement of DW-5 is also not helpful to the appellants' case.

15. The appellants in our opinion, have not established their plea of private defence by preponderance of probabilities. The appellants have not laid any foundation in cross-examination of the prosecution witnesses as well as in their statements under section 313, Cr. P.C. and by pointing out positive circumstances from the legally proved prosecution evidence which could establish their case of self-defence of property and person by preponderance of probabilities. This Court in catena of cases has held that a right of private defence given by the Penal Code is essentially one of defence or self protection and not a right of reprisal or punishment. It is subject to the restrictions indicated in section 88 which are so important as the right itself. In the instant case, the assault on both the deceased was exceedingly vindictive and maliciously excessive.

Under these circumstances, we are of the opinion that the appellants were not entitled for right of private defence and two persons were done to death by the appellants without there being any imminent danger to their property or lives.

16. There is no evidence on record much less to establish the defence version of acting in self-defence, which is a defence which was set up at a very late stage.

17. For the foregoing reasons, we are of the opinion that the appeals have no merits and are, accordingly, dismissed.

Appeals dismissed.

Yakub Ismailbhai Patel

v.

State of Gujarat

Criminal Appeal No. 62 of 2004

AIR 2004 SC 4209: 2004 AIR SCW 4955

Decided on: 31-8-2004

Coram: **K.G. Balakrishnan, J.**

Dr. AR. Lakshmanan, J.

FACTS

The accused committed murder of one Nizam. The trial court convicted the accused on the basis of evidence of sole eye-witness who was the friend of the deceased and sentenced him to life imprisonment. On appeal the High Court upheld the conviction and sentence. Hence, this appeal before the Supreme Court.

ISSUE

Who is an interested witness? Reliability of a sole witness.

HELD

The testimony of the sole eye-witness is wholly believable and worthy of inspiring confidence but is also sufficient by itself to prove the case against the appellant and that the credibility of this witness has not been impaired in the cross-examination by the appellant. The appellant has failed to establish his case of innocence. On the contrary, the prosecution has proved its case beyond any reasonable doubt. The sole eye-witness cannot be branded as a related or interested witness because he is merely a friend of the deceased. There is nothing significant to infer that there was enmity between himself and accused persons. The testimony of eye-witness cannot be brushed aside. He is believable and does inspires confidence. The appeal thus fails and is dismissed.

Judgment

Dr. AR. Lakshmanan, J.—The present criminal appeal arises out of the judgment and order dated 29-8-2003 passed by the High Court of Gujarat at Ahmedabad in Criminal Appeal No. 327 of 1998 wherein the High Court confirmed the conviction of the Appellant along with two other co-accused for offence under section 302 read with section 34 of the I.P.C. and sentenced them to imprisonment for life.

2. The brief facts of the present case are as under:

On 25-8-1995 at about 13.15 hrs. the Ahmedabad Railway Police received a Vardhi from one Abdulmajid that a knife blow has been inflicted on Nazim at Kankaria Loco Shed. On the strength of the said entry, Police Sub-Inspector went to the scene of occurrence, prepared inquest report of dead body and also drew panchnama of scene of occurrence. In the meantime, at about 17.40 hrs. complaint was given by Munna @ Gheti Mohamadshafi Shaikh. In the said complaint, it is stated that he happens to be a friend of Nizamuddin Ismailbhai (deceased) for the last 15 years and the said Nizamuddin has been allotted one quarter in B scale colony of Kankaria railway colony, but he was not residing there. He gave the quarter to his relative. Nearby the quarter of Nizamuddin, Yakubbhai Patel (accused No. 1) was residing. The Complainant also used to visit the said quarter along with Nizamuddin. On 24-8-1995, there was altercation and quarrel in between accused No. 1 and deceased in respect to the said quarter, as he wanted to get it evicted. On 25-8-1995, the day of the incident, while the said Munna @ Gheti was returning from the house of his friend, somewhere near Kankaria railway colony, he saw accused No. 1 and accused No. 2 along with other person. They were running. There was Jamaiya (kukari) in the hands of accused Nos. 1 and 2. Therefore, he went towards the fuel room of diesel shed, where he saw the dead body of Nizamuddin in a pool of blood lying near the railway track. One Raju was also there. In the inquiry, he could gather from the said Raju that accused Nos. 1 and 2 along with one another person had inflicted injuries on the person Nizamuddin and thus has resulted into death. The said Munna had also seen the injury on the throat and on the face of Nizamuddin.

3. During investigation, police recorded the statements of witnesses, panchanamas were drawn in respect of the clothes of the deceased, discovery of weapons at the instance of the accused persons and post mortem note of the deceased was collected. Incriminating articles were also collected for having scientific examination. Police arrested accused Nos. 1 and 2 and Tapan @ Tondi Shashdhar accused No. 3 on 19-9-1995. After completion of investigation, accused came to be charge-sheeted on 16-12-1995 before the Metropolitan Magistrate, Court No. 5, Ahmedabad. The said charge-sheet was for the alleged offences punishable under sections 302 and 304 of the I.P.C. and section 135 of the Bombay Police Act. It was numbered as Criminal Case No. 2833 of 1995. The Metropolitan

Magistrate, in turn, committed the said Criminal Case No. 2833 of 1995 of his file to the Court of Sessions Ahmedabad on 1-2-1996 and it was numbered as Sessions Case No. 101 of 1996. Charge was framed against all the three accused. They pleaded not guilty to the charges and claimed to be tried.

4. The prosecution, in order to prove the charge against the accused, examined 14 witnesses and also relied on documentary evidence which consisted of FIR, Panchanama of place of incident, recovery of weapons panchanama from the present appellants. The appellants have also examined D.W. 1 Munna @ Gheti Mohammadsami Shaikh and produced documentary evidence.

5. After the prosecution case was over, the appellants were questioned with regard to the evidence led by the prosecution against them and their statements were recorded under section 313 of the Code. In their further statements, all the appellants have denied the alleged part played by them in the commission of the offence. However, they gave application to examine the Complainant Munna @ Gheti Mohammadshafi Shaikh as defence witness.

6. The Additional Sessions Judge, after appreciating the oral and documentary evidence and arguments advanced by the respective counsel for the prosecution as well as the defence, held that on the day of incident *i.e.*, 25-8-1995 all the appellants had common intention to kill the deceased. It was further held that the deceased Nizamuddin died a homicidal death. In the light of this, the Additional Sessions Judge convicted all the appellants and sentenced them, as stated above, which has given rise to the appeal before the High Court. The High Court, after considering the entire evidence and the facts and circumstances of the case, found themselves in complete agreement with the reasoning and findings of the Sessions Judge and dismissed the appeal and gave liberty to the trial Court to proceed against the witness Munna @ Gheti under section 344 of the Cr. P.C. Aggrieved by the order of the High Court, the appellant has preferred the special leave petition before this Court. Leave was granted on 12-1-2004.

7. We heard Mr. Huzefa Ahmadi, learned counsel appearing for the Appellant ably assisted by Mr. Nakul Dewan and Mr. Ejaz Maqbool and Mr. Madhukar, learned Counsel for the Respondent ably assisted by Ms. Sadhana Sandhu and Ms. Hemantika Wahi. We have been taken through the pleadings, the evidence let in and the documents produced by learned counsel appearing on either side.

8. Mr. Huzefa Ahmadi, learned counsel appearing for the appellant, made the following submissions:

(a) the Courts below have relied upon the sole testimony of PW-2 and, therefore, no reliance can be placed on the statement of PW-1;

(b) the Courts have disbelieved the statement of PW-1 and have based the conviction solely on the ocular testimony of PW-2;

(c) No other eye-witness supports the case;

(d) In any event, it is evident that the statements of PW-1 and PW-2, far from establishing their respective presence near the railway tracks are, in fact, contradictory. In order to establish the above contention, learned counsel for the appellant drew our attention to the following extract from the judgment of the High Court.

"Thereafter, he saw the body of deceased Nizamuddin lying in a pool of blood. He saw Raju standing near the body for Nizamuddin. Raju told the witness that Yakub Patel and other accused persons gave blow to Nizamuddin and ran away. Subsequently, Raju and witness went to police station to lodge complaint which is given mark 10/1.

The witness came after some time and he saw the body of Nizamuddin at a distance of 200 ft. from the office. He did not see any blood on way to his office. Munna @ Geti was standing near deceased Nizamuddin before witness went there."

9. According to learned counsel for the appellant, the following is evident from the above extract:

There is clear dichotomy between the statements of PW-1 and PW-2 as regards who was there first at the railway tracks near the body;

If, indeed, the sole eye-witness PW-2 is to be believed, then it is PW-1 who reached the railway tracks first and not *vice versa*. Therefore, PW-1's statement that he had seen three persons running away while he was approaching the railway tracks and that he was told by the PW-2 that said persons killed the deceased is wholly unbelievable.

10. Learned counsel for the appellant further submitted that no T.I. Parade was conducted for accused No. 1. Learned counsel also pointed out the discrepancy between medical and ocular evidence. It was submitted that while the witnesses deposed that the accused had used jamiyas/kukaris which are blunt edged weapons, the medical evidence and the wounds show that sharp edged weapons were used. Learned counsel drew our attention to pages 17, 19, 22 and 23 of Volume-I of the paper-book.

11. It was further submitted that the weapon of offence was alleged to be kukari/jamiya which is a blunt weapon whereas the medical evidence shows that there were as many as 24 wounds caused by the sharp edged weapons. It was, therefore, submitted that the High Court in view of the discrepancy between the medical and ocular evidence ought not to have relied upon the ocular evidence to convict the accused.

12. The learned counsel brought to our notice the following discrepancies in the case of the prosecution:

Statement of PW-2:

> The case of PW-2 is that on the request of the deceased, he accompanied the deceased to his office in order to enable the deceased to file a sick note. However, PW-2 had stated in his deposition that the deceased had not signed the muster roll, which the High Court has recorded as under:
>
> "When they went to diesel-shed on scooter, Nizamuddin did not sign the muster roll".

13. The statement of PW-2, is however, belied by the fact that the muster roll was signed by the deceased. The High Court has recorded this as under:

> "As per muster roll exh. 66 it is clear that on 25-8-1995 the deceased was present on his duty."

14. He would submit that in view of the High Court noting the discrepancy, it ought not to have continued to place reliance on the statement of PW-2.

15. It was further submitted that PW-2 is not an employee of the railway and otherwise not a person who would ordinarily be at the scene of the offence. It was his submission that because the deceased was sick, at 7.30 AM he took the deceased to drop a sick note. The case of the prosecution is that both the persons were at one office for two and a half hours and then in another office for another two and a half hours and were, therefore, together from 12.30 AM to 1.00 PM when the alleged incident took place.

16. According to learned counsel for the appellant, it is inconceivable to believe that:

i. A person who is sick and needs to be taken to office by a friend in order to drop a sick note, will continue to remain present in office;

ii. Even if the deceased had in fact, decided to stay on, it is unbelievable that his friend would continue to remain with him and not attend to his daily work.

iii. Lastly, it is not as if the case of the prosecution is that the deceased had changed his mind about the sick note, or that he was feeling better on reaching his office. PW-2 has stated that the deceased did not sign the muster roll, a fact which has not proved to be untrue.

SCENE OF THE OFFENCE:

17. In the deposition of PW-12, Police Sub-Inspector, the scene of the offence has been stated to be between two railway tracks. According to learned counsel for the appellant, this is contrary to the deposition of PW-2, who states that the deceased was attacked in the diesel-shed 200 meters away. Learned counsel invited our attention to appreciate the deposition of PW-12, the Investigating Officer.

18. He has admitted that Fuel Room, gate of Fuel Room and the tracks of railway are distinct places. He volunteers that though, it may be called distinct, but it is nearby. He has admitted that no blood sample was obtained from the Fuel Room. He has admitted that he has not shown date and time of preparation of report exh. 48 when he reached at Loco Diesel Shed, dead body was not there. Dog squad was available however no trace was found out.

19. According to the learned counsel for the appellant, there is no explanation of how the body came to be found 200 meters away. No investigation was done on that behalf and even the dog squad could not determine the trace. Therefore, it is submitted that the prosecution version is not believable.

No other Eye-witness supports the case:

20. Learned counsel for the appellant submitted that PW-2 in his deposition has stated that there were four other railway employees who were present at the scene of offence and, therefore, their deposition becomes necessary for unfolding the narrative.

21. In the present case, out of the four alleged eye-witnesses, the prosecution only called upon PW-3 and PW-9 to depose as eye-witnesses and even these two eye-witnesses did not support the case of the prosecution. Thus it is submitted that the failure of the prosecution to call all material witnesses leads to an adverse inference against the prosecution under section 114: illustration (g) of the Indian Evidence Act.

THE STATEMENT OF P.W. 1 IS UNRELIABLE:

22. The learned counsel for the Respondent submitted that the statement of PW-1 supports the case in identifying the accused persons. It was also his submission that the statement of PW-1 established the presence of PW-2 at the scene of the offence. According to learned counsel for the appellant the said submission is devoid of merits for the following reasons;

(a) the Courts below have relied upon the sole testimony of PW-2 and, therefore, no reliance can be placed on the statement of PW-1 at this stage;

(b) the Courts have disbelieved the statement of PW1 and have based the conviction solely on the ocular testimony of PW-2;

(c) In any event, it is evident that the statements of PW-1 and PW-2, far from establishing their respective presence near the railway tracks are, in fact, contradictory.

23. The learned counsel for the appellant made two legal propositions for consideration of this Court:

THE TESTIMONY OF A SINGLE EYE-WITNESS MUST BE ENTIRELY RELIABLE FOR A CONVICTION:

24. According to Mr. Huzefa Ahmadi, the test for relying on the testimony of a sole eye-witness is based on the rule of caution, expounded by this Court in a catena of judgments. He placed reliance on the following judgments:

(1) *Joseph* v. *State of Kerala,* (2003) 1 SCC 465 which prescribes that the evidence of other witnesses must corroborate the single eye-witness. AIR 2003 SC 507: 2002 AIR SCW 4933: 2003 Cr LJ 813, Paras 13 and 14.

"When there is a sole witness to the incident his evidence has to be accepted with an amount of caution and after testing it on the touchstone of the evidence tendered by other witnesses or evidence as recorded. Section 134 of the Indian Evidence Act provides that no particular number of witnesses shall in any case be required for the proof of any fact and, therefore, it is permissible for a Court to record and sustain a conviction on the evidence of a solitary eye-witness. But, at the same time, such a course can be adopted only if the evidence tendered by such witness is cogent, reliable and in tune with probabilities and inspires implicit confidence. By this standard, when the prosecution case rests mainly on the sole testimony of an eye-witness, it should be wholly reliable. Even though such witness is an injured witness and his presence may not be seriously doubted, when his evidence is in conflict with other evidence, the view taken by the trial Court that it would be unsafe to convict the accused on his sole testimony cannot be stated to be unreasonable. Particularly, when the trial Court had given cogent reasons to acquit the accused, the High Court ought not to have interfered with the same merely because another opinion is possible and not that the finding concluded by the trial Court was impossible. The High Court did not follow the aforesaid standard but went on to analyse evidence as if the material before them was given for the first time and not in appeal.

(Paras 12 and 13)

(2) *Suresh Chaudhary* v. *State of Bihar*, (2003) 4 SCC 128: AIR 2003 SC 1981: 2003 AIR SCW 1483: 2003 Cr LJ 1717: 2003 AIR Jhar HCR 555.

In the above case, this Court while setting aside the sentence of conviction of two Courts below advocate the Rule of Caution.

(3) The Rule of Caution has also been advocated by this Court in *Shahbuddin Abdul Kahlik Shaikh* v. *State of Gujarat*, 1995 Supp (2) SCC 441.

(4) The aforesaid judgments are based on the judgment of this Court in *Vadivelu Thevar* v. *State of Madras*, AIR 1957 SC 614 wherein this Court has divided the appreciation of evidence into three categories, namely: (1) wholly reliable; (2) wholly unreliable; and (3) Neither wholly reliable nor wholly unreliable and thereafter stated that 'it becomes the duty of the Court to convict, if it is satisfied that the testimony of a single witness is entirely reliable." 1957 Cr LJ 1000.

(5) The above view emerges from the view of the Privy Council in *Mohamed Sugal Esa* v. *The King*, AIR 1946 PC 3.

"In England where provision has been made for the reception of unsworn evidence from a child it has always been provided that the evidence must be corroborated in some material particular implicating the accused. But in the Indian Act there is no such provision and the evidence is made admissible whether corroborated or not. Once there is admissible evidence a Court can act upon it, corroboration, unless required by statute, goes only to the weight and value of the evidence. It is a sound rule in practice not to act on the uncorroborated evidence of a child, whether sworn or unsworn, but this is a rule of prudence and not of law."

25. Mr. Ahmadi, in view of the above judgments and of the facts stated above, submitted that the statement of PW-2, sole eye-witness fails to meet the test of 'entire reliability' and therefore, cannot be the basis for convicting the accused and that the testimony of PW-2 to the effect that there were other employees present at the time of the occurrence is belied by the evidence of two of the said employees, who have deposed otherwise, and, therefore, the evidence of the other two witnesses far from corroborating the sole eye-witness account in fact belies it.

26. The learned counsel for the appellant then concentrated on the second legal proposition, namely, non-production of material witnesses leads to an adverse inference against the prosecution:

27. It was contended that it is the duty of the prosecution to produce all material witnesses and failure thereof leads to an adverse inference under section 114, illustration (g) of the Indian Evidence Act, 1857.

28. This Court in *Habeeb Mohammad* v. *State of Hyderabad,* (1954) SCR 475 (490) extracting from the judgment of the Privy Council in *Stephen Senivaratne* v. *The King,* AIR 1936 PC 289 stated as under:

> "Witnesses essential to the unfolding of the narrative on which the prosecution is based, must, of course, be called by the prosecution, whether in the result the effect of their testimony is for or against the case for the prosecution."

29. The above two judgments have been relied upon by this Court in the case of *State of Uttar Pradesh* v. *Jaggo* alias *Jagdish,* (1971) 2 SCC 42: AIR 1971 SC 1586: 1971 Cr LJ 1173.

30. It was submitted that while the prosecution is not necessarily required to call upon each and every witness, it is bound to call all witnesses who are material to the unfolding of the narrative and failure to do so, leads to an adverse inference. In the present case, the other two eye-witnesses did not support of the prosecution and it can thus be inferred that the other eye-witnesses would also not support the version of the prosecution and, in these circumstances, the Courts below have erred in relying upon the sole statement of PW-2 for convicting the accused.

31. Concluding his argument, Mr. Huzefa Ahmadi, submitted that the accused have spent over seven years in jail and if this Court is to allow the present appeal, it would only to trite to allow the appeal *qua* accused Nos. 2 and 3 who were unable to approach this Court. For this, the learned counsel for the appellant, relied on the judgment of this Court in *Suresh Chaudhary's* case, AIR 2003 SC 1981: 2003 AIR SCW 1483: 2003 Cr LJ 1717: 2003 AIR Jhar HCR 555, Para 14 wherein relying on precedents, the Court stated as under:

> "This Court in a catena of cases has held where on the evaluation of a case this Court reaches the conclusion that no conviction of any accused is possible, the benefit of doubt must be extended to the co-accused similarly situated though he has not challenged the order of conviction by way of an appeal. [See *Bijoy Singh* v. *State of Bihar,* (2002) 9 SCC 147]. This Court while rendering the above judgment has placed reliance on some other judgments of this Court in *Raja Ram* v. *State of Madhya Pradesh,* (1994) 2 SCC 568; *Dandu Lakshmi Reddy* v. *State of Andhra Pradesh,* (1999) 7 SCC 69 and *Anil Rai* v. *State of Bihar,* (2001) 7 SCC 318 wherein this Court had taken a similar view. Following the above dictum of this Court in the judgments noticed by us hereinabove, we are of the opinion since we have come to the conclusion that no conviction of any accused is possible based on the prosecution case as presented, it becomes out duty to extend the benefit of acquittal in these appeals also to a non-appealing accused, therefore, who is the first accused before the Sessions Court in Sessions Trial No. 417 of 1993 and who was the first appellant before the High Court in Crl. A. No. 88 of 1995 will also be acquitted of all the charges of which he is found guilty by the two courts below."

32. Concluding his argument, learned counsel submitted that the prosecution has failed of prove the case beyond reasonable doubt and, therefore, the accused appellant ought to be acquitted.

33. Learned counsel for the State of Gujarat Mr. Madhukar while justifying the judgments of the Courts below submitted that the body of the evidence produced by the prosecution against the appellant consisted of the following:

1. Testimony of eye-witness to the incident (PW-2);
2. Motive;
3. Evidence relating to Recovery of weapons at the instance of the accused;
4. Medical evidence;
5. Absence of accused from railway duty and their arrest only after 24 days of incident.

34. After narrating the case of the prosecution and the evidence and documents produced, he submitted that it has come in the evidence of PW-1 and PW-2 that both the witnesses were known to the deceased as well as the appellant accused and the testimony of both these witnesses has been relied upon by the trial Court and the High Court to base the conviction of the appellant.

35. He invited our attention to paras 20, 21 and 29 of the High Court's order and paras 50-53 of the Trial Court's order of PW-2 Akbar Khan @ Raju. This witness is an eye-witness to the incident. The two other eye-witnesses who were examined by the prosecution turned hostile during the trial and thus this witness was rendered in the position of being the sole eye-witness. We have perused the evidence of PW-2. It has given in his testimony that on the fateful day of the incident, he escorted the deceased to the railway office in order to enable him to place a sick note in the railway office. PW-2 has specifically stated in that while he has present in the railway office, the appellant along with the co-accused threatened and attacked the deceased with sharp dangerous weapons on his neck. It is the version of PW-2 that on witnessing this ghastly attack, he ran away from the spot out of fear. He came back from the hiding after sometime and saw the dead body of the deceased while PW-2 was near the body. He has stated to have met PW-1. In fact, PW-1 who is also the Complainant was accompanied by PW-2 to the Police Station for lodging of the complaint.

36. The testimony of this witness, in our opinion proves and corroborates the presence of the Complainant PW-1 and *vice-versa*. PW-2 does not claim to have seen the entire attack but has categorically deposed about having seen the initial attack by the appellant and co-accused with sharp-edged weapons on a vital organ of the deceased, namely, the neck.

37. The testimony of PW-2, in our view, is wholly believable and worthy of inspiring confidence but is also sufficient by itself to prove the case against the appellant and that the credibility of this witness has not been impaired in the cross-examination by the appellant. This witness has stuck to his police statement and the subsequent examination-in-chief in Court where he identified the appellant accused as well as the co-accused as the assailants of the deceased. This deposition, in our view, proved the intention of the accused to cause the death of the deceased inasmuch as he deposes that the assault was directed at the neck of the deceased. It is also not the case of the appellant that this witness was inimical to the appellant or that there was a reason for PW-2 to implicate the appellants falsely. The factum of his friendship with the deceased does not reduce PW-2 to the position of being an interested witness.

38. The learned counsel for the appellant has argued before this Court as well as the Courts below that the conduct of this witness in not saving the life of his friend, the deceased, renders him an improbable witness. In our view, the act of this witness in running away to save his own life and not going forward to help the deceased at the time of the incident is a most probable and natural human conduct which most men faced in such situation would resort to. In our view, the conduct of PW-2 in not having the courage to stop three persons armed with deadly sharp-edged weapons is not and cannot be a circumstances or a ground to disbelieve his testimony particularly when the rest of his testimony is tested with cross-examination.

39. Next we analyse the evidence of PW-1 Munna @ Gheti. Our attention was drawn to the various paras in the trial Court's order and the High Court's order of this witness. PW-1's evidence was relied upon by the trial Court and also by the High Court. The most important feature of the testimony of this witness is that he corroborates the presence of the eye-witness PW-2 at the spot. It is submitted that in face of the specific deposition of this witness, the PW-2 was present at the spot the doubts sought to be raised by the appellant in receipt of the sick note of the deceased and the subsequent staying back at the office are rendered irrelevant and insignificant. PW-1 has deposed that he was known to the deceased and the appellant and that there were altercation on 24-8-1995 between the appellant and the deceased in respect of the railway quarter. It is the version of this witness that on the day of the incident he saw the present appellant running away and also saw the deceased in the pool of blood. Raju was present there. PW-1 has deposed as prosecution witness that while he was returning from railway colony after meeting his friend at about 12.00 noon accused Nos. 1 and 2 and one another were being seen by him, they were running away. PW-1 has identified the appellants and the co-accused in the Court. Thus, it is clear from the testimony of Munnabhai @ Geti as a prosecution witness that although he is not an eye-witness of the incident, yet he throws light on the conduct of the accused on the day of the incident around the time of incident. His testimony together with the testimony of Investigating Officer corroborates the presence of PW-2 at the place of the incident.

40. Significantly this witness, later on filed an affidavit wherein he had sworn to the fact that whatever he had deposed before Court as PW-1 was not true and it was so done at the instance of Police.

41. The averments in the affidavits are rightly rejected by the High Court and also the Sessions Court. Once the witness is examined as a prosecution witness, he cannot be allowed to perjure himself by resiling from testimony given in Court on oath. It is pertinent to note that during the intervening period between giving of evidence as PW-1 and filing of affidavit in Court later he was in jail in a narcotic case and that the accused persons were also fellow inmates there.

42. It was argued by the learned counsel for the appellant that no identification parade was conducted for the accused. The Investigating Officer has stated in his testimony that the test identification parade was not necessary in the instant case. This apart, both the witnesses PW-1 and 2 have categorically stated in their deposition that they knew the appellant from the past.

RECOVERY

43. It is seen from the records that a weapon of offence has been recovered at the instance of the appellant from his own house. The testimony of the panch witness PW-6 in respect of the recovery and the appellant's identify therein has remained unshaken during extensive cross-examination and blood stains were also on the said weapon recovered at the instance of the accused.

MEDICAL EVIDENCE

44. We shall now see the medical evidence. There were as many as 24 injuries on the dead body of the deceased. The High Court says that all injuries were *ante*-mortem in nature an death was caused in this case due to haemorrhage and shock as a result of multiple injuries sustained and that the injuries were caused by sharp-edged and tipped penetrating weapon/weapons. After referring to the Muddamal articles Kukari and knives, the doctor has observed that the injury could be caused by mudammal articles kukari and knives. The High Court also specifically held that the ocular version in this case is not at the loggerheads with the medical evidence.

45. Certain discrepancies were pointed out by learned counsel for the appellant at the time of arguments. The learned counsel for the State while answering the said submission of the counsel for the appellant submitted that according to PW-2, the duration of attack which he witnessed before he ran away took place at the office and that there is evidence on record that blood was found at the spot where PW-2 states that he had witnessed the armed attack upon the deceased.

The presence of blood at the spot where PW-2 states the attack had taken place establishes the correctness of the version of this witness. In such an event, the mere failure to explain the presence of the dead body at an adjoining place does not disprove or contradict the prosecution case and in our opinion is certainly not fatal to the prosecution case.

46. Learned counsel for the State also made certain submissions on law and, in particular, the testimony of single eye-witness. Learned counsel for the State relied upon the legal principles as laid down in *Shivaji Sahabrao Bobade* v. *State of Maharashtra,* (1973) 2 SCC 793: AIR 1973 SC 2622: 1973 Cr LJ 1783, para 19 (three-Judge Bench) wherein it has been held as follows:

> "...Even if the case against the accused hangs on the evidence of a single eye-witness it may be enough to sustain the conviction given sterling testimony of a competent, honest man, although as a rule of prudence Courts call for corroboration. It is a platitude to say that witnesses have to be weighed and not counted since quality matters more than quantity in human affairs..."

47. The legal position in respect of the testimony of a solitary eye-witness is well-settled in a catena of judgments inasmuch as this Court has always reminded that in order to pass conviction upon it, such a testimony must be of a nature which inspires the confidence of the Court. While looking into such evidence this Court has always advocated the Rule of Caution and such corroboration from other evidence and even in the absence of corroboration if testimony of such single eye-witness inspires confidence then conviction can be based solely upon it. In the case on hand, the testimony of the solitary eye-witness stands corroborated by other circumstances and evidences and more particularly PW-1 whose testimony has been relied upon by both the Courts.

48. Learned counsel for the State next answered the submission of the learned counsel for the appellant in regard to the non-production of material witnesses. According to him, the witnesses which were necessary should unfold the narrative of the incident were cited and examined as witnesses. Two of the witnesses to the prosecution case present at the spot turned hostile. In such a scenario, it cannot be said that the prosecution must suffer adverse inference for any further non-production. It is not the case of the appellant that there were certain witnesses who were cited as witness in the charge-sheet but were later on dropped as witnesses by the prosecution during the trial. It was also pointed out to us and is pertinent to mention that once of the witnesses before the trial Court had been granted police protection by the trial Court on the ground of threats from the accused persons.

49. In our opinion, the appellant has failed to establish his case of innocence. On the contrary, the prosecution has proved its case beyond any reasonable doubt. We are of the opinion that the depositions that was given on record, namely, Akbar Khan @ Raju can be said to be reliable and that there is no reason to disbelieve him so far as the ocular aspect of the prosecution case is concerned. The witness Akbar Khan cannot be branded as a related or interested witness because he is merely a friend of the deceased. There is nothing significant to infer that there was enmity between himself and accused persons. His conduct appears to be consistent and natural in accompanying the deceased to his office at locoshed on the date of the incident thus the testimony of eye-witness Akbar Khan @ Raju cannot be brushed aside. He is believable and does inspires confidence.

50. Learned counsel for the appellant pointed out certain discrepancies which, in our opinion are trivial in nature but such discrepancies would not affect the case of conviction imposed on the appellant. The deposition of Dr. Patil who conducted the autopsy is worth to mention. There were in all 24 external injuries and 3 internal injuries on the head, chest and abdomen region. According to him, the injuries were caused by sharp edged deep penetrating weapons the victim had sustained multiple injuries and owing to the same there was haemorrhage which ultimately resulted into his death.

51. The cumulative effect of injuries found on the dead body were sufficient in the ordinary course of nature to cause death and the injury found out on the neck, a vital part of the body alone could have caused death. The evidence of the witnesses and the evidence on record sufficiently and convincingly upholds the narrative of the guilt of the appellant.

52. We, therefore, find ourselves in complete agreement with the reasoning and findings of the learned trial Judge and of the High Court. Therefore, the present appeal deserves to be dismissed and accordingly it is dismissed.

53. Before taking leave of the case, we would like to advert to the argument of the learned counsel for the appellant on the question of sentence. He submitted that the accused had spent over seven years in Jail. He relied on the judgment of this Court in *Suresh Chaudhary* v. *State of Bihar,* AIR 2003 SC 1981: 2003 AIR SCW 1483: 2003 Cr LJ 1717: 2003 AIR Jhar HCR 555. The above judgment is to the effect that if no conviction of any accused is possible, the benefit of doubt must be extended to the co-accused similarly situated though he has not challenged the order of conviction by way of an appeal.

54. In the instant case, we have come to the conclusion that the conviction and sentence imposed by the Courts below are correct and therefore the acquittal is not possible. We also hold that the prosecution has proved the case beyond any reasonable doubt. It is true that an order of sentence purely falls in the realm of judicial discretion and the prosecuting State is only duty bound to endeavour that the guilty had tried and convicted in accordance with law.

55. In the present case, the guilt of the appellant has been convincingly established. We are, therefore, unable to countenance the submission made by the learned counsel for the appellant on the submission of sentence.

56. The appeal fails and is therefore dismissed. The appellant to serve the remaining period of sentence.

Appeal dismissed.

Panchanan Mishra

v.

Digambar Mishra

Criminal Appeal Nos. 107-108 of 2005 [arising out of Spl. Leave Petn. (Cri.) Nos. 3315-3316 of 2004
AIR 2005 SC 1299

Decided on: 17-1-2005

Coram: **Ashok Bhan, J.**
Dr. AR. Lakshmanan, J.

FACTS:

The six accused persons are charged to commit murder. Among them two are absconding, one was not granted bail and other three were granted bail by the High court. Against the order granting bail the appellant filed appeal before the Supreme Court by special leave.

ISSUE:

Considerations in granting bail.

HELD:

There cannot be an inexorable formula in the matter of granting bail. The facts and circumstances of each case will govern the exercise of judicial discretion in granting or cancelling bail. The object underlying the cancellation of bail is to protect the fair trial and secure justice being done to the society by preventing the accused who is set at liberty by the bail order from tampering with the evidence in heinous crime. Once a person is released on bail in serious criminal cases where the punishment is quite stringent and deterrent the accused in order to get away from the clutches of the same indulge in various activities like tampering with the prosecution witnesses threatening the family members of the deceased victim and also create problems of law and order situation. In the instant case looking into the gravity of the crime, apprehension of tampering with the evidence and threats to the life of the complainant and other witnesses given by the accused, the High Court did not take into proper account the grave apprehension of the prosecution that there was a likelihood of the accused persons tampering with the prosecution witnesses. The appeals are allowed and the order passed by the High Court in granting bail stands set aside and cancelled.

Judgment

Dr. AR. LAKSHMANAN, J.—Leave granted in both the Special Leave Petitions.

2. Two Special Leave Petitions being Nos. 3315 and 3316 of 2004 were filed against the impugned non-speaking orders passed by the High Court of Patna in Criminal Appeal Nos. 50 of 2004 and 62 of 2004 granting the bail to accused Nos. 1 to 3 without considering the criminal history of the accused, the evidence available against them, the threats to the life of the complainant/appellant and his family members and likelihood to abscond from the criminal courts of justice and rendering the fair trial impossible. There are six accused in this case. They are:

1. Mahendra Mishra (no bail granted);
2. Rajendra Mishra and Jitendra Mishra (bail granted);
3. Digambar Mishra (bail granted);
4. Nagendra Mishra; and
5. Gopal Mishra (absconding/not on trial).

3. All the above accused persons have been charged for being members of an unlawful assembly and committing murder of Sunil Kumar Mishra and Chandra Shekhar Mishra and attempt to commit murder of Manoj Kumar Mishra, Anil Kumar Mishra and Panchanan Mishra. The accused were armed with the guns and they surrounded the brothers and the complainant/appellant. Digambar Mishra fired from his licensed gun at Sunil Kumar Mishra who fell down. Mahendra Mishra fired at Chandra Shekhar Mishra who also fell down. Gopal Mishra fired three shots from his country-made pistol on the complainant/appellant and the complainant managed to run towards his house raising an alarm. The complainant brought the two injured sons on a thela to Sardar Hospital, Munger but they died before any medical help could be given to them and they were declared dead. One of the deceased was an advocate, another was lecturer and one was appointed auditor.

4. The motive of the murder was on account of the occurrence which took place that the complainant/appellant had sold a land to Ramachandra Yadav and the accused persons felt annoyed at it and tried to grab those lands on the strength of their muscle power and there is also a litigation pending between the parties. Anil Mishra was also injured.

5. The accused Digambar Mishra, Rajendra Mishra, Jitendra Mishra and Mahendra Mishra were sent for trial and two accused, namely, Gopal Mishra and Nagendra Mishra were shown as absconded and did not turn up during the whole trial. The proceedings in respect of accused Nagendra Mishra and Gopal Mishra were separated *vide* order dated 20-11-2002 and the case of the rest of the accused was committed to the Court of Session.

6. The prosecution examined four eye-witnesses PW-1, PW-2, PW-4 and PW-5, who is an independent witness and whose house is adjacent to the house of the complainant. During the trial, it was established that PWs-1, 2, 4 and 5 are the natural and probable witnesses and their testimony was amply corroborated with each other. The identity of the accused persons during the cross-examination was also established. There is no dispute with reference to the place of occurrence, the time of occurrence and the manner of occurrence. The direct evidence of the eye-witnesses was corroborated by the medical evidence and the motive of the crime was also established. The presence of the eye-witnesses was also established at the time of occurrence. It was also proved that there was a *Satya Narayan Puja* at the house of the complainant before the occurrence.

7. The trial Court, on the basis of the evidence available, came to the conclusion that there is satisfactory evidence that Digambar Mishra instigated to commit the murder and at that point of time the common intention was developed and in pursuance of that common intention of the accused they fired at two deceased. They had also common intention to murder other persons available there and they fired on the complainant PW-2 and PW-1.

8. The trial Court convicted and sentenced the accused Mahendra Mishra, Rajendra Mishra and Jitendra Mishra for the offence under sections 148, 302 read with 34, 307 read with 34, I.P.C. and section 27 of the Arms Act. The accused Digambar Mishra was convicted and sentenced under section 109 read with section 302 and under section 307, I.P.C.

9. The criminal appeals were filed by the accused before the High Court. The High Court ordered the release of Digambar Mishra on bail in Criminal Appeal No. 50 of 2004 *vide* order dated 23-1-2004 and the other two accused, namely, Rajendra Mishra and Jitendra Mishra vide impugned order dated 30-1-2004 in Criminal Appeal No. 62 of 2004.

10. The non-speaking order passed by the High Court in Criminal Appeal No. 50 of 2004 and 62 of 2004 read thus:—

"In Criminal Appeal No. 50 of 2004

Issue notice and call for the lower court records.

On the point of bail, counsel submits that the appellant has been convicted under sections 302 and 307 with the aid of section 109 of the Penal Code. The prayer for bail is opposed on behalf of the informant, who has appeared on his own.

In the facts and circumstances, during pendency of this appeal, the appellant (Digambar Mishra) shall be released on bail on furnishing bond of Rs. 10,000 (ten thousand) with two sureties of the like amount each to the satisfaction of the trial Court *i.e.,* 3rd Addl. Sessions Judge, Munger in Sessions Trial No. 730 of 2002.

The realization of fine shall also remain stayed till disposal of the appeal.

In Criminal Appeal No. 62 of 2004

Issue notice and call for the records.

On the point of bail, counsel submits that the appellants are not assailants of the deceased. The prayer is opposed on behalf of the informant who has appeared on his own, and submits that from the evidence of PW-1 it will appear that these appellants had assaulted him.

In the facts and circumstances, during pendency of this appeal appellants namely Rajendra Mishra and Jitendra Mishra are ordered to be released on bail on their furnishing bail bonds of Rs. 10,000 with two sureties of the like amount each to the satisfaction of the trial Court *i.e.,* 3rd Addl. Sessions Judge, Munger in Sessions Trial No. 730/2002."

11. A reading of the above non-speaking order would only show the total non-application of mind by the Court to the gravity of the crime, the apprehension of tampering with the evidence and threats to the life of the complainant and other witnesses given by the accused. The High Court passed the impugned order in a mechanical fashion without proper application of mind and without going into the merits and evidence on record against the accused persons. The High Court failed to see and appreciate that the respondents herein who are the main accused Nos. 1 to 3 are the master-minds behind the crime committed. The High Court has not considered the material evidence available on record against the accused which *prima facie* establish the criminal liability of the respondents. The High Court also failed to see that the learned Sessions Judge, after taking into consideration, the seriousness and the gravity of the crime convicted the accused for the crime. This apart, three other vital factors have also been not taken note of by the High Court. They are the evidence of PWs-1, 2, 4 and 5 who are the eye- witnesses and whose testimony was amply corroborated with each other. Secondly, the identity of the accused persons during the cross-examination was also established. Thirdly, the direct evidence of the eye-witnesses was corroborated by the medical evidence and the motive of the crime was also established. The trial Court has held that there is satisfactory evidence that Digambar Mishra instigated to commit the murder and at that point of time and in pursuance of that common intention of the accused they fired at the two accused. The High Court also has not taken into account the several complaints and information reports before the trial and to the Police Authorities stating that the accused have killed his two sons out of six, the three accused were arrested and remanded to jail and other accused are absconding and evading their arrest and that one of the accused Digambar Mishra who is on bail has confirmed the group of criminals and comes to the house of the appellant and gives threatening to the eye-witnesses of the said order in order to pressurize them not to pursue the criminal case against them and that whenever these accused persons visit the house of the appellant, they are always armed with their guns.

12. The learned counsel for the respondent submitted that respondent No. 1 had already undergone 12 months of sentence, respondent Nos. 1 and 2 in Special Leave Petition No. 3316 of 2004 had already undergone 22 months of sentence approximately each and that the respondents have a meritorious case in criminal appeal and accordingly, the High Court while admitting the appeal have released the respondents on bail subject to certain conditions. It is further submitted that subsequent to the grant of bail order, there is no instance on record that the respondents have misused their release on bail and, therefore, there is no question of the respondents either trying to interfere with the course of justice or the attempt to tamper with the evidence or witnesses or to threaten or indulge in similar activities which would hamper the smooth investigation of trial. He would further submit that Annexure P2, an Information Petition No. 872(J) of 2004 under section 39 of the Cr. P.C. made by the appellant to the Court of CJM, Munger cannot be pressed into service and be made a ground for cancellation of bail granted by the High Court.

13. We have given our careful consideration on the rival submissions made by the counsel appearing on either side. The object underlying the cancellation of bail is to protect the fair trial and secure justice being done to the society by preventing the accused who is set at liberty by the bail order from tampering with the evidence in heinous crime and if there is delay in such a case the underlying object of cancellation of bail practically loses all its purpose and significance to the greatest prejudice and the interest of the prosecution. It hardly requires to be stated that once a person released on bail in serious criminal cases where the punishment is quite stringent and deterrent the accused in order to get away from the clutches of the same indulge in various activities like tampering with the prosecution witnesses threatening the family members of the deceased victim and also create problems of law and order situation.

14. In *Gurcharan Singh* v. *State (Delhi Administration)*, AIR 1978 SC 179: 1978 Cr LJ 129, this Court has observed that while granting bail the Court has to consider the nature and gravity of the circumstances in which the offence is committed, the position and status of the accused with reference to the victim and witnesses, the likelihood of the accused fleeing from justice, of repeating the offence, of jeopardizing his own life being faced with a grim prospect of the possible conviction in the case, of tampering with witness, the history of the case as well as of its investigation and other relevant grounds. It was further observed by this Court that the Sessions Judge did not take into proper account the grave apprehension of the prosecution that there was a likelihood of the accused persons tampering with the prosecution witnesses. In the peculiar nature of the case revealed from the allegations and the position of the accused in relation to the eye-witnesses it was incumbent upon the Sessions Judge to give proper weight to the serious apprehension of the proper case with regard to the tampering with the eye-witnesses, which was urged before him in resisting the application for bail.

15. In *State through the Delhi Administration* v. *Sanjay Gandhi,* AIR 1978 SC 961, this Court observed as under:

> "..........providing by the test of balance of probabilities that the accused has abused his liberty or that there is a reasonable apprehension that he will interfere with the course of justice is all that is necessary in order to succeed in an application for cancellation of bail."

16. In *Dolat Ram* v. *State of Haryana,* (1995) 1 SCC 349, it was observed by this Court as under:

> "Very cogent and overwhelming circumstances are necessary for an order directing the cancellation of the bail, already granted. Generally speaking, the grounds for cancellation of bail, broadly (illustrative and not exhaustive) are: interference or attempt to interfere with the due course of administration of justice or evasion or attempt to evade the due course of justice or abuse of the concession granted to the accused in any manner. The satisfaction of the Court, on the basis of material placed on the record of the possibility of the accused absconding is yet another reason justifying the cancellation of bail. However, bail once granted should not be cancelled in a mechanical manner without considering whether any supervening circumstances have rendered it no longer conducive to a fair trial to allow the accused to retain his freedom by enjoying the concession of bail during the trial. These principles, it appears, were lost sight of by the High Court when it decided to cancel the bail, already granted. The High Court it appears to us overlooked the distinction of the factors relevant for rejecting bail in a non-bailable case in the first instance and the cancellation of bail already granted."

17. Learned counsel for the respondent cited two decisions being *Dolat Ram* (supra) and *Mehboob Dawood Shaikh* v. *State of Maharashtra,* AIR 2004 SC 2890: (2004) 2 SCC 362, and submitted that bail once granted should not be cancelled in a mechanical manner without considering any supervening circumstances have rendered it no longer conducive to a fair trial to allow the accused to retain this freedom by enjoying the concession of bail during the trial.

He would also further submit the cancellation of bail is a harsh order because it takes away the liberty of the individual granted and is not likely to be resorted to and that this Court in exercise of its jurisdiction under article 136(1) of the Constitution of India does not ordinarily interfere with the grant of cancellation of bail. The argument advanced by learned counsel for the respondent is without substance and devoid of merit and against the consistent view taken by this Court in the judgment reported in *Gurcharan Singh* (supra) and *Sanjay Gandhi* (supra). In the instant case, the accused Digambar Mishra had been found and held guilty under section 109 read with sections 302 and 307, I.P.C. and he was sentenced to undergo rigorous imprisonment for life for the offence under section 109 read with sections 302 and 307, I.P.C. Likewise, the accused Rajendra Mishra,

Jitendra Mishra and Mahendra Mishra have been found guilty under sections 148, 302 read with sections 34, 307 read with section 34, I.P.C. and section 27 of the Arms Act and all of them were convicted and sentenced to undergo rigorous imprisonment for life for the offence punishable under section 302/34, I.P.C. and also sentenced to undergo various other sentences and also to pay the fine to the widows of the deceased.

18. Looking into the gravity of the crime, apprehension of tampering with the evidence and threats to the life of the complainant and other witnesses given by the accused, we are of the opinion that the High Court did not take into proper account the grave apprehension of the prosecution that there was a likelihood of the accused persons tampering with the prosecution witnesses. In the peculiar nature of the case revealed from the allegations and the position of the accused in relation to the eye-witnesses it was incumbent upon the High Court to give proper weight to the serious apprehension of the complainant which was urged before him in resisting the application for bail. The High Court, in our opinion, had failed to properly appreciate the entire position. Therefore, this Court will be justified under article 136 of the Constitution of India in interfering with the discretion exercised by the High Court in granting the bail of the accused persons. The High Court has not bestowed its attention on these above factors apart from others. There cannot be an inexorable formula in the matter of granting bail. The facts and circumstances of each case will govern the exercise of judicial discretion in granting or cancelling bail. The case on hand is one such which would justify our interference under article 136 of the Constitution with a discretion exercised by the High Court in granting bail to the respondents in this case. The appeals are allowed and the order passed by the High Court in granting bail in Criminal Appeal Nos. 50 of 2004 and 62 of 2004 stands set aside and cancelled and the Police Authorities are at liberty to re-arrest the accused and proceed further in accordance with law. Any observation made by us in this order in cancelling the bail will not prejudice the High Court in considering the appeal filed by the accused on its own merits and dispose of the same in accordance with law.

Appeals allowed.

Goa Plast (P) Ltd.

v.

Chico Ursula D'Souza

Criminal Appeal No. 1968 of 1996

AIR 2004 SC 408: 2003 AIR SCW 6803

Decided on: 20-11-2003

Coram: **B.P. Singh, J.**
Dr. AR. Lakshmanan, J.

FACTS:

The respondent issued cheques in favour of the appellant company for payment towards his liability for the amount misappropriated from the funds of the appellant company. The cheque was dishonoured by the bank on the ground that the respondent issued instructions to stop payment. A complaint was filed against the respondent under section 142 of the Negotiable Instruments Act, 1881 for offence committed under section 138 of the Act. The trial court acquitted the respondent holding that the petitioner failed to prove the liability of the respondent. On appeal to the High Court the appeal was dismissed. Aggrieved thereby, the appellant preferred appeal before the Supreme Court.

ISSUE:

1. Liability under section 138 of the Negotiable Instruments Act, 1881.

2. Scope of presumption under section 139 of the Negotiable Instruments Act, 1881.

HELD:

The object and the ingredients under sections 138 and 139 of the Act cannot be ignored. Proper and smooth functioning of all business transactions, particularly, of cheques as instruments, primarily depends upon the integrity and honesty of the parties. In our country, in a large number of commercial transactions, it was noted that the cheques were issued even merely as a device not only to stall but even to defraud the creditors. The sanctity and credibility of issuance of cheques in commercial transactions was eroded to a large extent.

In the instant case, the cheque issued by the respondent has been stopped for payment on his instructions and the cheque was returned to the appellant unpaid. Undoubtedly the respondent has committed an offence punishable under section 138 of the Act and is liable to be punished. The judgments of the High Court and the learned Judicial Magistrate are set aside. One month's time is granted to the respondent to pay a sum of Rs. 80,000 (twice the amount of the cheque) to the appellant. In default thereof, the respondent shall suffer simple imprisonment for six months.

Judgment

Dr. AR. LAKSHMANAN, J.—This appeal is preferred by the appellant/ complainant against the order of the High Court of Judicature at Bombay, Panaji Bench in Criminal Appeal No. 37/1995 whereby the High Court confirmed the order of acquittal dated 25-8-1995 passed by the Judicial Magistrate, First Class in Pvt. N.C. Case No. 149/93/8 for offence punishable under section 138 of the Negotiable Instruments Act.

2. The brief facts leading to the filing of the present appeal are as follows:

The respondent issued 10 post-dated cheques of Rs. 40,000 each in favour of the appellant totalling Rs. 4 lakhs for payment towards the liability of the amount misappropriated from the funds of the appellant-Company. The respondent wrote a letter to the appellant denying liability to pay the aforesaid sum for the reasons given in the letter dated 12-2-1993 (Annexure P-1). The appellant deposited the first cheque for encashment. The said cheque was dishonoured by the Bank on the ground that the respondent had issued instructions to stop payment. The appellant sent a legal notice to the respondent regarding the dishonour of the cheque demanding payment of Rs. 40,000 within 15 days. As the respondent did not comply with the aforesaid notice, a complaint was filed against the respondent under section 142 of the Negotiable Instruments Act (hereinafter referred to as "the Act") for offence punishable under section 138 of the Act. According to the appellant, the respondent/accused was working as Managing Director of the appellant-Company. The services of the respondent were discontinued from the month of July, 1992. The appellant examined its General Manager on their behalf to prove the complaint. The respondent in defence did not examine any witness. The respondent also did not step in the witness box so as to subject himself to the cross-examination. He only brought on record the letter dated 12-2-1993 written by him to the Company. True copy of the advice from the Bank dated 12-4-1993, true copy of the complaint dated 6-3-1996 and true copy of the deposition have been marked as Annexures P-2, P-3 and P-4.

3. The learned Judicial Magistrate, First Class *vide* order dated 25-8-1995 acquitted the respondent holding that the petitioner failed to prove the liability and also holding that the respondent had rebutted the statutory presumption under section 139 of the Act. Aggrieved by the said order, the appellant preferred Criminal Appeal No. 37 of 1995 to the High Court of Judicature at Bombay which also dismissed the appeal holding that the appellant had failed to prove the liability on the part of the respondent to pay the sum in question. Aggrieved by the judgment and order dated 12-1-1996 of the High Court of Bombay in Criminal Appeal No. 37/1995, the present appeal was preferred by the appellant.

4. We heard Shri Dhruv Mehta, learned counsel appearing for the appellant and Shri A.K. Sanghi, learned counsel appearing for the respondent.

5. Shri Dhruv Mehta, learned counsel appearing for the appellant submitted that the presumption has to be rebutted by leading evidence and not by mere explanation or statement and the mere issuance of a cheque in favour of the appellant-Company is sufficient to show that the respondent/accused owes liabilities of the appellant-Company. While construing the provisions of section 138 of the Act, besides the fact that the cheque issued by the respondent was dishonoured, nothing further is required to be proved by the complainant and it is for the accused to rebut the presumption under section 139 of the Act. He would further submit that merely by sending a letter or a communication to the appellant-Company is not sufficient unless and until the presumption is rebutted by leading evidence and that the presumption cannot be said to be rebutted. Shri Dhruv Mehta would further urge that it was incumbent on the respondent/accused to examine Rajan Kinnerkar as the respondent stated in his letter dated 12-2-1993 that Rajan Kinnerkar was responsible for the financial transactions of the Company and, therefore, he is responsible for the unexplained expenditure of the Company's Accounts. It was further contended that as soon as the respondent/accused presented or delivered the cheques to the appellant-Company, he admitted the liability and the cheque on presentation to the Bank being dishonoured the ingredients of section 138 of the Act are satisfied and the accused committed an offence punishable under section 138 of the Act.

6. Shri A.K. Sanghi, learned counsel appearing for the respondent/accused, submitted that the appellant/complainant scrupulously avoided in the complaint and in the examination-in-chief of PW-1 to state the relationship with the respondent/accused and there is also no whisper in the complaint as well as in the evidence led on behalf of the appellant regarding the receipt of the letter dated 12-2-1993. It was further submitted that the appellant has not placed before the trial Court any details or statement as to how the respondent is liable for any dues alleged to be against the respondent. Shri A.K. Sanghi would further submit that mere presentation or delivery of the cheque, in the instant case, to the appellant by the respondent will not amount to acceptance of the debt or liability and on the contrary, the respondent has given the entire history in his letter dated 12-2-1993 before presentation of the cheque in the month of April, 1993 to the Bank. It was further stated that the very letter was drafted by Rajan Kinnerkar and it was prepared, as directed by the appellant, as per the draft and, therefore, the respondent has rightly and specifically disowned the liability of Rs. 4 lakhs much less Rs. 40,000 involved in the instant appeal.

7. Before we advert to the respective contentions of the learned counsel appearing on either side, it is beneficial to quote section 138 and section 139 of the Act as it stood at the relevant time. Sections 138 and 139 of the Act read as under:

> "138. Dishonour of cheque for insufficiency, etc., of funds in the account.- Where any cheque drawn by a person on an account maintained by him with a banker for payment of any amount of money to another person from out of that account for the discharge, in whole or in part, of any debt or other liability, is returned by the Bank unpaid, either because of the amount of money standing to the credit of that account is insufficient to honour the cheque or that it exceeds the amount arranged to be paid from that account by an agreement made with that bank, such person shall be deemed to have committed an offence and shall, without prejudice to any other provision of this Act, be punished with imprisonment for a term which may extend to one year, or with fine which may extend to twice the amount of the cheque, or with both:

Provided that nothing contained in this section shall apply unless—

(a) the cheque has been presented to the bank within a period of six months from the date on which it is drawn or within the period of its validity, whichever is earlier.

(b) the payee or the holder in due course of the cheque, as the case may be, makes a demand for the payment of the said amount of money by giving a notice, in writing, to the drawer of the cheque, within fifteen days of the receipt of information by him from the bank regarding the return of the cheque as unpaid, and

(c) the drawer of such cheque fails to make the payment of the said amount of money to the payee or, as the case may be, to the holder in due course of the cheque, within fifteen days of the receipt of the said notice."

"139. Presumption in favour of holder:—

It shall be presumed, unless the contrary is proved, that the holder of a cheque received the cheque of the nature referred to in section 138 for the discharge, in whole or in part, of any debt or other liability."

8. We have perused the pleadings, annexures, the order passed by the learned Judicial Magistrate and the judgment rendered by the High Court. In our view, the High Court and the learned Judicial Magistrate failed to give effect to section 139 of the Act which creates a presumption unless the contrary is proved that the holder of cheque received the cheque for discharge in whole or in part of any debt or other liability. We have perused the contents of the letter dated 12-2-1993. Neither the said letter is proved nor its contents nor is the document produced in the proceedings of the Court it is pertinent to note that in the said letter, the respondent/complainant did not, however, deny the liability as such but merely shifted it on third person. The veracity of the contents of the letter could only be verified if the contents of the letter were proved. The High Court and the learned Judicial Magistrate have ignored the admission of the liability by the respondent who said that the liability did exist but he was not responsible for it. While considering this, the High Court and the learned Magistrate treated the proof adduced by the respondent, namely, the letter, denying the liability and that some other person is liable as sufficient to rebut the presumption under section 139 of the Act. As already noticed, the appellant examined its General Manager on his side. The respondent did not examine any witness and also did not step in the witness box so as to step himself for the cross-examination. The respondent has brought on record the letter dated 12-2-1993 written by him to the Company.

8A. In our view, the High Court and the learned Judicial Magistrate have clearly misunderstood the object behind section 138 of the Act. Sections 138 and 139 of the Act were enacted in view of the fact that cheques were issued for payment of admitted liability but the drawer used to dishonour the said liability by issuing instructions to the Bank for stop payment. To avoid the aforesaid and to create an element of credibility and dependability, the aforesaid sections were enacted which provide a criminal remedy of penalty if the ingredients of the sections are satisfied. The High Court, in our view, gave an interpretation which would defeat the very purpose for which the provisions were enacted. The impugned judgment wrongly interpreted section 139 of the Act which is a presumption in favour of the holder. Reading the judgment with section 139 of the Act, it would appear that the High Court has read in to section 139 of the Act what is not contained in the section. Many passages of the judgments of the High Court and of the learned Judicial Magistrate are direct off shoot of the wrong interpretation placed upon section 139 of the Act and the High Court and the learned Judicial Magistrate dwelt on extraneous factors and principles in order to bring the present case out of the purview of section 138 of the Act.

9. The High Court while discussing the object of the Chapter dealing with offences relating with dishonour of the cheque and extensively quoting commentary by Author Dr. P.W. Rege, however, has failed to consider the important aspect which is discussed at paragraph 16 which reads as under:

> "It is true that Negotiable Instruments Act has not failed to provide a remedy for the aggrieved party; but the foregoing provisions of the Act lay down a procedure which is in the first place very elaborate and since the remedy would be merely of a civil nature, the process to seek civil justice, in the second place becomes notoriously dilatory. To ensure promptitude in remedy against defaulters, therefore, was the only way in which the element of credibility and dependability could be re-introduced in the practice of issuing negotiable instruments in the form of cheques. The best way to do this was to provide a criminal remedy of penalty, which is just the thing that is sought to be done by the Amending Act."

10. To fulfil the objective, the Legislature while amending the Act has made the following procedure:

"(i) Under section 138 a deeming offence is created.

(ii) In section 139, a presumption is ingrained that the holder of the cheque received it in discharge of liability.

(iii) Disallowing a defence in section 140 that drawer has no reason to believe that cheque would be dishonoured.

(iv) An explanation is provided to section 138 to define the words "debt or other liability" to mean a legally enforceable debt or other liability".

11. If the aforesaid are borne in mind then the findings of the High Court are legally perverse, namely, that section 138 of the Act has application only in the case of transactions involving Mercantile relationship and the second being that the appellant has failed to prove the liability. Paragraph 18 of the judgment of the High Court contains both the findings which reads as under:

> "In this case no evidence or history being traced to show the relationship between the complainant and respondent accused. From the cross-examination it transpired that the respondent accused was working as the Manager of the Factory. Thus, relation were Master and Servant or employee or employer there being no business or commercial or mercantile relation between the parties."

12. The High Court in our opinion, has failed to appreciate that on the facts of the instant case, the liability was a legally enforceable debt or liability as per the explanation to section 138 of the Act therefore, the relationship between the appellant and the respondent was not at all a factor germane to the proceedings for an offence under section 138 of the Act. The liability was legally enforceable debt is clear from the finding of the High Court at paragraph 19 which is quoted below:

> "The Appellant-Company has attempted to short circuit the suit by compelling the accused respondent to pay the amount."

13. Both the Courts, in our view, failed to consider the important aspect as to the stop payment instructions issued by the respondent. Ordinarily, the stop payment instructions are issued to the Bank by the account holder when there is no sufficient amount in the account. In the present case, the reason for stopping the payment, however, can be manifold. It is essential that to issue stop payment instructions, there must be funds in the accounts in the first place. On this aspect, the Courts below have failed to see whether as on the date of signing of the cheque dated 20-7-1992, the date of presentation of the cheque dated 10-1-1993, the date of writing of letter dated 12-2-1993 and the date on which stop payment instructions were issued to the Bank the respondent has sufficient funds in the account. Both the Courts below have held that after issuing the letter, the respondent has stopped the payment, therefore, no *mala fide* can be attributed. It is pertinent to notice that the appellant made an application to the Bank Manager to ascertain whether or not there was sufficient amount in the account for the payment dated 2-6-1995. The learned Judicial Magistrate disallowed the said application without hearing the complainant holding that there is no dispute about the dishonour of the cheque by the accused, therefore, no purpose will be served by the Bank Manager as the dishonour is not in issue. Had the Bank Manager been examined it would have been clear whether the account had sufficient amount to pay the amount of the cheque or not. It would have enabled also to know on what date stop payment order was sent by the drawer to the Bank. The learned Magistrate committed a serious mistake in not allowing the application and the proceedings passed thereon have suffered from serious infirmity going to the root of the matter. The High Court and the learned Judicial Magistrate have also not noticed that the respondent was otherwise admitting the liability when the cheques were being issued. This was sufficient evidence to prove that there was a liability and as per the presumption under section 139 of the Act, the cheques issued, therefore, were towards the liability even as per the version of the respondent. The relevant section which is section 138 of the Act giving the ingredients of the offence. In the opening words of the section it is stated:

> "Where any cheques drawn by a person on an account maintained by him with a bank for payment of any amount of money to any person from out of that account for the discharge in whole or in part, of any debt or other liability."

14. Both the Courts below have ignored the admission of the liability by the respondent who stated that the liability did exist but he was not responsible for it. While considering this, the Courts below treated the proof adduced by the respondent, namely, letter denying liability and that some other person is liable for it, as sufficient to rebut the presumption under section 139 of the Act. The Courts below have also not considered that the accused had admitted that he was the Managing Director of the appellant-company when the liability arose.

15. Another reason given by the Courts below to reject the complaint was that the appellant has suppressed the fact about the letter dated 12-2-1993. In our view, there is no obligation on the part of the appellant to reply to such letter as per the scheme of section 138 of the Act.

16. Certain comments were made by the High Court in regard to the relationship of the parties. For the cases filed under section 142 of the Act for offence committed under the Act the relationship between the drawer and the drawee is not material because the liability admitted is one which can be legally enforced by way of suit.

17. We have perused the complaint also. On the point of pleadings in the complaint, the complainant narrated all the necessary facts required to constitute offence under section 138 of the Act, therefore, there was no question of suppression of facts in the case as held by the learned Judicial Magistrate and the findings endorsed by the High Court. The complainant narrated that the respondent owed the appellant a sum of Rs. 40,000. The appellant has received post-dated cheque for the said amount. The cheque was presented to the Bank and was returned with the remark 'stop payment'. The statutory notice was issued and was received by the respondent. The respondent not having complied with the demand made, complaint was filed.

18. We shall now advert to the rulings cited at the time of hearing. Learned counsel relied upon paragraphs 13 to 16 of the judgment of this Court in the case of *Modi Cements Ltd.* v. *Kuchil Kumar Nandi,* (1998) 3 SCC 249: AIR 1998 SC 1057: 1998 Cr LJ 1397 (three Judge Bench), which read as under:

> "It was, however, contended on behalf of the respondent that the decision in *Electronics Trade and Technology Development Corpn. Ltd.* does not support the appellant as far as the facts that emerged in the present cases inasmuch as the drawer had intimated to the bank on 8-8-1984 to stop the payment whereas the cheques were presented for encashment on 9-8-1994 although the same were drawn on 23-2-1994, 26-2-1994 and 28-2-1994. The learned counsel for the respondent strongly relied upon the following observations in *Electronics Trade and Technology Development Corpn. Ltd.,* AIR 1996 SC 2339: 1996 AIR SCW 840: 1996 Cr LJ 1692.
>
> "Suppose after the cheque is issued to the payee or to the holder in due course and before it is presented for encashment, notice is issued to him not to present the same for encashment and yet the payee or holder in due course presents the cheque to the bank for payment and when it is returned on instructions, section 138 does not get attracted."
>
> (Emphasis supplied)

The learned counsel for the appellant submitted that if the attention of the Court was drawn to the provisions of section 139 of the Act which according to him, had an important bearing on the point in issue, the Court would certainly not have made the above observations. The said section reads as under:

> "139. Presumption in favour of holder.—It shall be presumed, unless the contrary is proved, that the holder of a cheque received the cheque, of the nature referred to in section 138 for the discharge, in whole or in part, of any debt or other liability."

According to the learned counsel if the observations of the Court in *Electronics Trade and Technology Development Corpn. Ltd.*, AIR 1996 SC 2339: 1996 AIR SCW 840: 1996 Cr LJ 1692 to the effect,

> "Suppose after the cheque is issued to the payee or to the holder in due course and before it is presented for encashment, notice is issued to him not to present the same for encashment and yet the payee or holder in due course presents the cheque to the bank for payment and when it is returned on instructions, section 138 does not get attracted."
>
> is accepted as good law, the very object of introducing section 138 in the Act would be defeated.

We see great force in the above submission because once the cheque is issued by the drawer a presumption under section 139 must follow and merely because the drawer issues a notice to the drawee or to the bank for stoppage of the payment it will not preclude an action under section 138 of the Act by the drawee or the holder of a cheque in due course. The object of Chapter XVII, which is instituted as "OF PENALTIES IN CASE OF DISHONOUR OF CERTAIN CHEQUES FOR INSUFFICIENCY OF FUNDS IN THE ACCOUNTS" and contains sections 138 to 142, is to promote the efficacy of banking operations and to ensure credibility in transacting business through cheques, it is for this reason we are of the considered view that the observations of this Court in *Electronics Trade and Technology Development Corpn. Ltd.* in para 6 to the effect "Suppose after the cheque is issued to the payee or to the holder in due course and before it is presented for encashment, notice is issued to him not to present the same for encashment and yet the payee or holder in due course presents the cheque to the bank for payment and when it is returned on instructions, section 138 does not get attracted", does not fit in with the object and purpose for which the above chapter has been brought on the statute-book."

19. Learned counsel relied on paragraph 38 of the judgment of this Court in the case of *Hiten P. Dalal* v. *Bratindranath Banerjee*, (2001) 6 SCC 16: AIR 2001 SC 3897: 2001 AIR SCW 3861: 2001 CLC 1646: 2001 Cr LJ 4647 which reads as under:

> "The burden was on the appellant to disapprove (sic disprove) the presumptions under sections 138 and 139, a burden which he failed to discharge at all. The averment in the written statement of the appellant was not enough. Incidentally the defence in the written statement that the four cheques were given for intended transactions was not the answer given by the appellant to the notice under section 138. Then he had said that the cheques were given to assist the Bank for restructuring (Ext. H). It was necessary for the appellant at least to show on the basis of

acceptable evidence either that his explanation in the written statement was so probable that a prudent man ought to accept it or to establish that the effect of the material brought on record, in its totality rendered the existence of the fact presumed, improbable. [Vide *Trilok Chand Jain* v. *State of Delhi*, (1975) 4 SCC 761]. The appellant has done neither. In the absence of any such proof the presumption under sections 138 and 139 must prevail."

20. Learned counsel also relied on paragraph 7 of the judgment of this Court in the case of *K.N. Beena* v. *Muniyappan*, (2001) 8 SCC 458: AIR 2001 SC 2895: 2001 AIR SCW 4344: 2001 Cr LJ 4745: 2001 CLC 1754 which reads as under:

"In this case admittedly the 1st respondent has led no evidence except some formal evidence. The High Court appears to have proceeded on the basis that the denials/averments in his reply dated 21-5-1993 were sufficient to shift the burden of proof on to the appellant complainant to prove that the cheque was issued for a debt or liability. This is an entirely erroneous approach. The 1st respondent had to prove in the trial, by leading cogent evidence, that there was no debt or liability. The 1st respondent not having led any evidence could not be said to have discharged the burden of proving that the cheque was not issued for a debt or liability, the conviction as awarded by the Magistrate was correct. The High Court erroneously set aside that conviction."

21. Learned counsel placed reliance on paragraph 6 of the judgment of this Court in the case of *Goa Plast (P) Ltd.* v. *Chico Ursula D'Souza*, (2003) 3 SCC 232: AIR 2003 SC 2035: 2003 AIR SCW 1555: 2003 Cr LJ 1723: 2003 CLC 466 which reads as under:

"In the present case the issue is very different. The issue is regarding payment of a post-dated cheque being countermanded before the date mentioned on the face of the cheque. For the purpose of considering the issue, it is relevant to see section 139 of the Act which creates a presumption in favour of the holder of a cheque. The said section provides that:

"139. It shall be presumed, unless the contrary is proved, that the holder of a cheque received the cheque, of the nature referred to in section 138 for the discharge, in whole or in part, of any debt or other liability."

Thus it has to be presumed that a cheque is issued in discharge of any debt or other liability. The presumption can be rebutted by adducing evidence and the burden of proof is on the person who wants to rebut the presumption. This presumption coupled with the object of Chapter XVII of the Act which is to promote the efficacy of banking operation and to ensure credibility in business transactions through banks persuades; us to take a view that by countermanding payment of post-dated cheque, a party should not be allowed to get away from the penal provision of section 138 of the Act. A contrary view would render section 138 a dead letter and will provide a handle to persons trying to avoid payment under legal obligations undertaken by them through their own acts which in other words can be said to be taking advantage of one's own wrong. If we hold otherwise, by giving instructions to banks to stop payment of a cheque after issuing the same against a debt or liability, a drawer will easily avoid penal consequences under section 138. Once a cheque is issued by a drawer, a presumption under section 139 must follow and merely because the drawer issued notice to the drawee or to the bank for stoppage of payment it will not preclude an action under section 138 of the Act by the drawee or the holder of the cheque in due course. This was the view taken by this Court in *Modi Cements Ltd.* v. *Kuchil Kumar Nandi*, (1998) 3 SCC 249. On same facts is the decision of this Court in *Ashok Yeshwant Badave* v. *Surendra Madhavrao Nighojakar*, (2001) 3 SCC 726. The decision in *Modi* case overruled an earlier decision of this Court in *Electronics Trade and Technology Development Corpn. Ltd.* v. *Indian Technologists and Engineers (Electronics) P. Ltd.*, (1996) 2 SCC 739 which had taken a contrary view. We are in respectful agreement with the view taken in *Modi* case. The said view is in consonance with the object of the legislation. On the faith of payment by way of a post-dated cheque, the payee alters his position by accepting the cheque. If stoppage of payment before the due date of the cheque is allowed to take the transaction out of the purview of section 138 of the Act, it will shake the confidence which a cheque is otherwise intended to inspire regarding payment being available on the due date."

22. Reliance was also placed on paragraph 17 of the judgment of this Court in the case of *M.M.T.C. Ltd.* v. *Medchl Chemicals and Pharma (P) Ltd.*, (2002) 1 SCC 234: AIR 2002 SC 182: 2001 AIR SCW 4793: 2002 Cr LJ 266: 2002 CLC 146 which reads as under:

> "There is therefore no requirement that the complainant must specifically allege in the complaint that there was a subsisting liability. The burden of proving that there was no existing debt or liability was on the respondents. Thus they have to discharge in the trial. At this stage, merely on the basis of averments in the petitions filed by them the High Court could not have concluded that there was no existing debt or liability."

23. We are unable to agree with the reasonings adopted by the Courts below. The judgments of the High Court and the learned Judicial Magistrate are set aside. We hold that section 138 of the Act will be attracted in the facts of the case and a case for punishment under the provisions is made out.

24. In the instant case, the cheque issued by the respondent has been stopped for payment on his instructions and the cheque was returned to the appellant unpaid. In view of our discussion in the foregoing paragraphs and on the consideration of the facts and circumstances of the case and the law on the subject, we hold that the respondent shall be deemed to have committed an offence. When the matter was taken up for further hearing on 17-11-2003, learned counsel for the respondent submitted that this Court may consider the case of the respondent and the reason for his inability to pay the amount and may consider imposing lesser sentence by taking a lenient view. We are unable to countenance the said submission for the various reasons stated supra. We have no doubt that the respondent has committed an offence punishable under the provisions of section 138 of the Act and is liable to be punished. The transaction in question took place between the parties in the year 1993, therefore, section 138, as it stood at the relevant time, would be applicable to the present case. Section

138 provides imprisonment for a term which may extend to one year, or with fine which may extend to twice the amount of the cheque, or with both. Section 138 has now been amended and the penalty of imprisonment for a term which may extend to one year has been substituted to two years as provided by the Amending Act of 2002 and the fine which may extend to twice of the amount of the cheque. This has been prescribed as the punishment for the offence under section 138 of the Act.

25. The object and the ingredients under the provisions, in particular, sections 138 and 139 of the Act cannot be ignored. Proper and smooth functioning of all business transactions, particularly, of cheques as instruments, primarily depends upon the integrity and honesty of the parties. In our country, in a large number of commercial transactions, it was noted that the cheques were issued even merely as a device not only to stall but even to defraud the creditors. The sanctity and credibility of issuance of cheques in commercial transactions was eroded to a large extent. Undoubtedly dishonour of a cheque by the Bank causes incalculable loss, injury and inconvenience to the payee and the entire credibility of the business transactions within and outside the country suffers a serious set back. The Parliament, in order to restore the credibility of cheques as a trustworthy substitute for cash payment enacted the aforesaid provisions. The remedy available in a Civil Court is a long drawn matter and an unscrupulous drawer normally takes various pleas to defeat the genuine claim of the payee.

26. We, therefore, grant one month's time from this date to the respondent herein to pay a sum of Rs. 80,000 (twice the amount of the cheque) by way of Demand Draft drawn in favour of the appellant and payable at Goa (in the address given in the paper book). In default thereof, the respondent shall suffer simple imprisonment for six months.

27. In the result, the appeal stands disposed of.

Order accordingly.

State of West Bengal

v.

Babu Chakraborty

Criminal Appeal No. 426 of 1998

AIR 2004 SC 4324: 2004 AIR SCW 4995

Decided on: 2-9-2004.

Coram: **K.G. Balakrishnan, J.**

Dr. AR. Lakshmanan, J.

FACTS:

The respondent was found to be in possession of a huge amount of Heroin. The trial court convicted and sentenced the respondent to 10 years of rigorous imprisonment and imposed a fine of Rs. 1 lakh. On appeal, the High Court acquitted the respondent while making several strictures and observations against the police officials for not complying with certain mandatory provisions under the Narcotic Drugs and Psychotropic Substances Act, 1985 while conducting raids and awarded a compensation of Rs. 1 lakh to the respondent. Aggrieved thereby the State of West Bengal preferred an appeal before the Supreme Court.

ISSUE:

Police atrocities by non-compliance with the mandatory provisions under the Narcotic Drugs and Psychotropic Substances Act, 1985 relating to the recording of information and the ground of belief.

HELD:

There is no evidence or circumstance to show that there was any *mala fides* on the part of the police officers conducting raids. The officers who are discharging their statutory duties cannot be blamed when the action taken by the State Government and the officials concerned are for implementing the objects behind the Act by resorting the check and to direct the raids etc. While discharging their duties, the officials would have violated certain provisions. That does not, in our opinion, enables the High Court to pass strictures against the officials and order compensation. The strictures passed against them are wholly unjustified, and we have no hesitation in expunging the remarks. No compensation can be awarded to the accused in the facts and circumstances of this case. The impugned judgment shall stand in all other respects.

Judgment

Dr. AR. LAKSHMANAN, J.—1. This appeal is preferred by the State of West Bengal and two others to set aside the judgment of the Division Bench of the Calcutta High Court and also for expunging certain strictures passed against appellant Nos. 2 and 3, who belong to the Indian Police Service Cadre and a member of the West Bengal Police respectively. The High Court set aside the order of conviction and sentence passed by Additional Sessions in Sessions Trial No. 29 of 1990 convicting the respondent herein, Babu Chakraborthy, under section 21 of the Narcotic Drugs and Psychotropic Substances Act, 1985 (hereinafter referred as "the Act") and sentencing him for rigorous imprisonment for 10 years and pay a fine of Rs. 1 lakh in default of which one more year of imprisonment is to be undergone.

2. Briefly stated, the case of the prosecution is as under:

On obtaining of secret information, a raid was conducted at the house of the respondent/accused at about 21.45 hours under the supervision of appellant No. 2, K.L. Meena, the then Additional Superintendent of Police, Burdwan, accompanied by appellant No. 3, the Sub-Inspector and other persons and seized of Heroin. The accused was arrested for possession in contravention of section 8(c) of the Act.

3. According to the possession, necessary formalities as envisaged under section 50 of the Act was observed by the raiding Police party. Thereafter, the accused on his own produced 123 packets containing Diacetyl Morphine commonly known as Heroin. The said 13 polythene packets were seized under a seizure list prepared. Witnesses signed the seizure list. Subsequently, seized articles were sealed and labelled. G.D. entry No. 275 at the Police Station was made at 11.30 p.m. by the officer-in-charge of the said Police Station, who was not the member of the raiding party. G.D. entry No. 276 was made at 11.55 p.m. at the same Police Station where the accused was produced and the seized articles were handed over to the Excise Officer. The Excise Officials took charge of the accused for production before the Court. At about 7.00 a.m. on 6-5-1989, O.C. Memari Police Station sent wireless message to section P. Burdwan and other senior officers mentioning full details regarding arrest and seizure on being instructed by P.W. 4. The said message was received by the control room of section P. Burdwan at about 8.00 a.m. At about 4.00 p.m. on the same day, S.P. Burdwan sent a special message to Police, West Bengal, I.B., Crime, Commissioner, Burdwan Division, G.I.G. Burdwan Range, D.M. Burdwan etc., mentioning full details regarding the arrest and seizure.

4. The Additional Sessions Court, Burdwan in S.T. No. 29 of 1990 in Sessions Case No. 16 of 1990 convicted the accused and sentenced to 10 years' rigorous imprisonment and Rs. 1 lakh fine, in default of payment for another one year rigorous imprisonment. The accused preferred Criminal Appeal No. 461 of 1990 before the High Court of Calcutta. The High Court, on 3-10-1997, pronounced the impugned judgment allowing Criminal Appeal No. 461 of 1990 and acquitted the accused. While passing the said order, several strictures and observations were make against appellant Nos. 2 and 3. According to the counsel for the appellant, the said observations and strictures were made by the High Court without giving even an opportunity of being heard to the said appellants to explain their stand. Aggrieved by the impugned judgment, a Special Leave Petition was filed before this Court on 5-1-1998 and leave was granted by this Court on 6-4-1998. Interim stay of the direction regarding payment of Rs. 1 lakh as compensation was also made on 29-1-1998 and continued till date.

5. We heard Mr. Tapas Ray assisted by Ms. A. Subhashini, learned counsel for the appellant and Mr. K.V. Vishwanathan, learned counsel for the contesting respondent.

6. We have been taken through the judgment passed by the Sessions Court and of the High Court and the documents and annexures filed therein and also in this Court.

Mr. Tapas Ray, raised the following contentions:—

1. That the action taken by the appellants charging the offence for offence under section 21 of the Act is justified in the given circumstances. According to him, the ingredients of sections 41(2), 42(1)(2), 50, 51, 52, 54, 55 and 57 of the Act, are complied with. Under such circumstances, the High Court is not justified in setting aside the trial Court's judgment and releasing the accused;
2. That the High Court is not justified in directing the State of West Bengal to pay compensation of Rs. 1 lakh to the respondent reserving liberty to the State Government to realise the same from appellant No. 2, a member of the I.P.S.;

3. That the High Court has omitted to take note of the fact that the action taken by the officers under the Act is in good faith and is protected under section 69 of the Act.

7. Mr. K.V. Vishwanathan, learned counsel for the respondent, submitted that the judgment of the High Court is a well-considered one and that the High Court has found gross violation of the mandatory procedure prescribed in section 42(1) and proviso to section 42(1). Apart from this, several infirmities, inconsistencies and material contradictions as well as non-compliance of other mandatory provisions like sections 55 and 57 of the Act and section 102 of Cr. P.C. have also been found. Therefore, the judgment, by no stretch of imagination, can be characterized as a perverse judgment warranting interference in an appeal against acquittal.

8. Mr. Vishwanathan contended that the views expressed by the High Court on section 42 of the Act finds support from a large number of judgments of this Court and that this Court has held that the provisions of section 42(1) and the proviso to section 42(1) and section 42(2) are mandatory. According to the learned counsel, that any information has to be taken down in writing and that the proviso to section 42(1) of the Act has to be strictly complied with. The reason to believe that a search warrant or authorization cannot be obtained without affording opportunity for the concealment of evidence or facility for the escape of an Offender, has to be recorded with the grounds of his belief and he has to send a copy thereof to the immediate superior, where the search is after sunset and before sunrise. He relied on two judgments of this Court being *State of Punjab* v. *Balbir Singh*, (1994) 3 SCC 299; *State of Punjab* v. *Baldev Singh*, (1999) 6 SCC 172. It was further submitted that great significance has been attached to the mandatory nature of the provisions keeping in mind the stringent punishment prescribed in the Act. Arguing further, the learned counsel submitted that where mandatory provisions are not complied and where independent mahazar witnesses are not examined the accused would be entitled to be acquitted. At the time of hearing, the learned counsel has also pointed out other infirmities found by the High Court. They are: AIR 1994 SC 1872: 1994 AIR SCW 1802: 1994 Cr LJ 3702:

(i) In Exhibit-8, it is stated against Serial No. 2 regarding description of seal wax as West Bengal Excise seal No. Ex. 23 in red sealing wax. But curiously enough on left hand margin of Exhibit-8 a plain rubber stamp impression is seen. There is no such seal in red sealing wax as noted in Exhibit-8 at serial No. 2;

(ii) There is no explanation why the other search witness namely Swapen Samata did not sign on the lebels covering the seized articles being marked as Exhibits-4, 5 and 6;

(iii) PW-2 is wholly incompetent and unreliable witness regarding the search and seizure as in his cross-examination he has admitted that he conducted the search as per the direction of PW-4 without preparing any search Memo;

(iv) There is no explanation what prompted the PW-4 to locate the house of the accused 10 to 15 days prior to the date of raid. There is no answer to the pertinent question that if PW-4 was already in possession of the secret information what prevented him from raiding the house of the accused immediately;

(v) The West Bengal Notification No. 1573 Ex. dt. 5-11-1985 and Notification No. 1574, dt. 5-11-1985 do not show that PW-2 or PW-4 was authorized by the State Government under section 41(2) of the Act;

(vi) There is no evidence to show that the accused was informed of the grounds of his arrest by PW-2 or PW-4 as required under section 52(1) of the Act;

(vii) There is glaring inconsistencies and contradictions in the evidence of PW-2 and PW-4, the seizure list Ex. 7 and the G.D. entry Ex.-1, regarding the search and seizure of the contraband articles from the possession of the accused;

(viii) Nowhere from the evidence on record it appears that PW-1 the O.C. Memari P.S. has complied with the mandatory provisions of section 55 of the NDPS Act or for that matter PW-2 or PW-4 affixed their seals on the seized articles as per Ex. 7 given in custody of PW-1 as recorded in the GD entry as per Ex. 1;

(ix) It appears from the Ex. 10 that the sealed cover containing labelled paper packets were received from the laboratory on 3-8-89 by the Inspector of Excise, Kalan Katwa Range, Burdwan, but this sealed cover has not been produced before the trial Court to establish the identity of the samples seized by the Police;

(x) There was gross violation of section 57 of the NDPS Act, as the PW-4 did not make a full report of all the particulars of such arrest or seizure to his immediate official superior. Further, PW-2 and PW-4 have without any reasonable ground of suspicion, entered and searched the house of the respondent and have vexatiously and unnecessarily arrested him so as to proceed against section 58 of NDPS Act.

9. As far as the expunging of observation is concerned, where the observations are part and parcel of the reasoning, the Court may decline to expunge and further it is not the law that absence of notice alone is a ground for expunge particularly when the officers have appealed to the Court and had an opportunity to be heard.

10. The judgment of this Court in the case of *Lakshkari Ram* v. *Mast Ram Tanta*, (1998) 6 SCC 666; In the matter of: *K.A. Judicial Officer*, (2001) 3 SCC 54; *P.K.. Dave* v. *Peoples' Union of Civil Liberties (Delhi)*, (1996) 4 SCC 262, were cited for the above proposition.

11. Learned counsel for the respondent submitted that this Court in the case of *Daulat Ram* v. *State of Haryana*, (1996) 11 SCC 711 and *Mohd. Zahid* v. *Govt. of NCT of Delhi*, (1998) 5 SCC 419, held that in hearing an appeal against the conviction compensation can be awarded to the accused where ultimately he is acquitted and that this power is also available in the High Court since the High Court is having plenary power and there is no statutory bar. Additionally, the power is also traceable to section 482.

12. Concluding his arguments, Mr. Vishwanathan submitted that though the cases of *Rudul Sah* v. *State of Bihar,* (1983) 4 SCC 141; *Nilabati Behera* v. *State of Orissa,* (1993) 2 SCC 746; *D.K. Basu* v. *State of West Bengal,* (1997) 1 SCC 416, were cases under article 32 and the Court held that compensation for breach of fundamental rights by the Public Officials could be awarded in a proceeding under articles 32 and 226, that principle should be extended to section 482 also that the High Court hearing a criminal appeal should have power to order compensation to the accused for illegal incarceration. Hence, it is submitted that the High Court is perfectly justified in invoking section 482, Cr. P.C. while adjudicating appeal under section 374 read with section 386, Cr. P.C. and in ordering compensation.

13. As the last submission, Mr. Vishwanathan submitted that the respondent has undergone 7 years and 4 months in Jail and that even this Court finds that acquittal by the High Court is incorrect, in view of the period of 7 years and 4 months undergone, may declare the law or point out the lower Courts error, but still may not interfere since special circumstances are shown to exist.

14. As an alternative plea, Mr. Vishwanathan submitted that even if the acquittal is found to be incorrect, this Court following the principles laid down in *Chandra Singh* v. *State of Rajasthan,* (2003) 6 SCC 545: AIR 2003 SC 2889: 2003 AIR SCW 3518, may not direct the respondent to be taken into custody since he has already undergone 7 years 4 months for an alleged possession of 3 gms and 25 mgs of Heroin.

15. We have given our thoughtful consideration to the submissions made by both the learned counsel appearing on either side on facts and also on law. In the instant case, the respondent was charged for the offence under section 21 of the Act for the illegal possession of 3 gms and 25 mgs of Diacotyl Morphine, which is commonly known as Heroin in contravention of section 8(c) of the Act. The case of the prosecution was that PW-4, Additional S.P., received secret information and to work out the secret information, he along with PW-2, S.K. Dutta, went to the house of the respondent on 5-5-1989 and conducted a search of the house of the accused. What is important to notice is that the information was not taken down in writing, as required under law and as rightly contended by the learned counsel for the respondent. The search conducted at 9.45 p.m. after sunset and before sunrise was without complying with the proviso to section 42(1). Section 42(1) and the proviso to section 42(1) and section 42(2) is reproduced hereunder:

> "*42. Power of entry, search, seizure and arrest without warrant or authorisation.*—(1) Any such officer (being an officer superior in rank to a peon, sepoy or constable) of the departments of central excise, narcotics, customs, revenue intelligence or any other department of the Central Government including para-military forces or armed forces as is empowered in this behalf by general or special order by the Central Government, or any such officer (being an officer superior in rank to a peon, sepoy or constable) of the revenue, drugs control, excise, police or any other department of a State Government as is empowered in this behalf by general or special order of the State Government if he has reason to believe from persons knowledge

or information given by any person taken down in writing that any narcotic drug, or psychotropic substance, or controlled substance in respect of which an offence punishable under this Act has been committed or any document or other article which may furnish evidence of the commission of such offence or any illegally acquired property or any document or other article which may furnish evidence of holding any illegally acquired property which is liable for seizure or freezing or forfeiture under Chapter VA of this Act is kept or concealed in any building, conveyance or enclosed place, may between sunrise and sunset,—

(a) enter into and search any such building, conveyance or place;

(b) in case of resistance, break open any door and remove any obstacle to such entry;

(c) seize such drug or substance and all materials used in the manufacture thereof and any other article and any animal or conveyance which he has reason to believe to be liable to confiscation under this Act and any document or other article which he has reason to believe may furnish evidence of the commission of any offence punishable under this Act or furnish evidence of holding any illegally acquired property which is liable for seizure or freezing or forfeiture under Chapter VA of this Act; and

(d) detain and search, and, if he thinks proper, arrest any person whom he has reason to believe to have committed any offence punishable under this Act:

Provided that if such officer has reason to believe that a search warrant or authorisation cannot be obtained without affording opportunity for the concealment of evidence or facility for the escape of an offender, he may enter and search such building, conveyance or enclosed place at any time between sunset and sunrise after recording the grounds of his belief.

(2) Where an officer takes down any information in writing under sub-section (1) or records grounds for his belief under the proviso thereto, he shall within seventy-two hours send a copy thereof to his immediate official superior."

16. In view of the above, section 42(2) also stood violated. The proviso to section 42(1) requires that where an officer has reason to believe that a search warrant or authorization cannot be obtained without affording opportunity for the concealment of evidence or facility for the escape of an offender, he may enter and search such building, conveyance or enclosed place at any time before sunset and sunrise after recording the grounds of his belief.

17. We have perused the evidence led in, in this regard. Neither PW-4 nor PW-2 deposed that they had complied with the procedure under section 42(1) and the proviso to section 42(1) and section 42(2) before they conducted the search. It is alleged by them that on search certain Polythene Bags containing Heroin were recovered. According to them, two independent witnesses of the locality Swapan Kumar Samanta and Ramkaran Prasad were taken and they witnessed the search. But unfortunately, these witnesses were not examined and no attempts were made to summon them at the trial. In fact, PW-2-S.K. Dutta, on a specific question in cross-examination, deposed that no search memo was prepared and, PW-4 K.L. Meena said he does not remember if any search memo was prepared. Further, it is alleged that they came to Memari P.S. at 11.30 p.m. and Ex. 1 G.D. Entry was prepared. This G.D. Entry shows that the seized articles were recovered from the bedroom of the accused. The accused was also arrested on 5-5-1989. Thereafter, the case was made over to PW-3 and after receiving the report from the Central Public Health and Laboratories, the accused was sent up for trial. The trial Court convicted the accused and punished the respondent for offences under section 21 of the Act and sentenced him to undergo 10 years' rigorous imprisonment and pay a fine of Rs. 1 lakh.

18. The accused filed an appeal in the High Court and the High Court, after finding violation of section 42(1), proviso to section 42(1) and 42(2) of the NDPS Act and after finding several discrepancies acquitted the respondent and awarded compensation of Rs. 1 lakh. Strictures have also been passed on PW-4 and PW-2 and direction to the Magistrate to prosecute PW-4 and PW-2 was ordered.

19. As noticed earlier, the views of the High Court on section 42 of the Act finds support from a large number of judgments of this Court.

20. In the case of *State of Punjab* v. *Balbir Singh*, (1994) 3 SCC 299, a Bench of two-Judges of this Court observed as under:

> "Under section 42(1), the empowered officer if has a prior information given by any person, that should necessarily be taken down in writing. But if he has reason to believe from personal knowledge that offences under Chapter IV have been committed or materials which may furnish evidence of commission of such offences are concealed in any building etc., he may carry out the arrest or search without a warrant between sunrise and sunset and this provision does not mandate that he should record his reasons of belief. But under the proviso to section 42(1), if such officer has to carry out such search between sunset and sunrise, he must record the grounds of his belief.

To this extent, these provisions are mandatory and contravention of the same would affect the prosecution case and vitiate the trial.

(3) Under section 42(2), such empowered officer who takes down any information in writing or records the grounds under proviso to section 42(1) should forthwith send a copy thereof to his immediate official superior. If there is total non-compliance of this provision, the same affects the prosecution case. To that extent, it is mandatory. But if there is delay whether it was undue or whether the same has been explained or not, will be a question of fact in each case."

21. In the case of *State of Punjab* v. *Baldev Singh*, (1999) 6 SCC 172, a Constitution Bench of this Court observed in paragraphs 9 and 10 as under:

> "Sub-section (1) of section 42 lays down that the empowered officer, if has a prior information given by any person, he should necessarily take it down in writing and where he has reason to believe from his personal knowledge that offences under Chapter IV have been committed or that materials which may furnish evidence of commission of such offences

are concealed in any building etc., he may carry out the arrest or search, without a warrant between sunrise and sunset, and he may do so without recording his reasons of belief.

The proviso to sub-section (1) lays down that if the empowered officer has reason to believe that a search warrant or authorisation cannot be obtained without affording opportunity for the concealment of evidence or facility for the escape of an offender, he may enter and search such building, conveyance or enclosed place, at any time between sunset and sunrise, after recording the grounds of his belief. *Vide* sub-section (2) of section 42, the empowered officer who takes down information in writing or records the grounds of his belief under the proviso to sub-section (1), shall forthwith send a copy of the same to his immediate official superior. Section 43 deals with the power of seizure and arrest of the suspect in a public place. The material difference between the provisions of section 43 and section 42 is that whereas section 42 requires recording of reasons for belief and for taking down of information received in writing with regard to the commission of an offence before conducting search and seizure. Section 43 does not contain any such provision and as such while acting under section 43 of the Act, the empowered officer has the power of seizure of the article etc., and arrest of a person who is found to be in possession of any narcotic drug or psychotropic substance in a public place where such possession appears to him to be unlawful."

22. Great significance has been attached to the mandatory nature of the provisions, keeping in mind the stringent punishment prescribed in the Act. This Court has attached great importance to the recording of the information and the ground of belief since that would be the earliest version that will be available to a Court of law and the accused while defending his prosecution. This Court also held that failure to comply with section 42(1), proviso to section 42(1) and section 42(2) would render the entire prosecution case suspect and cause prejudice to the accused.

23. In the cases of *Abdul Rashid Ibrahim Mansuri* v. *State of Gujarat,* (2000) 2 SCC 513; *Koluttumottil Razak* v. *State of Kerala,* (2000) 4 SCC 465; *Beckodan Abdul Rahman* v. *State of Kerala,* (2002) 4 SCC 229 and in the case of *Chhunna* alias *Mehtab* v. *State of Madhya Pradesh,* (2002) 9 SCC 363, this Court has held that the non-compliance of the provisions of the proviso to section 42 of the Act which is mandatory, the action was held illegal and the conviction of the accused was set aside. This Court also held that the onus to prove compliance lies on the prosecution and in the absence of any prosecution evidence about the compliance with the mandatory procedure, the presumption would be that the procedure was not complied with.

24. In the case of *Saiyad Mohd. Saiyad Umar Saiyad* v. *State of Gujarat,* (1995) 3 SCC 610, this Court held that the prosecution is obliged to give evidence of the search and all that transpired in its connection. It is very relevant that the prosecution witnesses speak about the compliance about the mandatory procedure and if under the evidence to this effect is not given, the Court must assume that the person to be searched was not informed of the protection. The Court must find that the possession of illicit articles under the Act was not established. It has been held that when the officer has not deposed that he had followed the procedure mandated the Court is duty-bound to conclude that the accused had not had the benefit of the protection that the Act affords; that therefore, his possession of articles under Act is not established and that the pre-condition for his having satisfactorily accounted for such possession had not been met; and to acquit the accused.

25. The above statement of law has been affirmed in the Constitution Bench judgment of this Court in the case of *State of Punjab* v. *Baldev Singh,* (supra). AIR 1999 SC 2378: 1999 AIR SCW 2494: 1999 Cr LJ 3672.

26. Though these observations were made in a case to which section 50 applies, in view of the pronouncement of the judgment of three-Judges of this Court in *Abdul Rashid Ibrahim Mansuri* v. *State of Gujarat,* AIR 2000 SC 821: 2000 AIR SCW 375: 2000 Cr LJ 1384, the approach by the Court in interpreting the law for the non-compliance of section 42 and section 50 must remain the same. In this case, PW-2 and PW-4 and any other prosecution witness do not speak about the compliance with the mandatory provisions of section 42(1), proviso to section 42(1) and section 42(2).

27. It has been held that in any case where mandatory provisions are not complied with and where independent mahazar witnesses are not examined, the accused would be entitled to be acquitted and that any seizure in violation of the mandatory provisions would be inadmissible since these provisions are in the nature of statutory safeguards.

28. In the case of *Sajan Abraham* v. *State of Kerala,* (2001) 6 SCC 692, it was a chance recovery on the road and the observations made in the said judgment have to be confined to the facts of that case. The said judgment will not apply since in this case, the recovery is alleged from the house. For the same reason, the referral order in the case of *Narcotics Control Bureau* v. *Pradeep Nath Mathur,* (2003) 10 SCC 699, also need not detain this Court since the facts here are different from the case in *Sajan Abraham* v. *State of Kerala,* (supra) and a larger Bench of five-Judges and three-Judges have maintained that section 42 is mandatory under the present facts.

29. Replying to the arguments of Mr. Viswanathan, Mr. Tapas Ray, learned Senior Counsel, submitted that the operating portion of the impugned judgment clearly brings out the perversity in the judgment. According to him, the strictures that has been passed against the appellants by the Division Bench of the High Court are wholly unjustified and are liable to be expunged. He is right in his submission. In our view, the High Court was not justified and correct in passing observations/strictures against appellants 2 and 3 without affording an opportunity of being heard, and it is in violation of catena of pronouncements of this Court that harsh or disparaging remarks are not to be made against the persons and authorities whose conduct comes into consideration before Courts of law unless it is really necessary for the decision of the case. Likewise, the directions issued by the High Court to the trial Court to lodge a complaint to the Magistrate having jurisdiction for prosecuting appellants 2 and 3 for having committed an offence under section 58 of the Act read with sections 166 and

167 of the Indian Penal Code is not warranted. The observations made by the High Court are liable to be expunged and accordingly, we expunge the same including the direction to lodge a complaint against appellants 2 and 3.

30. As rightly pointed out by Mr. Tapas Ray, the observations of the High Court in the impugned judgment passing strictures against the appellants have been made while against the record of the case and penalize the two Police Officers who were discharging their official duties as per the law. The action taken by appellants 2 and 3 have been taken in the case of discharging of their official duties while discharging their duties, the official would have violated certain provisions. That does not, in our opinion, enables the Court to pass strictures against the officials and ordered compensation. There is no evidence or circumstance to show that there was any *mala fides* on the part of these officers.

31. Likewise, the direction issued by the High Court directing the State of West Bengal to pay compensation of Rs. 1 lakh to the respondent/accused giving liberty to the State to realize or to recover the whole of such compensation from appellant No. 2, Mr. K.L. Meena, a member of the Indian Police Service, is wholly unjustified.

32. In our view, officers who are discharging their statutory duties cannot be blamed when the action taken by the State Government and the officials concerned are for implementing the objects behind the Act by resorting the check and to direct the raids etc. The High Court has further penalized the State Government and its officers for such an action. Since the strictures passed against them are wholly unjustified, we have no hesitation in expunging the remarks.

33. Above all, the respondent/accused who was the appellant before the High Court did not take any plea in the memorandum of grounds attributing motive against the appellants, particularly, appellants 2 and 3. The High Court by pronouncing the impugned judgment has not followed the parameters laid down by this Court inasmuch as when the appellant before the High Court, the accused, has not taken the plea attributing motives to appellants 2 and 3 specifically. However, we hold that the High Court is right in giving a finding that non-compliance of the mandatory statutory provisions vitiates the prosecution. There was no reason for the police officials to implicate the accused falsely in this case. Even the accused has nowhere including in his statement under section 313, Cr. P.C. stated that the case was fabricated against him due to animosity or enmity by the police. Even in the criminal appeal filed before the High Court, the accused has nowhere complained that the case was falsely implicated against him.

34. The impugned judgment directing the State Government to pay Rs. 1 lakh as compensation to the accused caused a great prejudice to the State. There was no ground for coming to such conclusion. In this regard, the High Court also has omitted to take note of the fact that the action taken under the Act in good faith is protected under section 69 of the Act. The judgment of the High Court passing strictures against the professions/officials amounts to condemning the affected parties without being heard.

35. In paragraph supra, we have already discussed about the non-compliance of the mandatory provisions of the Act by the appellants 2-3. Under such circumstances, we are of the opinion that the judgment of the High Court cannot be characterized as perverse judgment warranting interference in appeal by this Court.

36. Hence, we are of the opinion that no compensation can be awarded to the accused in the facts and circumstances of this case. We, therefore, allow the appeal in part and set aside that part of the impugned judgment ordering compensation to the accused and also the direction to launch prosecution against PW-2 and PW-4 (2nd appellant) under section 58 of the NDPS Act. The impugned judgment shall stand in all other respects.

37. The appeal is partly allowed.

Appeal partly allowed.

M.C.D.

v.

State of Delhi

Criminal Appeal No. 660 of 2005 [arising out of SLP (Cri) No. 5754 of 2004]

AIR 2005 SC 2658: 2005 AIR SCW 2882

Decided on: 29-4-2005.

Coram: **Ashok Bhan, J.**
Dr. AR. Lakshmanan, J.

FACTS:

The second respondent was convicted by the trial court under sections 332 and 461 of the Delhi Municipal Corporation Act and sentenced him to six month's simple imprisonment and imposed a fine of Rs. 5000. Aggrieved thereby, the second respondent-accused filed an appeal before the Sessions Court, Delhi which dismissed the appeal. In a revision petition before the High Court it was held that the accused suffered the agony of trial lasting for 12 years. Besides that he has already undergone some period in custody. The High Court observed that there is no allegation that the petitioner-accused is a previous convict and held that the accused deserved the benefit of probation under section 4 of the Probation of Offenders Act and while maintaining the conviction of the respondent-accused set aside the sentence of imprisonment and fine. The appellant, aggrieved by the judgment of the High Court, preferred appeal by way of special leave petition before the Supreme Court.

ISSUE:

Grant of benefits under the Probation of Offenders Act without giving an opportunity to the Authorities by the High Court to file conduct report of the respondent-accused.

HELD:

Since the High Court has disposed of the criminal revision without giving an opportunity of filing counter-affidavit to the counsel for the appellant and that the respondent did not disclose the fact in the criminal revision filed before the High Court that he has also been convicted in another Criminal Case No. 202 of 1997, the judgment impugned in this appeal cannot be allowed to stand. The impugned order was set aside and the matter was remitted to the High Court for fresh disposal. The appeal was accordingly, allowed with costs of Rs. 10,000 to be paid by the second respondent to the appellant.

JUDGMENT

1. Leave granted.

2. Municipal Corporation of Delhi, aggrieved against the judgment and final order dated 26-3-2004 passed by the High Court Delhi in Criminal Revision Petition No. 185 of 2004 by which order the High Court gave the benefit of probation under section 4 of the Probation of Offenders Act, 1958 (hereinafter referred to as "POB Act") to the second respondent Gurcharan Singh but maintained the conviction, preferred the above appeal.

3. The brief facts leading to the filing of the above appeal are as under:

> One Mr. M.K. Verma (PW-4), Junior Engineer, Civil Line Zone, visited 189 Prem Gali, Punja Sharif, Mori Gate where he found unauthorized construction going at the first floor of the said plot. F.I.R. was prepared on the report of Mr. M.K. Verma who forwarded the F.I.R. before Zonal Engineer, who ordered to issue notice under section 343/344 of the Delhi Municipal Corporation Act, 1957 (for short the "DMC Act"). Subsequently, the second respondent along with Kuldeep Singh were prosecuted for commission of offences under sections 332 and 461 of the DMC Act before the designated Municipal Court.

4. The trial Court, after the conclusion of the trial, convicted the second respondent under sections 332 and 461 of the DMC Act and sentenced him to six month's simple imprisonment and imposed a fine of Rs. 5000 (Annexure P-1).

5. Aggrieved by that order, the second respondent-accused filed an appeal before the Sessions Court, Delhi. The said Court by an order and judgment dated 23-3-2004 dismissed the appeal by holding that there was no infirmity in the order passed by the trial Court (Annexure P-2).

6. Against the judgment and order dated 23-3-2004, the accused filed Criminal Revision Petition No. 185 of 2004 before the High Court Delhi. At the time of arguments, the advocate for the accused submitted before the High Court that the accused did not wish to challenge the conviction on merits and stated it a fit case of accused to be admitted to the benefit of POB Act on the ground that the accused faced trial for 12 years in the lower courts and remained in jail for three days.

7. The High Court *vide* its order dated 26-3-2004 held that the accused suffered the agony of trial lasting for 12 years. Besides that he has already undergone some period in custody. The High Court also observed that there is no allegation that the petitioner-accused is a previous convict and it further held that the accused deserved the benefit of probation under section 4 of the POB Act and while maintaining the conviction of the respondent-accused, the sentence of imprisonment and fine as awarded to him was set aside.

8. The appellant, aggrieved by the judgment of the High Court, preferred the above appeal by way of special leave petition before this Court.

9. We have perused the entire pleadings, orders and judgments passed by the lower Courts and also of the High Court, the other Annexures, in particular, Annexures P-1 and P-2, and records annexed to this appeal and also heard the arguments of Mr. Ashwani Kumar, learned Senior Counsel appearing for the appellant, Mr. Vikas Sharma, learned counsel appearing for respondent No. 1 and Mr. Jaspal Singh, learned Senior counsel, appearing for the second respondent.

10. Learned Senior Counsel appearing for the appellant submitted that the High Court, before extending the benefit of POB Act to the accused did not call for a report from the authorities to check upon the conduct of the accused-respondent as per section 4(2) of the POB Act and that the appellant-MCD was also not given time to file their counter-affidavit on the question of sentence. He further submitted that the High Court while passing the impugned order and judgment did not take into consideration that the accused respondent had been convicted in another Criminal Case No. 202 of 1997 by the Court of Metropolitan Magistrate, Patiala House, New Delhi. In the said case, the accused-respondent was convicted under sections 332/461 of the DMC Act and sentenced to six months' simple imprisonment with a fine of Rs. 5,000.

11. Learned Senior Counsel appearing for the appellant further submitted that there was no good reason for letting the respondent off by granting to him the said benefit of POB Act, particularly keeping in view the large scale irregularity and unauthorized constructions carried by the builders in Delhi despite strict direction of the Municipal authorities and Courts passing various orders from time to time against the unauthorized constructions. It was further submitted that the High Court should not have waived off the payment of fine amount by the accused-respondent and that the High Court ought to have taken into consideration that the respondent has been in jail for only three days and had not put in substantial period in custody.

12. It was further submitted by learned Senior Counsel appearing for the appellant that the court shall not direct release of offender unless it is satisfied that the offender or his surety, if any, has a fixed place of abode or regular occupation in the place over which the court exercises jurisdiction or in which the offender is likely to live during the period for which he enters into the bond. It was also contended that before making any order under section 4(1) of the POB Act, the Court shall take into consideration the report, if any, of the probation officer concerned in relation to the case which the High Court has miserably failed to do so. Therefore, learned Senior Counsel appearing for the appellant, prayed that order dated 26-3-2004 in Cri. Revn. Petn. No. 185 of 2004 be set aside and appropriate orders be passed in this appeal.

13. Learned Senior Counsel appearing for the contesting respondent submitted that the order of the High Court does not require any reconsideration by this Court and that the High Court while extending the benefit of POB Act had clearly recorded in the order that the counsel for the State of Delhi is not averse to the grant of benefit of probation to the answering respondent and, therefore, the requirement under section 4(2) of the POB Act has been waived off by the State and that the High Court took into consideration the fact that the answering respondent has faced the agony of the trial for over 12 years and has also undergone some period in custody and while maintaining the conviction of the answering respondent, the benefit of probation was extended to him. It was, therefore, submitted that the High Court passed the said order in the presence of the counsel of all the parties.

14. Learned Senior Counsel appearing for the second respondent submitted that in S.T. No. 202 of 1997, a judgment was given by the Metropolitan Magistrate on 10-9-2002 and the respondent filed an Appeal No. 374 of 2002 before the Court of Session, Patiala House, New Delhi challenging the said order of conviction and in that appeal, the Court of Additional Sessions Judge, Patiala House, suspended the sentence during the pendency of the appeal upon furnishing a personal bond for a sum of Rs. 25,000 with one surety of the like amount to the satisfaction of the trial Court. It was, therefore, submitted that the sentence/imprisonment awarded by the Metropolitan Magistrate has been suspended under section 389 of the Criminal Procedure Code by the Court of Additional Sessions Judge, Delhi in view of the pendency of the appeal against the order of conviction is a continuation of proceedings, and therefore, there is no conviction against the answering respondent so long as the same is not decided by the Court of Session. It was also submitted that the requirement of calling of a report from the Probationer Officer under section 4(2) of the POB Act has been waived off by the counsel for the State of Delhi and that the counsel for the MCD also did not raise any objection before the High Court. It was further contended that the respondent has not contested the revision in the High Court on merits and confined his submission to the benefit of section 4 of the POB Act being extended to him. Therefore, there is no occasion for the High Court to go into the issue of extent of constructions being raised by the answering respondent. He further contended that the trial Court has committed serious error in exercising jurisdiction while not granting the benefit of probation to the answering respondent and the order of the trial Court was, therefore, rightly and justifiable modified by the High Court.

15. Concluding his arguments, he submitted that the respondent has been released after compliance of the order passed by the High Court by furnishing the bond of good conduct and security to the satisfaction of the Additional Court of Metropolitan Magistrate, Delhi and there is no report of any misconduct or breach of the bond of good conduct by the answering respondent since the date of the order of the High Court, therefore, the order of the High Court is not liable to be interfered with.

16. In the above background, two questions of law arise for consideration by this Court:

"1. Whether the High Court was correct in extending the benefit of the Probation of Offenders Act, 1958 to the accused-respondent without calling for a report from the Authorities relating to the conduct of the respondent as per section 4 of the Act.

2. Whether the High Court was correct in passing the impugned judgment in view of the fact that the respondent has been convicted in another Criminal Case No. 202 of 1997 by the trial Court, New Delhi."

17. Before proceeding further, it would be beneficial to reproduce section 4 of the Probation of Offenders Act, 1958 which is extracted below for ready reference:—

Power of Court to release certain offenders on probation of good conduct:—

1. When any person is found guilty of having committed an offence not punishable with death or imprisonment for the life and the court by which the person is found guilty is of opinion that, having regard to the circumstances of the case including the nature of the offence and the character of the offender, it is expedient to release him on probation of good conduct, then, notwithstanding anything contained in any other law for the time being in force, the Court may, instead of sentencing him at once to any punishment direct that he be released on his entering into a bond, with or without sureties, to appear and receive sentence when called upon during such period, not exceeding three years, as the Court may direct, and in the meantime to keep the peace and be of good behaviour:

   Provided that the Court shall not direct such release of an offender unless it is satisfied that the offender or his surety, if any, has a fixed place of abode or regular occupation in the place over which the Court exercises jurisdiction or in which the offender is likely to live during the period for which he enters into the bond.

2. Before making any order under sub-section (1), the Court shall take into consideration the report, if any, of the Probation Officer concerned in relation to the case."

18. It is the specific case of the appellant herein that the High Court has not afforded to the appellant an opportunity to file counter-affidavit. The appellant would have filed the orders passed by the criminal Courts convicting the respondent herein had an opportunity been given to the appellant. The High Court while passing the impugned order and judgment did not take into consideration that the accused respondent has been convicted in another Criminal Case No. 202 of 1997 by the Court of Metropolitan Magistrate, Patiala House, New Delhi. In the said case, the accused has been convicted under sections 332/461 of the DMC Act and sentenced to six months' simple imprisonment with fine of Rs. 5000. In our view, there was no good reason for letting the respondent off by granting to him the said benefit of POB Act particularly, keeping in view the large scale irregularity and unauthorized constructions carried by the builders in

Delhi despite strict direction of the Municipal authorities and despite of the Courts passing various orders from time to time against the unauthorized construction. The High Court also failed to take into consideration that the respondent has been in jail for three days and had not put in substantial period in custody. The High Court *vide* its order impugned in this appeal has observed that there is no allegation that the respondent is a previous convict. In fact, as could be seen from the Annexures filed along with this appeal, the respondent has been convicted for offence under sections 332 and 461 of the DMC Act.

19. The Trial Court heard the respondent on sentence also and passed the following order:

"Convict in person with counsel

Heard on sentence.

It is contended that he is first offender. He is not a previous convict nor habitual offender. He has faced trial since 1991. He is aged about 57 years. He is not doing any business due to his bad health.

Considering the above facts and circumstances, and gravity of the nature of the offence *i.e.*, extent of construction raised by the accused for commercial as 11 shops at ground floor and 11 shops at first floor, I am not inclined to release the accused/convict on probation. Hence request declined.

In the interest of justice, sentence of six months' simple imprisonment, with fine of Rs. 5,000 I.D. one month simple imprisonment is imposed upon the convict for offence under sections 332/461 DMC Act. Fine deposited. Convict remained for sentence."

20. The Additional Sessions Judge, New Delhi also in Civil Appeal No. 7 of 2002 (Annexure P-2) dismissed the appeal as there is no infirmity in the order of the trial Court and uphold the conviction order passed by the trial Court on the point of sentence. The appellate Court held that no interference is required in the order passed by the trial Court regarding point of sentence. Since the appellant-MCD was not given any opportunity by the High Court to file conduct report of the respondent, the order impugned in this appeal is liable to be set aside.

21. This apart, the respondent did not also disclose the fact in the criminal revision filed before the High Court that he has also been convicted in another Criminal Case No. 202 of 1997 by the Court of Metropolitan Magistrate, Patiala House, New Delhi. Thus, the contesting respondent has come to the High Court with unclean hands and withholds a vital document in order to gain advantage on the other side. In our opinion, he would be guilty of playing fraud on the Court as well as on the opposite party. A person whose case is based on falsehood can be summarily thrown out at any stage of the litigation. We have no hesitation to say that a person whose case is based on falsehood has no right to approach the Court and he can be summarily thrown out at any stage of the litigation. In the instant case, non-production of the order and even non-mentioning of the conviction and sentence in the Criminal Case No. 202 of 1997 tantamounts to playing fraud on the Court. A litigant who approaches the Court is bound to produce all documents which are relevant to the litigation. If he withholds a vital document in order to gain advantage on the other side he would be guilty of playing fraud on the Court as well on the opposite party. The second respondent, in our opinion, was not justified in suppressing the material fact that he was convicted by the Magistrate on an earlier occasion. Since the second respondent deliberately suppressed the crucial and important fact, we disapprove strongly and particularly, the conduct of the second respondent and by reason of such conduct, the second respondent disentitled himself from getting any relief or assistance from this Court. We, however, part with this case with heavy heart expressing our strong disapproval of the conduct and behaviour but direct that the second respondent to pay a sum of Rs. 10,000 by way of cost to the appellant herein.

22. We have already reproduced section 4 of the POB Act. It applied to all kinds of offenders whether under or above 21 years of age. This section is intended to attempt possible reformation of an offender instead of inflicting on him the normal punishment of his crime. The only limitation imposed by section 6 is that in the first instance an offender under twenty-one years of age, will not be sentenced to imprisonment. While extending benefit of this case, the direction of the Court has to be exercised having regard to the circumstances in which the crime was committed, the age, character and antecedents of the offender. Such exercise of discretion needs a sense of responsibility. The offender can only be released on probation of good conduct under this section when the Court forms an opinion, having considered the circumstances of the case, the nature of the offence and the character of the offender, that in a particular case, the offender should be released on probation of good conduct. The section itself is clear that before applying the section, the Magistrate should carefully take into consideration the attendant circumstances. The second respondent is a previous convict as per the records placed before us. Such a previous convict cannot be released in view of section 4 of the POB Act. The Court is bound to call for a report as per section 4 of POB Act but the High Court has failed to do so although the Court is not bound by the report of the Probationer Officer but it must call for such a report before the case comes to its conclusion. The word "shall" in sub-section (2) of section 4 is mandatory and the consideration of the report of the Probationer Officer is condition precedent to the release of the accused as reported in the case of *State* v. *Naguesh G. Shet Govenkar,* AIR 1970 Goa 49 and a release without such a report would, therefore, be illegal 1970 Cr LJ 465.

23. In the case of *Ram Singh* v. *State of Haryana,* (1971) 3 SCC 914, a Bench of two Judges of this Court in paragraph 16 of the judgment observed as under:

> "Counsel for the appellants invoked the application of Probation of Offenders Act. Sections 4 and 6 of the Act indicate the procedure requiring the Court to call for a report from the Probation Officer and consideration of the report and any other information available relating to the character and physical and mental condition of the offender. These facts are of primary importance before the Court can pass an order under the Probation of Offenders Act. This plea cannot be entertained in this Court."

24. In the case of *R. Mahalingam* v. *G. Padmavathi,* 1979 Cr LJ (NOC) 20 (Mad), the Court observed as under:

"If any report is filed by the Probation Officer, the Court is bound to consider it. Obtaining such a report of the Probation Officer is mandatory since the sub-section (1) of section 4 says that the Court shall consider the report of the Probation Officer. Words "if any" do not mean that the Court need not call for a report from the Probation Officer. The words "if any" would only cover a case where notwithstanding such requisition, the Probation Officer for one reason or the other has not submitted a report.

Before deciding to act under section 4(1), it is mandatory on the part of the Court to call for a report from the Probation Officer and if such a report is received, it is mandatory on the part of the Court to consider the report. But if for one reason or the other such a report is not forthcoming, the Court has to decide the matter on other materials available to it.

In the instant case, the Magistrate passed order releasing the accused on probation without taking into consideration their character. Held, the requirement of section 4(1) was not fulfilled and, therefore, the case remanded."

25. Since the High Court has disposed of the criminal revision without giving an opportunity of filing counter-affidavit to the counsel for the MCD and that the respondent did not disclose the fact in the criminal revision filed before the High Court that he has also been convicted in another Criminal Case No. 202 of 1997, the judgment impugned in this appeal cannot be allowed to stand. We, therefore, have no hesitation in setting aside the order impugned and remit the matter to the High Court for fresh disposal strictly in accordance with law.

26. The appeal is, accordingly, allowed with costs of Rs. 10,000 to be paid by the second respondent to the appellant, as indicated in paragraph supra.

Appeal allowed.

Rajiv Ranjan Singh 'Lalan'

v.

Union of India

Writ Petn. (Cri.) Nos. 197-198 of 2004, 2006 AIR SCW 4287

Decided on: 21-8-2006

Coram: **K.G. Balakrishnan, J.**

Dr. AR. Lakshmanan, J.

S.H. Kapadia, J.

FACTS:

The petitioners, by way of a Public Interest Litigation, alleged that there were serious irregularities by Income Tax Appellate Tribunal, ITAT in disposing of the cases against respondent Nos. 4 and 5 who were formerly Chief Ministers of the State of Bihar for having assets disproportionate to income. The petitioners also alleged that the public prosecutor who was conducting the Criminal case against the respondent Nos. 4 and 5, was removed by the Director of the CBI presumably under pressure from the accused and one 'U' was appointed and he was a Deputy Superintendent of Delhi Police and had commenced his law practice only recently. The petitioners also alleged that the respondent Nos. 4 and 5 were unnecessarily interfering in the course of justice and managed to change the public prosecutor who was diligently discharging his duties.

ISSUE:

1. Irregularities by Income Tax Appellate Tribunal in disposing of cases.
2. Interference in the course of justice.

HELD:

PIL is not maintainable to probe or enquire into the returns of another taxpayer except in special circumstances. The allegations made by the petitioners that there were serious irregularities in disposing of the cases of respondent Nos. 4 and 5 are not factually correct. The Chief Justice of the Patna High Court is requested to convene a meeting of Administrative Judges and have a fresh look at the evaluation in the case of posting of Sri Paswan as Special Judge for C.B.I.

Judgment

K.G. BALAKRISHNAN, J. (Dr. AR. Lakshmanan, J., Concurring) (Majority View).—These writ petitions are filed as Public Interest Litigation by the two petitioners herein who were Members of the Parliament at the time of filing the petitions. Respondent Nos. 4 and 5 were formerly Chief Ministers of the State of Bihar. It is alleged by the petitioners that they filed writ petitions before the High Court of Patna alleging large-scale defalcation of public funds and falsification of accounts involving hundreds of crores of rupees in the Department of Animal Husbandry in the State of Bihar and pursuant to these allegations, several cases were registered by the Police and investigation of these cases was later handed over to the Central Bureau of Investigation. In an earlier petition filed before this Court on 19-3-1996, this Court directed that the investigation shall be monitored by the Division Bench of the Patna High Court and in that Order, it was indicated that the CBI Officers entrusted with the investigation shall inform the Chief Justice of Patna High Court from time to time of the progress made in the investigation and if they needed any directions in the matter of conducting the investigation, obtain them from him and it was also said that the learned Chief Justice may either post the matter for directions before a Bench presided over by him or constitute any other appropriate Bench. It was also directed that the State Government shall co-operate in assigning adequate number of Special Judges to deal with the cases expeditiously so that no evidence may be lost.

2. The petitioners allege that consequent upon change of the Government in the Centre, attempts have been made to delay and interfere with the judicial process. It is alleged that the public prosecutors who were handling the cases were removed and to protect the interests of respondent Nos. 4 and 5, convenient prosecutor was appointed.

3. The respondent No. 5 is an accused in a case registered under the Prevention of Corruption Act, 1988. The case is filed pursuant to the FIR registered as

No. R.C. 5[A] 498/AHD-Pat dated 19-8-1998. The allegation in that case is that respondent No. 5 as Chief Minister of Bihar between 1990 to 1996 had acquired assets disproportionate to his known sources of income. Charge-sheet was filed in the Court of the Special Judge, CBI, Patna on 4-4-2000 under section 13(1)(e) of the Prevention of the Corruption Act, 1988. Respondent No. 4 also was charge sheeted in the same case for abetment under section 109 of the I.P.C. read with section 13(2) and section 13(1)(e) of the Prevention of Corruption Act, 1988. This case has been re-numbered as Special Case No. 5/1998 and is pending trial in the Court of the Special Judge, CBI, Patna. The petitioners allege that certain income tax cases of respondent nos. 4 and 5 were pending before the Income Tax Appellate Tribunal (ITAT) and one Mr. D.K. Tyagi who was a member of the ITAT had been hearing those cases and that respondent nos. 4 and 5 found it difficult to pursue the hearings before the said ITAT member and hence at their influence Mr. Tyagi was sent on deputation and he was replaced by one Mr. Mohanaranjan who was on the verge of retirement. It is further alleged that the new member along with another member heard these cases within two weeks and orders were pronounced in favour of respondent Nos. 4 and 5. It is also alleged that respondent No. 3, namely, the Central Board of Direct Taxes did not prefer appeal in these cases though the decision went against the revenue. This, according to the petitioners, was to help respondent Nos. 4 and 5 in the cases filed against them based on the allegation that they acquired assets disproportionate to their known sources of income.

4. The petitioners have also alleged that the Special Case No. 5/1998 pending before the Special Judge, CBI was at the final stage of hearing and that the Director, CBI, presumably under pressure from the accused changed the prosecutor and appointed one Shri Oma Shankar Singh who was only a retired Deputy Superintendent of Delhi Police and had no experience of conducting the prosecution. According to the prosecution, this was done at the fag end of the prosecution case to help the accused. The petitioners have made allegations against respondents 1 to 3 also that they were acting arbitrarily and interfering in the judicial process to benefit the respondent Nos. 4 and 5. The petitioners have alleged that respondent Nos. 4 and 5 obtained stay of proceedings of the case pending before the Special Judge from this Court suppressing some material facts. It is alleged that the respondent Nos. 4 and 5 still wield influence and power and, therefore, this Court should monitor the trial of the case pending before the Special Judge, CBI, at Patna.

5. In these Writ Petitions, the petitioners have prayed mainly four reliefs. The first relief prayed is to issue an appropriate writ, order or direction monitoring the conduct of the trials relating to fodder scam cases proceedings against respondent nos. 4 and 5 in the State of Bihar and State of Jharkhand. The second prayer is to appoint the very same prosecutor who had been conducting prosecution earlier and to direct the High Court to see that no prosecutor or CBI Officer attached with the investigation and trial of the case should be removed, harassed or victimized for discharging their duties. The petitioners have also prayed that at least one inspector be provided for each fodder case. The petitioners have also prayed for cancellation of bail granted to respondent Nos. 4 and 5. Petitioners have further prayed for a direction to respondents 1 to 3 to file an appeal against the orders passed by the ITAT.

6. During the pendency of these Writ Petitions, the Counsel for the petitioners alleged that the Special Judge who was trying the case involving respondent nos. 4 and 5, was being replaced by another Special Judge. The allegation was that one Shri Yogender Prasad was the CBI Special Judge and he was being replaced by one Shri Muni Lal Paswan and this according to the petitioners was deliberately done to help the respondent Nos. 4 and 5. In view of the allegations made by the petitioners, this Court on 1-8-2005 directed the Registrar General of the Patna High Court to send details and files as to when Judge Shri Yogender Prasad was promoted as a District Judge and all papers regarding posting of the subsequent officer Shri Muni Lal Paswan. As regards the posting of Shri Muni Lal Paswan as a Special Judge, this Court again passed an Order on 26-10-2005 and the Registrar of the High Court was directed to give further clarification in the matter. The Registrar General of the High Court of Patna appeared in person before us and filed an affidavit giving out the details leading to the decision of the Standing Committee of the High Court to post Shri Muni Lal Paswan as a Special Judge, CBI case Patna.

7. In view of the allegations made by the petitioners in respect of the cases pending before the ITAT, the President of the ITAT was directed to send all papers pertaining to the constitution of the Bench of Shri P. Mohanarajan and Shri M.K. Sarkar which disposed of the various appeals pending before the ITAT. The President of the ITAT has submitted a report and also produced relevant papers before us.

8. In view of the allegation made by the petitioners regarding the appointment of a new prosecutor in place of earlier prosecutor, this Court directed the 3rd respondent to produce the entire files including the notations pertaining to the appointment of Shri Oma Shankar Sharma as Prosecutor.

9. Refuting the allegations contained in the Writ Petition, detailed counter-affidavits have been filed by the respondents. In the joint counter-affidavit of respondent Nos. 4 and 5, they have alleged that the writ petitions contain vague and indefinite allegations and they are made with political motive to satisfy their personal grudge and that this is an abuse of the process of the Court. The respondents have alleged that the Public Interest Litigation shall not be used for private or political motives or for other consideration. It is also alleged that Special Case No. 5/98 pending before the Special Judge is a case registered under sections 13(2) and 13(1) of the Prevention of Corruption Act and it has nothing to do with the 'fodder scam' case. The various allegations made in the Writ Petitions have been denied specifically.

10. We heard the learned Senior Counsel Shri Mukul Rohtagi for the petitioner and Solicitor General appearing for respondents 1 to 3 and also the learned counsel for respondent Nos. 4 and 5. At the time of the arguments, the learned Counsel for the petitioners submitted that the petitioners in the present facts and circumstances of the case only pray for appointment of an appropriate prosecutor to conduct the case pending before the Special Judge and that the bail of the respondent nos. 4 and 5 be cancelled and Respondent No. 3 be directed to file appeals against the orders passed by the ITAT. The petitioners also submitted arguments to the effect that the appointment of the present Special Judge was not done properly. No specific prayer was made by the petitioners to change the Presiding Officer. They, however, submitted a request that High Court may be directed to reconsider the appointment and posting of Shri Muni Lal Paswan as a Special Judge.

11. We shall first consider the prayer of the petitioners as to whether any irregularities have been committed in the matter of disposal of cases against respondent Nos. 4 and 5 by the Income Tax Appellate Tribunal, Patna. The petitioners have alleged that Shri D.K. Tyagi, who had been hearing the cases of respondent Nos. 4 and 5 and proving to be difficult during the course of the hearing, was curiously sent on deputation and was replaced by Shri Mohanarajan, who was on the verge of the retirement, to head the Tribunal. It is further alleged that Shri Mohanarajan picked up only two cases pertaining to respondent Nos. 4 and 5 even though the matter had been heard fully by another bench, and within two weeks, the cases were heard and allowed in favour of the assessees namely respondent Nos. 4 and 5, and that he had no background of the case and had not disposed of any other matter. The petitioners alleged that after the disposal of these cases by the Tribunal, steps were not taken to file appeal against these orders and that was done at the instance of respondent Nos. 4 and 5.

12. The entire allegations made by the petitioners are denied. The President of the Income Tax Appellate Tribunal submitted a report regarding the manner in which income tax cases of respondent Nos. 4 and 5 were disposed of by the Tribunal. The President has stated that he took over as the President of ITAT on 31-10-2003 and at that time a petition filed by Respondent No. 5 for transfer of cases from Patna to Delhi was pending. The Department after considering the legal aspects declined to transfer the cases of respondent No. 5 to Delhi. It was suggested and noted on the files "it may perhaps be worthwhile to consider constituting a Special Bench for early disposal of these appeals". Shri D.K. Tyagi sent a representation on 12-1-2004 praying that he may be transferred to Delhi as his mother was 80 years old and with deteriorating health and that he was anxious to arrange marriage of his daughter and his son was studying at Delhi. There were some other developments also as Shri D.K. Tyagi had left India without permission and a show-cause notice was issued to him. He filed an explanation and came over to Delhi to personally explain the things and he was allowed to remain at Delhi for some period and the President of the ITAT, with a view to inculcate judicial discipline, decorum and proper behaviour from the Bench, made Shri Tyagi to sit in Delhi Bench of the ITAT along with the seniormost.

Accountant Member. There were also other circumstances whereby Shri Tyagi wanted his transfer from Patna to avoid recurrence of another incident in view of the repeated confrontations with the Bar. It was under these circumstances Shri Mohanarajan was directed to camp at Patna in June, 2004. Another member Shri Aggarwal also expressed his inability to camp at Patna. Shri P. Mohanarajan along with Shri M.K. Sarkar who was a senior member of the Tribunal, dealt with the cases of respondent Nos. 4 and 5. The President has also refuted an allegation that Shri Sarkar was selected to camp at Delhi only for a short period to dispose of this case. He has brought to our notice that the Bench disposed of 11 appeals of respondent No. 5 and several other cases and that 136 cases were disposed of during that period and the list of such cases and details are given at Annexure I.

13. As regards non-filing of the appeals against the order passed by ITAT, the Chief Commissioner of Income Tax-VIII in New Delhi had filed affidavit wherein it is stated that the question was referred to the Central Board of Direct Taxes for consideration and he had sought opinion from the Ministry of Law. The Central Board of Direct Taxes and the Ministry of Finance obtained the opinion of the Ministry of Law to the effect that no substantial questions of law arose out of the judgments of the ITAT in the cases of respondent Nos. 4 and 5 for filing appeals before the High Court and thus instructions were issued not to appeal against these cases.

14. The allegations made by the petitioners that there were serious irregularities in disposing of the cases of respondent Nos. 4 and 5 are not factually correct. The very foundation of the allegation is that Shri Tyagi, member of the Appellate Tribunal was transferred from Patna to Delhi at a time when he was hearing appeals is factually incorrect. It is also not correct to say that appeals were disposed of by the member of the Tribunal who was on the verge of retirement. The petitioners could not point out any procedural irregularity in the manner in which these appeals were disposed of. After going through the affidavits and reports and various other papers, we are satisfied that the allegations made by the petitioners are not true. The petitioners have prayed that this Court should direct the authorities to file appeal against the orders passed by ITAT in the cases of respondent Nos. 4 and 5. In a collateral proceedings like this, the petitioner cannot seek any remedy of Writ of *Mandamus* directing the authorities to file appeals against such orders. An appeal is a statutory remedy available to the Department and the third party like Writ Petitioner cannot seek such remedies in collateral proceedings like this. Moreover, the petitioners could not point out anything to show that there were serious procedural irregularities on the part of the Department in not filing the appeal. The Department had taken opinion of the Central Board of Direct Taxes as well as the Ministry of Finance and the Ministry of Finance had sought the opinion of the Ministry of Law. The petitioners have not made any specific allegation that these decisions were taken at the behest of respondent Nos. 4 and 5 or any undue influence was exerted to take such decisions. The allegations made by the petitioners are vague and indefinite. Therefore, the prayer for Writ of *Mandamus* to direct the respondent Nos. 1 to 3 to file an appeal against the ITAT orders cannot be allowed and is liable to be rejected.

15. The next prayer of the petitioners is that the Special Judge who is dealing with the CBI cases at Patna was not properly appointed by the High Court of Patna and another Judge who was dealing with this case was suddenly transferred to help respondent Nos. 4 and 5. It may be noticed, at the outset, that no such allegations have been made in the original Writ Petition. The petitioners filed

IA as Criminal Miscellaneous Petition Nos. 6589-6590 of 2005 wherein certain allegations have been made. Subsequent to this filing of these interim petitions, the original writ petition was not amended and no prayer was incorporated in the relief portion as to whether the present Special Judge is to be removed or not. In the interlocutory application as Criminal Miscellaneous Petition Nos. 6589-6590 of 2005, the petitioners alleged that taking undue advantage of the ongoing summer vacations, in an attempt to over reach the orders passed by this Hon'ble Court which was already seized of the matter in its entirety, the Patna High Court on the administrative side, has directed the transfer of the Special Judge (AHD), Patna. Such act according to the petitioners amounts to contempt of this Hon'ble Court and the petitioners reserved their right to initiate appropriate proceedings for contempt against the persons responsible for the same. The petitioners sought for stay of the transfer of the then Special Judge Shri Yogender Prasad. This Court on 1-8-2005 passed the following order:

> "At the request of the learned counsel appearing for the parties, the petitions are fixed for hearing on 20th September, 2005.
>
> In the meantime, the prosecution arguments may continue but thereafter the trial to remain stayed and defence argument not to start without further orders of this Court.
>
> The Registrar General of the Patna High Court to send the details and files when Judge Yogender Prasad was promoted as a District Judge and all papers regarding posting of the present incumbent Shri Muni Lal Paswan."

16. This Court declined to grant stay of transfer of Special Judge Shri Yogender Prasad as he was promoted to the post of Principal Sessions Judge. This Court also passed an Order on 26-12-2005 wherein the details regarding the appointment of the present incumbent Shri Muni Lal Paswan were sought from the High Court. The entire records relating to the appointment of Shri Muni Lal Paswan as a Special Judge CBI, Patna have been produced in this case including the Confidential Registers of the various officers. On perusal of these records, we find that the Standing Committee of the High Court took a decision to post Shri Muni Lal Paswan as the CBI Special Judge, Patna. Six senior most Judges of the High Court of Patna constituted the Standing Committee of the High Court and the decision was taken in the meeting of the Committee held on 22nd June, 2005. The decision of the Standing Committee is recorded as follows:

> "Having considered the relevant service records of the officers concerned as also taking into consideration the fact that no allegation petition has been received against Sri Muni Lal Paswan, Additional District Judge, Sahara. It is resolved that let him (Sri Muni Lal Paswan) be posted as Special Judge for C.B.I. (Fodder Scam Cases) at Patna. It is further resolved upon consideration of the relevant service records of the officers concerned that Shri J.P. Ratnesh, Additional District Judge, Patna, be posted as Special Judge, C.B.I. (South Bihar) and Sri Ram Niwas Prasad, Additional District Judge, Patna, as Special Judge for Vigilance Case (Court No. 1).

In view of the urgency of the matter, the officer is directed to take necessary steps for issue of notification immediately."

17. Though the petitioners have not made any allegations in the Writ Petitions, at the time of argument, the learned Senior Counsel stated that Shri Muni Lal Paswan was having poor record and he was not senior to be appointed as a Special Judge. We have perused the Confidential Register of Shri Muni Lal Paswan which was made available to us. Of course, the Confidential Register of this Officer was available only upto 2003. For some period, he was working on deputation and the inspecting judge had not recorded the confidential registers for that period, though the confidential registers of other officers were available to the Standing Committee. The Confidential Reports of Shri Muni Lal Paswan from 1981 to 2003 have been produced in Court. We have perused the Confidential Register of this Officer and it has been repeatedly recorded that this Officer has maintained honesty and integrity during the period under report. About his conduct and integrity, nothing adverse is reported against him. Of course, in some of the years, this Officer has been graded as 'Category B' with regard to his judicial performance. These are all matters considered by the Standing Committee which consists of senior Judges of the High Court. The appointment of this Officer is not challenged by the petitioners and no pleadings also made in the main Writ Petition. By filing a Criminal Miscellaneous Application, the petitioners have made series of allegations which are not borne out by any records. If at all, the petitioners had any grievance regarding the appointment of any particular Officer, the proper remedy was to approach the High Court and to bring this fact to the notice of the Chief Justice. Under the above circumstances, we do not find any material on record to show that there was any illegality or serious infraction of any procedure in the appointment of the present CBI (Special Judge), Patna and the appointment as such cannot be challenged in a collateral proceedings and this Court cannot go into the question of appointment of a Special Judge which is exclusively within the domain of the High Court under article 235 of the Constitution. Therefore, the oral appeal of the petitioners for the change of the Officer of the Special Judge cannot be granted.

18. The learned Counsel for the petitioners also alleged that the public prosecutor who was conducting the case No. 5/98 against the respondent Nos. 4 and 5 was removed by the Director of the CBI presumably under pressure from the accused and one Uma Shankar Singh was appointed and he was a Deputy Superintendent of Delhi Police and had commenced his law practice only recently. The petitioners alleged that the respondent Nos. 4 and 5 were unnecessarily interfering in the course of justice and managed to change the public prosecutor who was diligently discharging his duties.

19-20. In the rejoinder affidavit filed on behalf of the petitioners, the petitioners reiterated their allegation and stated that Shri L.R. Ansari who had been conducting the disproportionate assets case, had examined 225 witnesses, was sent elsewhere and some other public prosecutor was appointed. Refuting all these allegations, a counter-affidavit was filed on behalf of respondent No. 2 CBI. In the counter-affidavit, it is stated that disproportionate assets case against respondent Nos. 4 and 5 was being conducted by Shri L.R. Ansari, right from the beginning. He had examined 132 witnesses from the prosecution and the defence had also examined 93 witnesses. Arguments on behalf of the petitioners were completed on 14-7-2004 and the arguments on behalf of the defence started on 19-7-2004 and as the case was practically over, it was decided to avail Shri Ansari's service in other Animal Husbandry cases.

It is also stated that if found necessary, Mr. Ansari would be called to give any reply at the end of the case. As regards Shri Oma Shankar Sharma, it is submitted that he had started his practice as an Advocate on 23-2-1968 and he was appointed as a Prosecutor in 2-1-1973 in Delhi and conducted several cases before criminal courts in New Delhi. He was promoted as Senior-cum-Additional Public Prosecutor on 16-10-1992 and conducted several important cases including TADA cases. He was appointed as a Legal Adviser to the Commissioner of Police, Delhi and continued upto 31-8-2003.

21. From the averments made in the counter-affidavit, it is clear that the earlier prosecutor Shri Ansari had completed the cases and examined all the witnesses for the prosecution as well as for the defence and he had also submitted his entire arguments to the Special Judge. Therefore, the contention of the petitioners that the prosecutor was purposely changed to give benefit to respondent Nos. 4 and 5 is not correct. There is no allegation to prove that respondent Nos. 4 and 5 had in any way interfered with the appointment of the Public Prosecutor. The petitioners could not produce any documents to show that the allegations made in the original petitions were true.

22. The learned Counsel for the respondent Nos. 4 and 5 submitted that the original petition is a politically motivated move to malign respondent Nos. 4 and 5 and this sort of public interest litigation should not be entertained by the Court and placed reliance on the series of decisions passed by this Court. It may be noticed that the case No. 5/98 has been filed against the respondent Nos. 4 and 5 alleging that they had amassed wealth disproportionate to their known sources of income while holding the post of Chief Minister of the State of Bihar. Both the petitioners are not in any way connected with this case. They are not de facto complainant in this case. It is for the prosecution to prove its case and the respondent Nos. 4 and 5 to deny that the allegations are not true and they did not have the disproportionate income as alleged by the prosecution. It is a criminal litigation exclusively between respondent Nos. 4 and 5 and the State. It is also important to note that in a case of this nature, nobody else has got any right to interfere especially by way of public interest litigation or else such public interest litigation would only hamper the course of justice and may cause prejudice to the accused by denying a fair trial. In this case, as early as 2004, 132 witnesses were examined on the side of the prosecution and 93 witnesses were examined on the defence side. Arguments of the prosecution were over as early as in 14-7-2004 and the defence arguments continued upto 19-7-2004. Because of the present public interest litigation, the trial could not be conducted. It is equally important to note that though the petitioners have alleged series of irregularities, but they are not supported by basic facts having solid foundation.

23. This Court in *Janata Dal* v. *H.S. Chaudhary*, (1992) 4 SCC 305 held that in a criminal case, a person who has no interest shall not invoke the jurisdiction of the Court by intervening in the proceedings and a person acting *bona fide* and having sufficient interest in the proceeding alone has *locus standi* to file a public interest litigation and a person for personal gain or private profit or political motive, or any oblique consideration has no such right to file public interest litigation.

24. The respondent Nos. 4 and 5 relied on *Ashok Kumar Pandey* v. *State of West Bengal,* (2004) 3 SCC 349. That is a case where petition was filed under article 32 of the Constitution purportedly in public interest but the prayer was to the effect that the death sentence imposed on one 'D' by the Sessions Court, affirmed by the Calcutta High Court and the Supreme Court, needed to be converted to a life sentence because there had been no execution of the death sentence for a long time. Therein, this Court said that a person acting *bona fide* and having sufficient interest in the proceeding alone can initiate public interest litigation and that the court must not allow its process to be abused for oblique considerations.

25. In *Union of India* v. *Sushil Kumar Modi,* (1998) 8 SCC 661, a three-Judge Bench of this Court held that once a charge-sheet is filed in the competent court after completion of the investigation, the process of monitoring by the monitoring Court for the purpose of making the CBI and other investigative agencies concerned perform their function of investigating into the offences concerned comes to an end; and thereafter it is only the court in which the charge-sheet is filed which is to deal with all matters relating to the trial of the accused, including matters falling within the scope of section 173(8) of the Code of Criminal Procedure.

26. In the instant case, the petitioners have approached this Court by filing this public interest litigation under article 32 of the Constitution at the time when the recording of the prosecution evidence was almost over and the trial of the case reached a final stage. If at all, the petitioners had any grievance regarding the removal of the public prosecutor, they should have submitted their grievance before the Special Judge or before the High Court. It is already noticed that the petitioners had no direct connection with this case. They were absolutely strangers as regards the criminal cases against respondent Nos. 4 and 5 which was pending before the Special Judge. This unnecessary interference in the criminal case may cause, sometimes, damage to the prosecution case and at times may cause serious prejudice to the accused also. In any view of the matter, this sort of interference in the criminal prosecution would only deny a fair trial to the accused.

27. The petitioners in the writ petitions have prayed to re-engage the same prosecutor who was handling the case in the Trial Court from the very beginning of the trial. The earlier prosecutor had already been deployed to conduct some other case and we do not think that there is any necessity to give any direction to the CBI. However, the CBI would be at liberty to make use of the services of the earlier Prosecutor Shri Ansari. The second prayer of the petitioners that the present Special Judge is to be replaced by another Judicial Officer also cannot be granted as the appointment of the Judge has been validly made by the High Court. In the petition, there was no allegation against the present Judicial Officer warranting his removal from the post.

28. The petitioners prayed for a Writ of *Mandamus* directing the respondent Nos. 1 to 3 to file appeal against the orders passed by the ITAT. The petitioners have not made out any case for issuing any such Writ of *Mandamus*. The respondent Nos. 1 to 3, after following the due procedure, have decided not to file an appeal against the order passed by ITAT and we do not find any reason to give any direction to file appeal.

29. The last prayer of the petitioners is that the bail granted to respondent Nos. 4 and 5 is liable to be set aside. The petitioners could not prove anything that these respondents have interfered in the course of justice and they misused the privilege of bail extended to them. The petitioners have also no case that they are likely to flee from justice. The petitioners have not made out any case for cancellation of their bail.

30. The prayers sought for in the Writ Petitions cannot be allowed and the Writ Petitions being without any merits are liable to be and dismissed accordingly. All interim orders passed in the Writ Petitions are vacated.

31. Dr. AR. LAKSHMANAN, J. (Concurring with K.G. Balakrishnan, J.):—I had the privilege of perusing the judgment proposed by my learned Brother – Hon'ble Mr. Justice K.G. Balakrishnan. While respectfully concurring with the conclusion arrived by the learned Judge, I would like to add the following few paragraphs:

The first petitioner is a Member of Parliament and the second petitioner is the Deputy Chief Minister of Bihar. The above writ petition, ostensibly in public interest, has been filed by them for the following relief:

a. issue an appropriate writ, order or direction monitoring the conduct of the trials relating to the fodder scam case proceeding against respondent Nos. 4 and 5 in the State of Bihar and State of Jharkhand;

b. issue an appropriate writ, order or direction directing the Director, CBI to reinstate the prosecutors who were handling the cases in the Trial Court and the High Court and directing that no prosecutor or any CBI officer attached with the investigation and the trial of these scam cases should be removed, harassed or victimized for discharging their duties, without specific orders from this Hon'ble Court;

c. issue an appropriate writ, order or direction directing the Director, CBI to provide the logistics and ensure that it is represented by at least one Inspector in each of the 7 courts by Special Judge, CBI in the State of Jharkhand which is trying the fodder scam cases so that no adjournments are sought and granted;

d. issue an appropriate writ, order or direction cancelling the bail granted to respondent Nos. 4 and 5.

e. issue an appropriate writ, order or direction directing the respondent No. 1 and/or 3 to file an appeal against the order passed by the Hon'ble Income Tax Appellate Tribunal."

32-33. On our direction, the Registrar General of the Patna High Court was present in Court on 26-7-2006. He filed an affidavit and also explained the procedure followed in the appointment of Shri Munni Lal Paswan as a special Judge to try the disproportionate assets cases with reference to the records.

34. We heard Mr. Mukul Rohatgi and Mr. Kailas Vasudev learned senior counsel for the petitioners and Mr. Ram Jethmalani, learned senior counsel assisted by Mr. P.H. Parekh and Mr. G.E. Vahanvati, learned Solicitor General and Mr. Mohan Parasran, learned ASG for the respondents.

35. Mr. Mukul Rohatgi and Mr. Kailash Vasudev, learned senior counsel made elaborate submissions on the question of maintainability of the writ petitions and also submitted that Mr. Munni Lal Paswan was promoted recently and posted at Patna for disposing of the case filed against respondent Nos. 4 and 5 and that the said Munni Lal Paswan is not a desirable person to be posted in the said post to conduct the case. He also requested that the Public Prosecutors who were proving to be inconvenient to respondent Nos. 4 and 5 are being supplanted with chosen ones. Like that, Member (Judicial) in the Income-tax Appellate Tribunal – Mr. R.K. Tyagi who had been hearing the appeal of respondent Nos. 4 and 5 was curiously sent on deputation and was replaced by Mr. Mohanarajan, a person who was on the verge of retirement to head the Tribunal. Within 2 weeks, the matter was heard and allowed in favour of the assessees. He also submitted that the case relating to disproportionate assets before the Special Judge, CBI is at the final stage of hearing. The Director, CBI has started changing the prosecutors mid-way when the case was nearing completion and that the public prosecutor who was conducting the cases from the very beginning has been replaced by Shri Om Shankar Singh, a retired Deputy Superintendent of Delhi Police who has commenced law practice recently. It is also submitted that respondent Nos. 4 and 5 are deliberately protracting the trial by taking unnecessary adjournments which, by itself, would be a ground for cancellation of bail. He further submitted that by virtue of the new political equations between the party in power in the State of Bihar and at the Centre, respondent No. 5 one of the main accused in the fodder scam now has substantial administrative control and political say in the functioning of the Government of India and that the CBI and the Central Board of Direct Taxes, respondent Nos. 2 and 3 have become a party in an effort to shield respondent Nos. 4 and 5. He continued to submit that this Court shall monitor the case since the accused are using State machinery to block the judicial process and subvert the trial and dilatory tactics being adopted by the accused to delay the trial on one pretext or the other. He also submitted that the prosecutors or investigators connected with the fodder scam matters in the State of Bihar who have till date been discharging their functions in the trial Court should not be disturbed, replaced or sidelined.

36. Mr. Rohatgi, in support of his contentions, invited our attention to the various documents, annexures, income-tax records and the paperbooks.

37. Appearing for respondent Nos. 4 and 5, Mr. Ram Jethmalani, learned senior counsel argued that the petition had been filed only to achieve personal or political gain, no case had been made out for the cancellation of bail to Mr. Lalu Prasad Yadav and his wife and this court should not monitor the trial as it would send wrong signals. He also cited many decisions with regard to the maintainability of the writ petitions at the instance of practicing politicians. He sought dismissal of the writ petitions with exemplary costs.

38. Appearing for the CBI, learned Solicitor General G.E. Vahanwati denied point by point the allegations of the petitioners made in their pleadings with reference to various documents and records and proved to our satisfaction that the statements made by the petitioners are not true and correct and have been made with an ulterior motive. Learned Solicitor General further submitted that there had been no interference by Mr. Lalu Prasad Yadav or his wife in any of the matters whether in the appointment of Judges or in the change of the prosecutor or on the decision not to file an appeal in the income-tax cases. The learned Solicitor General cited *T.N. Godavarman Thirumulpad (98)* v. *Union of India,* (2006) 5 SCC 28 (Hon. Y.K. Sabharwal, C.J., Arijit Pasayat and S.H. Kapadia, JJ.) and submitted that howsoever genuine a case brought before the Court by a public interest litigant may be, the Court has to decline its examination at the behest of a person who, in fact, is not a public interest litigant and whose *bona fides* and credentials are in doubt and that no trust can be placed by the Court on a *mala fide* applicant in public interest litigation. Learned Solicitor General submitted now it is time to give a severe warning and sound alert since these are basic issues which are required to be satisfied by every public interest litigant. He also cited paras 25 and 26 in support of the contention that the writ petition is not maintainable at the instance of the political rivals. 2006 AIR SCW 2082.

39. Mr. Ram Jethmalani in regard to the maintainability of the writ petition cited the following decisions:

40. *Janata Dal* v. *H.S. Chowdhary,* (1992) 4 SCC 305: 1993 AIR SCW 248:

> "It is thus clear that only a person acting *bona fide* and having sufficient interest in the proceeding of PIL will alone have a *locus standi* and can approach the court to wipe out the tears of the poor and needy, suffering from violation of their fundamental rights, but not a person for personal gain or private profit or political motive or any oblique consideration. Similarly, a vexatious petition under the colour of PIL brought before the court for vindicating any personal grievance, deserves rejection at the threshold."

41. *Dattaraj Nathuji Thaware* v. *State of Maharashtra,* (2005) 1 SCC 590 and invited our attention to paras 4, 5, 9, 10, 12 and 14.

42. *Ashok Kumar Pandey* v. *State of West Bengal,* (2004) 3 SCC 349:

> "12. Public interest litigation is a weapon which has to be used with great care and circumspection and the judiciary has to be extremely careful to see that behind the beautiful veil of public interest an ugly private malice, vested interest and/or publicity-seeking is not lurking. It is to be used as an effective weapon in the armoury of law for delivering social justice to citizens. The attractive brand name of public interest litigation should not be used for suspicious products of mischief. It should be aimed at redressal of genuine public wrong or public injury and not publicity-oriented or founded on personal vendetta. As indicated above, Court must be careful to see that a body of persons or a member of the public,

who approaches the court is acting *bona fide* and not for personal gain or private motive or political motivation or other oblique consideration. The Court must not allow its process to be abused for oblique considerations. Some persons with vested interest indulge in the pastime of meddling with judicial process either by force of habit or from improper motives. Often they are actuated by a desire to win notoriety or cheap popularity. The petitions of such busybodies deserve to be thrown out by rejection at the threshold, and in appropriate cases, with exemplary costs."

43. *S.P. Gupta* v. *Union of India,* 1981 (Supp) SCC 87: AIR 1982 SC 149:

"24. But we must be careful to see that the member of the public, who approaches the Court in cases of this kind, is acting *bona fide* and not for personal gain or private profit or political motivation or other oblique consideration. The Court must not allow its process to be abused by politicians and others to delay legitimate administrative action or to gain a political objective. Andre Rabie has warned that "political pressure groups who could not achieve their aims through the administrative process" and we might add, through the political process, "may try to use the Courts to further their aims". These are some of the dangers in public interest litigation which the Court has to be careful to avoid. It is also necessary for the Court to bear in mind that there is a vital distinction between *locus standi* and justiciability and it is not every default on the part of the State or a public authority that is justiciable. The Court must take care to see that it does not overstep the limits of its judicial function and trespass into areas which are reserved to the Executive and the Legislature by the Constitution. It is a fascinating exercise for the Court to deal with public interest litigation because it is a new jurisprudence which the Court is evolving, a jurisprudence which demands judicial statesmanship and high creative ability. The frontiers of public law are expanding far and wide and new concepts and doctrines which will change the complexion of the law and which were so far as embedded in the womb of the future, are beginning to be born."

44. Mr. Rohatgi submitted that this Court should monitor the conduct of the trial relating to the fodder scam cases against respondent Nos. 4 and 5.

45. *Union of India* v. *Sushil Kumar Modi,* (1998) 8 SCC 661:

"6. This position is so obvious that no discussion of the point is necessary. However, we may add that this position has never been doubted in similar cases dealt with by this Court. It was made clear by this Court in the very first case, namely *Vineet Narain* v. *Union of India,* (1996) 2 SCC 199 that once a charge-sheet is filed in the competent court after completion of the investigation, the process of monitoring by this Court for the purpose of making the CBI and other investigative agencies concerned perform their function of investigating into the offences concerned comes to an end; and thereafter it is only the court in which the charge-sheet is filed which is to deal with all matters relating to the trial of the accused, including matters falling within the scope of section 173(8) of the Code of Criminal Procedure. We make this observation only to reiterate this clear position in law so that no doubts in any quarter may survive. It is, therefore, clear that the impugned order of the High Court dealing primarily with this aspect cannot be sustained." (Emphasis supplied)

46. It is thus clear from the above judgment that once a charge-sheet is filed in the competent Court after completion of the investigation, the process of monitoring by this Court for the purpose of making the CBI and other investigative agencies concerned perform their function of investigating into offences concerned comes to an end and thereafter, it is only the Court in which the charge-sheet is filed which is to deal with all matters relating to the trial of the accused including matters falling within the scope of section 173(8).

47. We respectfully agree with the above view expressed by this Court. In our view, monitoring of pending trial is subversion of criminal law as it stands to mean that the Court behind the back of the accused is entering into a dialogue with the investigating agency. Therefore, there can be no monitoring, after the charge-sheet is filed.

48. This Court issued a direction on 22-2-2005 to the President of the Income-tax Appellate Tribunal to submit a detailed report in regard to the allegations made by the petitioners. Pursuant to the directions of this Court, the President of ITAT filed a detailed report dated 9-3-2005. A perusal of which shows that there is not an iota of truth in the allegation and all the aforesaid averments are completely baseless. As noticed earlier, certain allegations were made against Mr. R.K. Tyagi and Mr. Mohanarajan whom, according to the petitioners, were due for retirement was appointed to head the Tribunal. It was further stated that on 2-7-2004 Mr. R.K. Tyagi who had been hearing the appeal of respondent Nos. 4 and 5 was sent on deputation for 2 weeks and was replaced by Mr. Mohanarajan, a person who was on the verge of the retirement to head the Tribunal and that the said Mohanarajan picked up only the cases pertaining to respondent Nos. 4 and 5 and heard the matter and allowed in favour of the assesses and that no appeal has been filed against the said order.

49. On 22-2-2005, an order was passed by this Court directing the Union of India to produce before this Court the proposal of CBI dated 20-7-2004 and the entire file including notations pertaining to the appointment of Mr. Uma Shankar Sharma as prosecutor. The President, ITAT was directed to send to this Court all papers pertaining to constitution of the Bench of Mr. Mohanarajan and Mr. M.K. Sarkar and also to sent copies/order sheets of ITA Nos. 233-237 of 2000 etc. etc. The President, ITAT was directed to state whether Mr. R.K. Tyagi was sent on deputation for two weeks during the period the other two persons were appointed and if so why and on whose behalf he was sent on deputation.

50. On 9-3-2005, Mr. Vimal Gandhi, President, ITAT submitted his report. Flash figures of investigation, disposal and dependency of appeals for the month of April, 2004 and the position as on 1-5-2004 with reference to the various benches in the country was furnished (Annexure-2). It is seen from the report that Mr. D.K. Tyagi, JM, Patna had left India without obtaining permission as required under the rules and he was accordingly issued a show cause notice to explain about the acts of indiscipline. This was done in early June. Mr. Tyagi also explained the circumstances under which he had gone abroad etc. The

President acceded to his request on compassionate grounds and permitted him to remain in Delhi without any T.A., D.A. for 1 month from June, 21 onwards. The President, ITAT, therefore, has stated that it is not correct to suggest that Tyagi was shunted out of Patna by him.

51. Insofar as Mohanarajan is concerned, the President has explained the position with regard to Mohanarajan and M.K. Sarkar. He said Mr. Mohanarajan joined the Tribunal as Judicial Member in November, 1995 and posted at Jabalpur, Chennai, Patna and Bangalore and he served in Patna from 2-9-2002 onwards till he was transferred to Bangalore in March, 2003. He is sobre in nature and that he is to retire on 6-11-2009 and he had never sat with Mr. Sarkar earlier. When Mr. Agarwal's inability to tour Patna was made known to the President in Bangalore, Mohanarajan's name came to his mind as an appropriate person to replace Mr. D.K. Agrawal and he was accordingly directed to camp at Patna in June, 2004 and that the camp was organized accordingly. Insofar as Mr. M.K. Sarkar is concerned, he before joining the Appellate Tribunal Mr. Sarkar was asked managed to Patna and other Benches on camp till regular members were available as pendency at Kolkata was also low. The details of tour of Sarkar to Patna in 2004 has also been furnished.

52. The learned Solicitor General then invited our attention to Annexure-7 filed along with the report of the President, ITAT. Respondent No. 4 Mr. Lalu Prasad, by his letter dated 15-10-2003, addressed a letter to the President, ITAT, New Delhi requesting for transfer of appeals filed before Patna Bench of the Tribunal to Delhi Bench in his case. On 17-10-2003, the President made a note on the said letter to call for comments/objections, if any, from the Department/ Patna Bench by fax. Mr. Lalu Prasad has stated in the said letter that since he is elected as a Member of Rajya Sabha and performed duties as a Member of Rajya Sabha he has to be present in Delhi and, therefore, the appeals may be transferred from Patna to Delhi Bench. By Annexure-8, the Patna Bench gave its response on 31-12-2003 stating that the legal aspect of the matter was being examined and that a final report will follow soon. By Annexure-9 dated 8-1-2004, the Directorate General of Income-tax Patna addressed a letter to Assistant Registrar, ITAT Patna Bench as to whether constituting a Special Bench for early disposal of the appeals of Shri Lalu Prasad. Annexure-9 was in reply to the ITAT Patna Bench letter dated 11-11-2003 and during that time the present Government was not in power. By Annexure-10 the DGIT by their letter dated 23-4-2004 stated that it would not be possible to agree to transfer the appeals of Mr. Lalu Prasad from ITAT, Patna Bench to ITAT, Delhi Bench and it may be worthwhile to consider constituting a Special Bench for early disposal of these appeals. It is seen from Annexure-12 dated 11-3-2004 signed by M.A. Bakshi, V.P. ITAT, Chandigarh-one that it may not be necessary to constitute a Special Bench for disposal of the appeals relating to Mr. Lalu Prasad.

53. In regard to the prayer for cancellation of the bail at the instance of the petitioner, we are of the opinion that the said request cannot at all be countenanced. Our attention was drawn to order dated 14-7-2003 passed by this Court which reads thus:

"We have been extending bail from time to time for a period of six months in order to monitor the trial. In our view, it is not now necessary to do so any further. We, therefore, order that the bail which has been granted by this Court will continue for the duration of the case on the same terms and conditions. We clarify that it will be open to the C.B.I to apply for cancellation of bail in accordance with law in this court. Further, if it is found that the petitioner is deliberately protracting the trial or taking unnecessary adjournments then that by itself would be a ground for cancellation of bail."

54. Mr. Rohatgi submitted that respondent Nos. 4 and 5 are interfering with the cause of justice so far as conduct of the trial and IT proceedings are concerned and, therefore, the bail granted to them is liable to be cancelled. This submission has no merits in view of the arguments advanced by learned Solicitor General inviting our attention to the various documents and annexures etc., to the effect that the respondent Nos. 4 and 5 have never interfered with the conduct of trial or with the IT proceedings. It is stated that respondent Nos. 4 and 5 are deliberately protracting the trial by taking unnecessary adjournments. Then that itself would be a ground for cancellation of bail. This argument has no substance. It is a fact that the matter was adjourned at the instance of the defence on various occasions. Court itself has adjourned the matter for various reasons. We, therefore, cannot hold that the delay is solely attributable to respondent Nos. 4 and 5 which, in our opinion, cannot be a ground for cancellation of bail when it is not proved that any of the bail conditions has been violated. The delay is attributable to both the prosecution and the defence and also to the Court. Therefore, respondent Nos. 4 and 5 cannot be held responsible for the delay.

55. Mr. Rohatgi argued that Munni Lal Paswan should be changed from the present place and some other officer should be posted there. Mr. Ram Jethmalani, at the time of hearing, explained to this Court as to how and under what circumstances the earlier incumbent of the office – Mr. Yogendra Prasad was shifted at his own request and that how Munni Lal Paswan was promoted recently and posted at Patna for the conduct of the matters. We summoned the Registrar General of Patna High Court on 26-7-2006. The Registrar General Madhusudhan Singh has also filed an affidavit in regard to the three queries raised by us. The Registrar General explained to this Court in regard to the practice in the High Court of Patna and how the matter is placed before the Standing Committee and the remarks of the inspecting Judges and the guard files which are maintained separately of each officers which were made available to the Standing Committee. The said fact also finds mention in the decision dated 22-6-2005 of the Standing Committee. In regard to query No. 3 the Registrar has submitted as follows:—

"That in regard to Query No. 3 of this Hon'ble Court as mentioned in the order dated 26-7-2006, I respectfully say and submit that the remarks of the Hon'ble Inspecting Judge in case of Shri Jawahar Prasad Ratnesh was of the year 1985, 1986-87, 1988, 2001, 2003 and 2005 (and remarks recorded by P.O., Industrial Tribunal, Patna in 1998). In respect of Shri Ram Niwas Prasad, the remarks recorded by the Hon'ble Inspecting Judge was of 1985, 1986, 1997 and 2002. As regards Shri Munni Lal Paswan, the remarks recorded by the Hon'ble Inspecting Judge was of 1985 and 1990 and by Vice-Chairman, Industrial Tribunal, Patna Bench in 1997."

56. We have perused the records submitted by the High Court in regard to the officers including Munni Lal Paswan. There is absolutely no adverse entry against Munni Lal Paswan and that poor record if any is not the record of integrity and that no gradation has been given to officers after 1997 onwards including Paswan.

57. We have perused the proceedings of the meetings of the Standing Committee held on 22-6-2005 in the chambers of the Hon'ble Chief Justice which reads thus:

Proceedings of the meeting of the Standing Committee held on 22nd June, 2005 in the Chambers of the Hon'ble the Chief Justice:

Agenda...

Decision...

To consider the matter regarding Postings if three Special Judges at Patna for C.B.I. (Fodder Scam Cases), C.B.I. (South Bihar) and Vigilance Cases (Court No. 1) in Place of Shri Yogendra Prasad, Mungeshwar Sahoo and Jitendra Mohan Sharma, respectively (P.FXXVII-5-98). Having considered the relevant service records of the officers concerned and also taking into consideration the fact that no allegation petition has been recieved against Sri Munni Lal Paswan, Additional District Judge, Saharsa. It is resolved that let him (Sri Munni Lal Paswan) be posted as Special Judge for C.B.I. (Fodder Scam Cases) at Patna. It is further resolved upon consideration of the relevant service records of the officers concerned that Sri J.P. Ratnesh, Additional District Judge, Patna, be @page-SCW 4307 posted as Special Judge, C.B.I. (South Bihar) and Sri Ram Niwas Prasad, Additional District Judge, Patna as Special Judge for Vigilance Case (Court No. 1). In view of the urgency of the matter, the office is directed to take necessary steps for issue of notification immediately.

Sd/- Nagendra Rai, Actg. C.J.

Sd/- I.P. Singh, J.A.D. 1

Sd/- R.N. Prasad, J.A.D. II

Sd/- Barin Ghosh, J.

Sd/- M.L. Vis.., J.

Sd/- Rajendra Prasad, J."

58. It is thus seen from the above that all the relevant service records of the officers concerned including Munni Lal Paswan was placed before the Standing Committee which took into consideration the fact that no allegation petition has been received against Munni Lal Paswan, Addl. District Judge. It was resolved that Munni Lal Paswan be posted as Special Judge, CBI Fodder Scam Cases at Patna. The Registrar General had also stated at the time of hearing that the resolution of the Standing Committee was also placed before the Full Court which also approved the same.

59. Article 233 of the Constitution of India deals with subordinate Courts. The appointment of persons, posting and promotion of District Judges in any State shall be made by the Governor of the State in consultation with the High Court exercising jurisdiction in relation to such State. Likewise, under Article 235 the control over district courts and courts subordinate thereto including the posting and promotion of and the grant of leave to persons belonging to judicial service of a State and holding any post inferior to the post of District Judge shall be vested in the High Court.

60. The appointment of lawyers is the prerogative of the Government and the prosecuting agency. The petitioners are trying to find fault with every attempt with every steps taken. Cases like this the delay is inevitable.

61. It is also settled law that appointment of advocates, public prosecutors etc., is the prerogative of the Government in power and court has no role to play.

62. In the above case, the Standing Committee has taken a decision to appoint Munni Lal Paswan and other officers after scrutinizing the records, ACRs etc., in accordance with articles 233 and 235 of the Constitution of India which is the prerogative right of the Standing Committee and the High Court and when a decision is taken it is not for this Court to scrutinize the correctness of the decision that too at the instance of third parties.

63. In regard to the prayer of the petitioner to direct the Government of India to file the appeal in the income-tax matters, we are of the opinion that the said prayer also cannot at all be countenanced. In this regard, section 260A(1) and (2)(a) may be referred to which reads as under:

> "*260A. Appeal to High Court.*—(1) An appeal shall lie to the High Court from every order passed in appeal by the Appellate Tribunal, if the High Court is satisfied that the case involves a substantial question of law.
>
> (2) The Chief Commissioner or the Commissioner or an assessee aggrieved by any order passed by the Appellate Tribunal may file an appeal to the High Court and such appeal under the sub-section shall be—
>
> (a) filed within one hundred and twenty days from the date on which the order appealed against is received by the assessee or the Chief Commissioner or Commissioner;
>
> (b) ******
>
> (c) ******"

64. In this regard, counter-affidavit filed on behalf of the Under-Secretary to the Government of India, Ministry of Finance may be usefully referred to. It is stated in the said counter-affidavit that the matter has been fully considered and legal opinion was sought by BCIT investigation, Patna and that the opinion of the learned ASG was received stating that there is no substantial question of law for filing an appeal and that the consideration of this aspect had been done properly and independently and there have been no extraneous consideration.

65. This apart, another affidavit was filed by Mr. L.K. Sighvi, the Chief Commissioner of Income-tax (VIII), New Delhi, para 1:

> "I was the Director General IT (Inv.), Patna during the relevant period when decision was taken regarding filing of appeals pertaining to the ITAT

orders in the cases of Smt. Rabri Devi and Shri Lalu Prasad Yadav before the Hon'ble High Court at Patna. Considering the facts and circumstances of the case and the fact that the present petition was pending before this Hon'ble Court, I thought it fit to refer the matter to the CBDT for consideration and seeking opinion from the Ministry of Law. The CBDT and the Ministry of Finance obtained the opinion of the Ministry of Law to the effect that no substantial questions of law arose out of the judgments of the ITAT in the cases of Smt. Rabri Devi and Shri Lalu Prasad Yadav for filing appeals before the Hon'ble High Court. Accordingly, instructions were issued by me that appeals would not be filed in respect of these cases.

66. It is thus seen that the Government of India has taken into consideration the views of the Ministry of Law, Ministry of Finance to the effect that no substantial questions of law arise out of the judgments of the ITAT in the case of respondent Nos. 4 and 5 for filing appeals before the High Court and that instructions were issued that appeals would not be filed in respect of those cases.

67. Certain allegations have been made against CBDT and the Public Prosecutors, Members of the Income-tax Tribunal etc. None of them were made parties before us. Therefore, the allegations made against them are one-sided and cannot be looked into at all. We cannot also say that all these authorities have acted in a *mala fide* manner.

68. In our opinion, public interest litigation meant for the benefit of the lost and lonely and it is meant for the benefit of those whose social backwardness is the reason for no access to the Court. We also say that PILs are not meant to advance the political gain and also settle their scores under the guise of a public interest litigation and to fight a legal battle. In our opinion, the liberty of an accused cannot be taken away except in accordance with the established procedure of law under the Constitution Criminal Procedure and other cognate Statutes. We are also of the opinion that PIL is totally foreign to pending criminal proceedings. The records placed before us would only go to show that respondent No. 4 had no hand in any of these matters whether in the appointment of Judges or in the change of the prosecutor or on the decision not to file an appeal in the income-tax cases.

69. For the foregoing reasons, we hold that both the writ petitions have no merit and is liable to be dismissed and accordingly we do so.

70. In the circumstances, we order no costs. Before concluding, we say that the petitioners are waging a political battle against respondent Nos. 4 and 5 through the medium of Public Interest Litigation. The venue for political battle, in our opinion, can never be this Court by filing a writ petition under article 32 of the Constitution of India.

71. S.H. KAPADIA, J. (Dissenting):—I have had the privilege of reading the opinions of Brother Justice Balakrishnan and Brother Justice Lakshmanan, I have to record my respectful dissent with the views expressed by my learned brothers.

72. In these writ petitions under article 32 of the Constitution, filed to enforce article 14 of the Constitution, following three issues arise for determination:

(a) Whether the writ petitions were maintainable as Public Interest Litigation;

(b) Whether there was failure of statutory and public duty on the part of the Revenue in not preferring an appeal to the High Court under section 260A of the Income-tax Act, 1961; and

(c) Whether the procedure adopted at the time of posting Mr. Munni Lal Paswan, ADJ as Special Judge, CBI, Patna (Fodder Scam Cases) on 22-6-2005, needs to be relooked by the Patna High Court.

(a) Whether the Writ Petitions Were Maintainable as Public Interest Litigation:

BACKGROUND FACTS:

73. Large-scale defalcation of public funds, fraudulent transactions and falsification of accounts, of around Rs. 500 crores, came to light in the Animal Husbandry Department of the State of Bihar. This Scam took place during the period 1977 to 1996. A similar situation existed in the Education, Corporation and Fisheries Departments. By judgment dated 11-3-1996 delivered by the Division Bench of the Patna High Court in Writ Petition No. 459 of 1996 the High Court, in exercise of its powers under article 226 of the Constitution, took away the investigation from the State police and entrusted it to CBI. The said decision of the Patna High Court was challenged by the State *vide* Civil Appeal Nos. 5177-81 of 1996. By judgment dated 19-3-96, this Court observed that the exercise of the power under article 226 in a public interest litigation was not to give any advantage to a political party or group of people but it was done to investigate corruption in public administration, misconduct by the bureaucracy, fabrication of official records and misappropriation of public funds. Therefore, this Court refused to interfere with the impugned judgment of the Patna High Court [See: *State of Bihar* v. *Ranchi-ila Samta Party,* (1996) 3 SCC 682: 1996 AIR SCW 1582].

74. In the case of *Union of India* v. *Sushil Kumar Modi,* (1996) 6 SCC 500, certain allegations were made against the then Director, CBI, in the context of investigations into the above Fodder Scam. The relevant paragraphs 11 and 14 of the said judgment are quoted hereinbelow:

> "11. We deem it proper to emphasise that every officer of the CBI associated with the investigation has to function as a member of a cohesive team which is engaged in the common pursuit of a fair, honest and complete investigation into the crimes alleged. It is needless to further emphasise that the exercise has to be performed objectively and fairly, mindful of the fact that the majesty of law has to be upheld and the 'rule of law' preserved, which does not discriminate between individuals on the basis of their status, position or power. The law treats everyone as equal before it and this has to be kept in view constantly in every State action to avoid violation of the 'right to equality' guaranteed in article 14 of the Constitution.
>
> 14. It appears necessary to add that the Court, in this proceeding, is concerned with ensuring proper and honest performance of its duty by the CBI and not the merits of the accusations being investigated, which

are to be determined at the trial on the filing of the charge-sheet in the competent court, according to the ordinary procedure prescribed by law. Care must, therefore, be taken by the High Court to avoid making any observation which may be construed as the expression of its opinion on merits relating to the accusation against any individual. Any such observation made on the merits of the accusation so far by the High Court, including those in Para 8 of the impugned order are not to be treated as final, or having the approval of this Court. Such observations should not, in any manner influence the decision on merits at the trial on the filing of the charge-sheet. The directions given by this Court in its aforesaid order dated March 19, 1996 have to be understood in this manner by all concerned, including the High Court."

PLEADINGS

75. On 31-8-2004 the present Writ Petition (Crl.) Nos.197-198 of 2004 were filed for enforcement of article 14 of the Constitution. Briefly, it is alleged that the Union of India (respondent No. 1) and other respondents (including respondent Nos. 4 and 5) are allegedly committing acts of misfeasance in relation to the corruption cases pending before the Special Judge, CBI, Patna as well as in the appeals preferred by the accused before the Income Tax Appellate Tribunal. Respondent No. 4 is Smt. Rabri Devi, former Chief Minister of Bihar and respondent No. 5 is Mr. Lalu Prasad, former Chief Minister of Bihar. In the writ petitions it is alleged that trial Judge as well as the Member (Judicial) of the Income Tax Appellate Tribunal who are found to be inconvenient are being transferred and supplanted with the chosen ones. That, even the judgment of the Income Tax Appellate Tribunal (for short, 'the Tribunal') allowing the appeal in favour of the assessees for the assessment years 1986-87 to 1996-97, though involving substantial questions of law, has not been challenged by the Revenue by filing appeals under section 260A of the Income-tax Act, 1961 (for short, 'the I.T. Act') in order to protect some of the respondents-accused.

76. Respondent Nos. 4 and 5 as well as Union of India have categorically denied the allegations made by the petitioners. It is the case of the respondents that irresponsible statements have been made in the petitions without having any basis; that, political battles were being fought in the name of public interest litigation (for short, 'PIL') by politicians and that respondent Nos. 4 and 5 had no role to play either in the transfer of lawyers in the criminal case, in the transfer of the trial Judge or in the constitution of the Special Bench of the Tribunal. They have further submitted that they have no role to play in Revenue Department not going in appeal to the High Court under section 260A of the I.T. Act. It is submitted that the Revenue Department took the opinion of Additional Solicitor General of India who has certified that no substantial questions of law arise for determination by the High Court under section 260A of the I.T. Act. Accordingly, it is submitted by the respondents that the writ petitions deserve to be dismissed with heavy costs.

SUBMISSIONS

77. Mr. Ram Jethmalani, learned senior counsel appearing on behalf of respondent Nos. 4 and 5, raised the preliminary objection stating that PIL has no role to play in pending criminal proceedings. He submitted that if the petitioner is a politician and if it is found that the object is to win political battle then PIL should be dismissed with costs. He submitted that in the present case the PIL is politically motivated; that, in the present petitions there is no breach of article 14 and, therefore, it deserves to be dismissed with strictures against the petitioners. Learned senior counsel submitted that PIL is meant for the benefit of the lost and lonely who have no access to courts or the legal system. Learned senior counsel submitted that when the provisions of the Constitution are violated and loss is caused to a group of persons who are handicapped then PIL is maintainable, if it is shown that they have no access to legal system. It is submitted that respondents 4 and 5 are the accused persons before the criminal court and the liberty cannot be taken away except by the procedure established by law; that, the Criminal Procedure Code requires that the guilt of the accused must be determined by a Special Judge in the present case which is the court of exclusive jurisdiction and if anybody, aggrieved by the decision of the Special Judge, is free to hold appeal. Learned senior counsel submitted that the assessment orders passed by the Revenue Department under the I.T. Act cannot be used to prove holding of disproportionate assets by respondent Nos. 4 and 5. He submitted that in the present case the CBI pressurized the assessing officer to pass assessment order against respondent Nos. 4 and 5. Learned senior counsel further alleged that in some cases even the Commissioner of Income Tax (Appeals) was persuaded to make order of assessment against respondent Nos. 4 and 5 and in such circumstances and even otherwise orders of assessment cannot form the basis of trials dealing with accusation of disproportionate assets by respondent Nos. 4 and 5. Learned senior counsel submitted that in fact a bare perusal of the decision of the Tribunal in the present case indicates although the appeal is allowed in favour of the assessees the Tribunal has decided every point against the assessee and in the circumstances the Department was right in not moving the High Court in appeal under section 260A of the I.T. Act. Learned senior counsel further urged that respondent Nos. 4 and 5, who are the accused in the criminal trial, should be allowed to pursue their defence. Learned senior counsel stated that admittedly there was a Scam and misappropriation of public property but that should not give right to the petitioners to obstruct the course of justice or obstruct the rights given to the accused under Criminal Procedure Code, Evidence Act and the Constitution.

78. Learned senior counsel submitted three propositions in the context of the parameters of the PIL. He submitted that firstly, every criminal trial has to proceed according to the procedure established by law and every deviation from that procedure, even if by a judicial order could violate article 21 of the Constitution; secondly, in every PIL the *locus standi* of the petitioner should be examined at the threshold; and thirdly, the source of his information must be subjected to strict scrutiny. Learned senior counsel submitted that if any of the three conditions are not fulfilled then PIL should be dismissed. In this connection, learned senior counsel relied upon the judgments of this Court in support of his above submissions.

79. In the case of *Janata Dal* v. *H.S. Chowdhary*, (1992) 4 SCC 305, this Court observed that violation of a fundamental right is the sine qua non of the exercise of the right conferred by Article 32; that, PIL is part of the process of participatory justice and in a competition between courts and streets the rule of law must win and, therefore, the rule of *locus standi* must be liberalized to meet the challenges of the times. This Court, further, noted the judgment in *A.R. Antulay* v. *Ramdas Sriniwas Nayak,* (1984) 2 SCC 500, in which it has been observed that *locus standi* of the complainant is a concept foreign to criminal procedure jurisprudence except where the statute creates an offence which provides for the eligibility of the complainant to set the criminal case in motion.

80. In para 92 of the said judgment the concept of PIL has been explained. Any member of the public having sufficient interest can maintain an action for judicial redress for public injury arising from breach of duty or violation of the Constitution. This is absolutely essential for maintaining the rule of law, furthering the cause of justice and achieving the constitutional goals, subject to a caveat which states that the member of the public who approaches by way of PIL should be acting *bona fide* and not for personal gain, private profit or political motivation.

81. In the case of *Union of India* v. *Sushil Kumar Modi,* (1998) 8 SCC 661, this Court has held that once a charge-sheet is filed in the competent court after completion of investigation the process of monitoring for the purposes of making the CBI and other investigating agencies to perform their function comes to an end and, thereafter, it is only the court in which the charge-sheet is filed has to deal with all matters relating to the trial of the accused, including matters falling within section 173(8) of Cr. P.C. Relying on this judgment, learned senior counsel for respondent Nos. 4 and 5 stated that in the present case the charge-sheet has been filed and, therefore, the process of monitoring has ended. It is urged that since the charge-sheet has been filed the criminal trial should be allowed to take its own course without any further interference from any court outside the trial court.

82. In the case of *Dattaraj Nathuji Thaware* v. *State of Maharashtra,* (2005) 1 SCC 590, the Division Bench of this Court on facts found that the petitioner was a lawyer who had filed PIL. He was a blackmailer. In the circumstances the PIL was dismissed with costs. It is in that light, that the Division Bench of the Court speaking through Pasayat, J. stated the parameters of PIL. Learned senior counsel for respondent Nos. 4 and 5 has referred to para 4 of the said judgment in support of his contention that PIL is maintainable to help poor and needy who have no access to the legal system. I quote hereinbelow para 4 of the said judgment.

> "4. When there is material to show that a petition styled as a Public Interest Litigation is nothing but a camouflage to foster personal disputes, the said petition is to be thrown out. Before we grapple with the issue involved in the present case, we feel it necessary to consider the issue regarding public interest aspect. Public Interest Litigation which has now come to occupy an important field in the administration of law should not be "publicity interest litigation" or "private interest litigation" or "politics interest litigation" or the latest trend "paise income litigation". The High Court has found that the case at hand belongs to the last category. If not

properly regulated and abuse averted, it becomes also a tool in unscrupulous hands to release vendetta and wreak vengeance, as well. There must be real and genuine public interest involved in the litigation and not merely an adventure of knight errant borne out of wishful thinking. It cannot also be invoked by a person or a body of persons to further his or their personal causes or satisfy his or their personal grudge and enmity. Courts of justice should not be all-owed to be polluted by unscrupulous litigants by resorting to the extraordinary jurisdiction. A person acting *bona fide* and having sufficient interest in the proceeding of public interest litigation will alone have a *locus standi* and can approach the Court to wipe out violation of fundamental rights and genuine infraction of statutory provisions, but not for personal gain or private profit or political motive or any oblique consideration. These aspects were highlighted by this Court in *The Janta Dal* v. *H.S. Chowdhary,* (1992) 4 SCC 305 and *Kazi Lhendup Dorji* v. *Central Bureau of Investigation,* 1994 Supp (2) SCC 116. A writ petitioner who comes to the Court for relief in public interest must come not only with clean hands like any other writ petitioner but also with a clean heart, clean mind and clean objective. [See *Ramjas Foundation* v. *Union of India,* 1993 Supp (2) SCC 20 and *K.R. Srinivas* v. *R.M. Premchand* (1994) 6 SCC 620; 1993 AIR SCW 248; 1994 AIR SCW 2190; 1992 AIR SCW 3460.]

83. To the same effect is the ratio of the decision of the Division Bench of this Court in the case of *Gurpal Singh* v. *State of Punjab,* (2005) 5 SCC 136. In the said judgment it has been held that PIL will not lie in cases of personal and political rivalry. While laying down the parameters the Division Bench speaking through Pasayat, J. observed that in the PIL nobody should be allowed to make wild and reckless allegations spoiling the characters of others; that, PIL is not maintainable in cases of personal vendetta. However, in the said judgment it has been held that the court can act if it is satisfied with the correctness or the nature of the information given by the petitioner.

84. Mr. Goolamhusein E. Vahanvati, Learned Solicitor General of India, appearing for Union of India, adopted the arguments advanced by Mr. Ram Jethmalani, learned senior counsel, on the preliminary issue. He, however, added that in the present case reckless allegations have been made without any basis against important functionaries, Judges and authorities under the I.T. Act. He submitted that the petitioners cannot destroy the service careers of the Government officers without any reason on basis except for their own political rivalry with respondent No. 5. He submitted that there is no violation of law or the Constitution, particularly, when Mr. Yogender Prasad, the earlier trial Judge who had extensively heard the matter, was promoted as District Judge. Learned counsel further submitted that constitution of the Special Bench by the President of the Tribunal was done in the circumstances spelt out in the various affidavits; that the matter was required to be expeditiously heard which led to the constitution of the Special Bench; and that decision was not arbitrary, as alleged. There is nothing on record to indicate that favoured judges/members were appointed and that inconvenient judges/members were dispensed with to favour the accused in the present case.

85. Learned senior counsel relied upon the judgment of this Court in the case of *T.N. Godavarman Thirumulpad (98)* v. *Union of India,* (2006) 5 SCC 28, where this Court speaking through learned Chief Justice of India has held *vide* para 26 as follows:

> "26. For the last few years, inflow of public interest litigation has increased manifold. Considerable judicial time is spent in dealing with such cases. A person acting *bona fide* alone can approach the court in public interest. Such a remedy is not open to an unscrupulous person who acts, in fact, for someone else. The liberal rule of *locus standi* exercised in favour of *bona fide* public interest litigants has immensely helped the cause of justice. Such litigants have been instrumental in drawing attention of this Court and High Courts in matters of utmost importance and in securing orders and directions for many under-privileged such as, pavement dwellers, bonded labour, prisoners' conditions, children, sexual harassment of girls and women, cases of communal riots, innocent killings, torture, long custody in prison without trial or in the matters of environment, illegal stone quarries, illegal mining, pollution of air and water, clean fuel, hazardous and polluting industries or preservation of forest as in the *T.N. Godavarman Thirumulpad (I)* v. *Union of India,* (1997) 2 SCC 267. While this Court has laid down a chain of notable decisions with all emphasis at their command about the importance and significance of this newly developed doctrine of PIL, it has also hastened to sound a red alert and a note of severe warning that courts should not allow their process to be abused by a mere busybody or a meddlesome interloper or wayfarer or officious intervener without any interest or concern except for personal gain or private profit or other oblique consideration. [See *Janata Dal* v. *H.S. Chowdhary,* (1992) 4 SCC 305; 1997 AIR SCW 1263; 1993 AIR SCW 248.]

FINDINGS:

86. At the outset, it needs to be noted that in this case we are concerned not with the merits of the allegations but with the decision-making process, be it in the posting of Mr. Munni Lal Paswan, Special Judge, CBI, Patna or in the matter of the Revenue Department not moving in appeal to the High Court under section 260A of the I.T. Act despite there being substantial questions of law arising from the impugned judgment of the Tribunal. It is submitted on behalf of the petitioners that the present writ petitions should be seen in the context of the earlier two decisions of the Supreme Court under which investigations were handed over to CBI as an amount of around Rs. 500 crores stands misappropriated in the Fodder Scam. It is the case of the petitioners that the present case should be seen in the light of the directions given by the Supreme Court in the cases of *Ranchi-ila Samta Party* (supra) and *Sushil Kumar Modi* (supra).

87. The present petitions are filed on the alleged acts of misfeasance. The test which one has to apply to decide the maintainability of the PIL concerns sufficiency of the petitioner's interest. Under this test it is necessary to consider the subject matter to which the PIL relates. It is wrong in law for the court to judge the applicant's interest without looking at the subject-matter of his complaint. If the petitioner shows failure of public duty, the court would be in error in dismissing his PIL.

88. In the case of *Inland Revenue Commissioners* v. *National Federation of Self-employed and Small Business Ltd.*, 1982 AC 617, a declaration was sought that the Revenue had acted unlawfully in granting amnesty to the trade union of casual workers and accordingly a writ of *mandamus* was sought to assess and collect income-tax from casual workers according to law. In the Divisional Court when the motion for judicial review came, the point of *locus standi* was treated as a preliminary point. The Divisional Court refused the leave saying that the petitioner had no power to bring such an action. The Court of Appeal by majority reversed the decision of the Divisional Court and made a declaration that the applicants have sufficient interest to apply for judicial review. Upholding the decision of the Division Court it was held by the House of Lords that the question of sufficient interest of the petitioner cannot be considered in the abstract. It must be taken together with the legal and factual context. It was held that the management of tax recovery falls within the domain of the Revenue but if that act of management is found to be based on exercise of its authority for extraneous reasons, then judicial review would certainly lie. It was held that the Revenue Department was in-charge of assessment and collection of taxes for the welfare of the State; that, it was responsible for good management under the statute; that, if it was found that the Board was proposing to exercise its authority or if the Board was refraining itself from exercising its power not for good reasons of good management but for some extraneous or ulterior reasons then that action or inaction by the Board would be ultra vires and such a matter would be a proper matter for judicial review. In this respect the following observation made by the House of Lords at pages 636-637 is quoted hereinbelow:

> "It is, in my view, very much to be regretted that a case of such importance to the development of English public law under this new procedure should have come before this House in the form that it does as a result of what my noble and learned friend, Lord Wilberforce, has described as the unfortunate course that was taken in the courts below when, leave to apply for judicial review having been previously granted *ex-parte*, the application itself came on for hearing. This has had the result of deflecting the Divisional Court and the Court of Appeal from giving consideration to the questions (1) what was the public duty of the Board of Inland Revenue of which it was alleged to be in breach, and (2) what was the nature of the breaches of that duty that were relied upon by the federation. Because of this, the judgment of the Court of Appeal, against which appeal to your Lordships' House is brought, takes the form of an interlocutory judgment declaring that the federation "have a sufficient interest to apply for judicial review herein."
>
> As my noble and learned friend has pointed out, these two omitted questions need to be answered in the instant case before it is possible to say whether the federation have "a sufficient interest in the matter to which the application relates," since, until they are answered, that matter cannot be identified. This is likely also to be the case in most applications

for judicial review that are not on the face of them frivolous or vexatious. Your Lordships have accordingly heard full argument on both these questions.

As respects the statutory powers and duties of the Board of Inland Revenue, these are described and dealt with in several of your Lordships' speeches. It would be wearisome if I were to repeat what already has been, and later will be, better said by others. All that I need say here is that the board are charged by statute with the care, management and collection on behalf of the Crown of Income-tax, corporation tax and capital gains tax. In the exercise of these functions the board have a wide managerial discretion as to the best means of obtaining for the national exchequer from the taxes committed to their charge, the highest net return that is practicable having regard to the staff available to them and the cost of collection. The board and the inspectors and collectors who act under their directions are under a statutory duty of confidentiality with respect to information about individual taxpayers' affairs that has been obtained in the course of their duties in making assessments and collecting the taxes; and this imposes a limitation on their managerial discretion. I do not doubt, however, and I do not understand any of your Lordships to doubt, that if it were established that the board were proposing to exercise or to refrain from exercising its powers not for reasons of "good management" but for some extraneous or ulterior reason, that action or inaction of the board would be *ultra vires* and would be a proper matter for judicial review if it were brought to the attention of the court by an applicant with "a sufficient interest" in having the board compelled to observe the law."

(Emphasis supplied)

89. Applying the above test we have to ascertain in the present case whether the decision of the Government in not preferring the appeal to the High Court under section 260A of the I.T. Act constituted inaction on the part of the Department. This question needs to be answered not in an abstract but having regard to position in law and having regard to the facts of the present case.

(b) Whether there was Failure of Statutory and Public Duty on the Part of the Revenue in Not Preferring an Appeal to the High Court under section 260A of the Income-Tax Act, 1961

The facts of the case of the assessee, Smt. Rabri Devi, are as follows:

On 14-10-1996 the assessee filed voluntary returns for assessment years 1995-96 and 1996-97. On 14-11-1996 she filed voluntary returns for assessment years 1986-87 to 1994-95 declaring various incomes which had escaped assessment as she had not filed her returns earlier. The assessee also applied for waiver of interest and penalty under section 273A of the I.T. Act. In the voluntary returns, the assessee disclosed income derived from dairy farming, agriculture and rent from house property. Upon receipt of returns for the assessment years 1995-96 and 1996-97 the Assistant Commissioner of Income Tax issued notice of defecting returns under section 139 of the I.T. Act in which it was alleged that regular books of accounts were not maintained; that, return was not accompanied by a statement indicating the amount of turnover, gross receipts, gross profits and net profits from business/profession. The assessee also received notices under section 148 of the I.T. Act for the period 1986-87 to 1994-95. The Assessing Officer recorded the reasons for reopening the assessment for each of the above years. For example, the reasons for reopening the assessment for the year 1986-87 are as follows:

"A notice under section 131A of the I.T. Act' 61 was issued to the husband of the assessee, asking him to furnish, among other things, details of income of other family members and details of assets owned by such family members. In reply to the said notice the assessee' husband submitted that the assessee had been deriving rental income from house property at Sheikhoura since 1983-84 and from dairy farms since 1975. Subsequently, the assessee on 25-10-96 filed details of her immovable and movable properties before the ADIT (Inv.), Patna. From a perusal of this, it is noticed that the assessee has made substantial investments in residential house at Sheikhoura, in agricultural land at Saran and Patna and land at Danapur, Patna. It is also noticed that she has made substantial investments in FDs, Kisan Vikas Patras and National Savings Certificates, besides having a number of bank a/cs. The assessee has also contributed to the construction of her husband's house property at Phulwari.

Despite having made such large investments, the assessee has never filed Income-tax returns, nor has she be assessed to Income-tax in past. Recently, the assessee had filed a petition under section 273-A of the I.T. Act 61 before the CIT, Patna. Pursuant to this petition, she had also filed a disclosure of income Rs. 70,000 for the A/Y in question in order to explain the capital required for the investment that she has made.

All these information in our possession give us reason to believe that at the very least a sum of Rs. 70,000 has escaped assessment for the A/Y 1986-87. Owing to the failure of the assessee to file return within stipulated time limit and to disclose material facts relevant to have assessment at the appropriate time.

As more than four years from end of the assessment year have lapsed, approval is solicited from DCIT, Range-1, Patna to issue notice under section 148 of the I.T. Act, 61. It is clarified that notice under section 148 of the I.T. Act is issuable as income escaping assessment exceeds the amount stipulated in section 149(1)(b).

Sd/- Nikhil Choudhary 20-11-96

Asst. Commissioner of Income-tax,

Spl. Inv. Circle-1, Patna."

90. I need not go into further details regarding the alleged undisclosed income for each assessment year. Suffice it to state that additions have been made by the Department to the income of the assessee under various orders passed by the Assessing Officer and the Commissioner of Income Tax (Appeals). These orders were challenged by the assessee before the Tribunal.

91. By the impugned judgment the appeals filed by the assessee were allowed by the Tribunal. While allowing the appeal of the assessee the Tribunal held that the case involved highly intricate issues; that, these issues were extremely difficult to understand; that, but for the assistance of the learned advocates on both sides it was difficult to adjudicate such disputes. At the same time the Tribunal without any basis castigated the officers of the Department including the Commissioner (Appeals) saying that rampant additions were made to destroy the case of the assessees and to destroy the political career of respondent No. 5 (*See*: para 40 of the judgment of the Tribunal). Similarly, the Tribunal has castigated the higher officers of the Department saying that they were biased and that they had acted at the behest of the Centre in clubbing the income of respondent No. 4 with that of respondent No. 5 who was going through political crisis (*See*: para 54 of the said judgment).

92. There is no basis given in the impugned decision of the Tribunal for making such strong observations against the officers of the Revenue. Although the High Court under section 260A of the I.T. Act would not have enquired into the sufficiency of materials or substituted its judgment for that of the Tribunal in regard to facts, nevertheless, if the conclusion drawn by the Tribunal is without any basis or based on irrelevant considerations then the High Court was required to interfere under section 260A.

93. PIL is not maintainable to probe or enquire into the returns of another taxpayer except in special circumstances. It is the ratio of the decision of House of Lords in the case of National Federation of Self-employed (supra). However, when Scams take place, accusation of disproportionate assets are required to be looked into.

94. In the case of *M.C. Mehta* v. *Union of India,* (Taj Trapezium Matter) (2003) 8 SCC 696, the Division Bench of this Court not only directed CBI to investigate the cases against the bureaucrats but also to enquire the outflow of Rs. 17 crores released by the State of U.P. in respect of project undertaken by NPCC. In that matter the income-tax returns of the former Chief Minister and other officials were ordered to be collected by this Court. They were directed to be collected from various income-tax authorities. The point to be noted is that the source of the funds plays a crucial role in investigations by CBI in matters involving misappropriation of public funds. Departments have to work in tandem. The evidentiary value of the collected material in the criminal trial is a matter different from the collection of information by the officers of the Revenue Department. In the present case officers of the Revenue have been condemned by the aforesaid judgment of the Tribunal. Comments have been made without any basis and yet till today appeals have not been filed by the Government under section 260A of the I.T. Act. As stated above, even the Tribunal has observed in its judgment that complicated legal issues were involved in the matter; that, even the members of the Tribunal found it very difficult to understand those issues, particularly, matters involving interpretation of sections 131, 131(1A), 273A and 147/148 of the I.T. Act. If the issues were so difficult for the members to understand, one fails to appreciate why high-ranking officers of the Department were castigated by the Tribunal. This Court has noticed in number of cases that even an innocuous statement of the Tribunal against the Revenue Officers is challenged before the higher courts on the ground that such observations are aspersions against the officers who have performed their duty and that they need to be expunged. Surprisingly, in this particular case till today no such appeal has been filed under section 260A of the I.T. Act. There is one more reason which is required to be mentioned. The judgment of the jurisdictional Tribunal on the scope and interpretation of the above sections which the Tribunal itself says involve complex legal issues, is binding on assessing officers and the appellate authority within that jurisdiction. If so, one fails to understand why the Department has not moved in appeal under section 260A of the I.T. Act. In the circumstances of this case, Union of India should apply its mind afresh and take its decision keeping in mind the factors referred to hereinabove. 2003 AIR SCW 6997.

95. Before concluding, it may be noted that arguments have been vehemently advanced on behalf of respondent No. 1 saying that these petitions need to be dismissed as the petitioners have made irresponsible statements against judicial officers and members of the Tribunal whose service records are sought to be tarnished. Applying the same yardstick one fails to understand as to why the Revenue has not moved in appeal even when its own higher officers are branded as biased in deciding matters against respondent Nos. 4 and 5. Their service records are as important as the service records of members of the trial court or the judicial officers.

(c) Whether the Procedure Adopted at the Time of Posting Mr. Munni Lal Paswan, Adj as Special Judge, CBI, Patna (Fodder Scam Cases) On 22-6-2005, Needs to be Relooked by the Patna High Court

96. Institutional autonomy of the High Court on its administrative side under article 233 and article 235 is a well-known concept. It is based on public trust and confidence. Existence of the power, as a concept, is different from exercise of power. Promotions and posting of judicial officers fall within its domain on its administrative side. At the same time it is important to note that choice of the candidate falls in the domain of public law and, therefore, that choice has to be exercised on some standard, failing which judicial review steps in. Standards of evaluation in matters of promotion and posting have to be uniformly applied otherwise arbitrariness comes in. Integration of the evaluation process has to be maintained. If different standards or no standards are applied it breaks the integrity of the process which brings in discrimination and arbitrariness which violates article 14 and therefore judicial review.

97. In the present case we are required to see whether the standards applied to evaluate Mr. J.P. Ratnesh and Mr. Ram Niwas Prasad, trial Judges, appointed as Special Judges *vide* Minutes of the meeting of the Standing Committee dated 22-6-2005 were equally applied while posting Mr. Munni Lal Paswan as Special Judge, CBI, Patna (Fodder Scam Cases).

98. By order dated 26-10-2005 this Court directed the Registrar General, Patna High Court, to forward this Court A.C.Rs. recorded by the Inspecting Judges of the High Court in the case of Mr. Munni Lal Paswan. In reply the Registrar General has stated as follows:

"The A.C.Rs., recorded by the Hon'ble Inspecting Judges in the years 1985, 1990 and by the Chairman of CAT in 1997, have been placed before the Supreme Court. Besides them no ACRs of Sri Munni Lal Paswan have ever been recorded by the Hon'ble Inspecting Judges. The A.C.Rs. of Additional District and Sessions Judges are recorded by the Hon'ble Inspecting Judges."

(Emphasis supplied)

99. Mr. Munni Lal Paswan was promoted to the post of ADJ on 17th June, 2003. Therefore, when Mr. Paswan was promoted as ADJ there was no categorization available.

100. In the report submitted by the Registrar General to this Court on 18-12-2005 pursuant to our order dated 26-10-2005, the Registrar General has forwarded the consolidated statement showing the Outturn of the work done by Mr. Paswan during the period 1998, 1999, 2000, 2001, 2002, 2003, 2004 and 2005 (partly). This statement refers to various parameters like disposal, remarks of P.O., remark of D.J. etc. as approved by the court. At this stage, I do not wish to comment about the remarks mentioned therein. These remarks have been approved by the District Judge and by the Courts. These remarks are heavily weighted against Mr. Paswan. It is not clear whether these remarks were ever noticed by the Committee and if not they need to be relooked by the High Court.

101. One more aspect needs to be stressed. There is a prescribed form in which the C.Rs. are recorded. That form indicates various parameters, namely, knowledge of law, whether the officer is hardworking, the rating to be given in respect of the judgments, namely, A+(outstanding), A (very good), B+(good), B (satisfactory). The point to be noted is that apart from honesty and integrity there are other parameters to be fulfilled by the judicial officers and that is where the disposals, ability and all other relevant factors come.

102. On 26th July, 2006 this Court put up the following three questions in the form of order to the Registrar General of the Patna High Court:

"1. Is it the practice in the High Court of Patna to prepare gradation/ remarks of the Judicial Officers by the Inspecting Judges?

2. As regards the three officers, including Shri M.L. Paswan, who were appointed as Special Judges on 22-6-2005 by the Standing Committee of the High Court, whether any remarks/gradation expressed by the Inspecting Judges were available to the Standing Committee?

3. Whether the gradation/remarks of the Inspecting Judges were made as regards these three officers?"

103. In reply, the Registrar General of the Patna High Court stated as follows in paras 2 to 4:

"2. That in regard to Query No. 1 of this Hon'ble Court as mentioned in the Order dated 26-7-2006, I respectfully say and submit that there is a practice in the High Court of Patna to record remarks of Judicial Officers by the Hon'ble Inspecting Judges of the concerned Judgeships which is known as Annual Confidential Remarks. The Annual Confidential Remarks recorded by the Hon'ble Inspecting Judges which includes knowledge of law, integrity, behaviour with Bar, general reputation, industriousness, efficiency, behaviour towards superiors and subordinate colleagues and categorization made by the Hon'ble Inspecting Judges and net result categorization is to be placed before the Standing Committee where the gradation is given to the Officer by the Hon'ble Standing Committee.

3. That in regard to Query No. 2 of this Hon'ble Court as mentioned in the Order dated 26-7-2006, I respectfully say and submit that the 3 Officers, namely, Shri Jawahar Prasad Ratnesh, Shri Ram Niwas Prasad and Shri Munni Lal Paswan who were appointed as Special Judge on 22-6-2005 by the Standing Committee, the remarks of the Hon'ble Inspecting Judges as maintained in the Guard Files which are maintained separately of each officers, were available to the Hon'ble Standing Committee. The said fact also finds mention in the decision dated 22-6-2005 of the Hon'ble Standing Committee.

4. That in regard to Query No. 3 of this Hon'ble Court as mentioned in the Order dated 26-7-2006, I respectfully say and submit that the remarks of the Hon'ble Inspecting Judge in case of Mr. Jawahar Prasad Ratnesh was of the year 1985, 1986-87, 1988, 2001, 2003 and 2005 (and remarks recorded by P.O., Industrial Tribunal, Patna in 1998). In respect of Shri Ram Niwas Prasad, the remarks recorded by the Hon'ble Inspecting Judge was of 1985, 1986, 1997 and 2002. As regards Shri Munni Lal Paswan, the remarks recorded by the Hon'ble Inspecting Judge was of 1985 and 1990 and by Vice-Chairman, Industrial Tribunal, Patna Bench in 1997."

(Emphasis supplied)

104. Reading para 4 it is clear that the remarks of Inspecting Judge, in the case of Mr. J.P. Ratnesh, were duly updated when they were placed before the Standing Committee of the High Court. In respect of Mr. Ram Niwas Prasad the remarks recorded by the Inspecting Judge for the years 1985, 1986, 1997 and 2002 were updated and placed before the Standing Committee of the High Court. However, in case of Mr. Munni Lal Paswan the remarks of the Inspecting Judge duly recorded are only of 1985 and 1990. Mr. Munni Lal Paswan was promoted as ADJ on 17-6-2003. He was posted as Special Judge on 22-6-2005. Therefore, it is clear that there is no gradation/categorisation of the confidential reports of Mr. Munni Lal Paswan by the Inspecting Judge of the High Court particularly after becoming ADJ.

105. In the case of *High Court of Punjab and Haryana, through Registrar General* v. *Ishwar Chand Jain,* (1999) 4 SCC 579 this Court has held as follows:

"32. Since late this Court is watching the spectre of either judicial officers or the High Courts coming to this Court when there is an order prematurely retiring a judicial officer. Under article 235 of the Constitution the High Court exercises complete control over subordinate courts which include District Courts. Inspection of the subordinate courts is one of the most important functions which the High Court performs for control over the subordinate courts. The object of such inspection is for the purpose of assessment of the work performed by the Subordinate Judge, his capability, integrity and competency. Since Judges are human beings and also prone to all the human failings inspection provides an opportunity for pointing out mistakes so that they are avoided in future and deficiencies, if any, in the working of the subordinate court, remedied. Inspection should act as a catalyst in inspiring Subordinate Judges to give the best results. They should feel a sense of achievement. They need encouragement. They work under great stress and man the courts while working under great discomfort and hardship. A satisfactory judicial system depends largely on the satisfactory functioning of courts at the grass-roots level. Remarks recorded by the Inspecting Judge are normally endorsed by the Full Court and become part of the annual confidential reports and are foundations on which the career of a judicial officer is made or marred. Inspection of a subordinate court is thus of vital importance. It has to be both effective and productive. It can be so only if it is well-regulated and is workmanlike. Inspection of subordinate courts is not a one-day or an hour or a few minutes' affair. It has to go on all the year round by monitoring the work of the Court by the Inspecting Judge. A casual inspection can hardly be beneficial to a judicial system. It does more harm than good. As noticed in the case of Registrar, *High Court of Madras* v. *R. Rajiah,* AIR 1988 SC 1388: (1988) 3 SCC 211 there could be ill-conceived or motivated complaints. Rumour-mongering is to be avoided at all costs as it seriously jeopardizes the efficient working of the subordinate Courts.

33. Time has come that a proper and uniform system of inspection of subordinate courts should be devised by the High Courts. In fact the whole system of inspection needs rationalization. There should be some scope of self-assessment by the officer concerned. We are informed that the First National Judicial Pay Commission is also looking into the matter. This subject, however, can be well-considered in a Chief Justices' Conference as the High Court itself can devise an effective system of inspection of the subordinate courts. The Registrar General shall place a copy of this judgment before the Hon'ble Chief Justice of India for him to consider if the method of inspection of subordinate courts could be a matter of the agenda for the Chief Justices' Conference."

(Emphasis supplied)

106. The above judgment emphasizes the importance of the remarks given by the Inspecting Judge. The object of Inspection is to assess the work performed, capability, competency besides integrity of the candidate. Those gradations/categorisations given by Inspecting Judges are required to be placed before the Full Court. In the present case, that exercise is done for two out of three judicial officers when they were posted. However, it appears from the affidavit of the Registrar General that no gradation/categorisation has been done after 1990 by the Inspecting Judge *vis-a-vis* the judgments of Mr. Munni Lal Paswan.

107. It is important to bear in mind that in the matter of economic scams be it security transactions or fodder scams or Taj corridor it is the economic interest of the country which is at stake. These cases are highly complicated in which complicated questions are involved and, therefore, posting plays a vital role.

108. In the circumstances, it seems that the procedure followed by the High Court in the meeting on 22-6-2005 has lost sight of the above criteria. In the circumstances, a request is being made to the Chief Justice of the Patna High Court to convene an urgent meeting of Administrative Judges and complete the exercise of giving appropriate gradation/categorisation after looking at the judgments and orders delivered by the concerned judge, Mr. Paswan. I may make it clear that this is just a request to the High Court and not a direction so that the evaluation standards are commonly applied to all the three candidates.

109. Before concluding it may be pointed out that this decision is confined strictly to the decision-making process and it is not concerned with the merits of the allegations made in the petitions. The allegations made in the petitions are not only against the accused, they are also directed against number of functionaries. It is, therefore, made clear that this decision is only to rectify the procedure of decision-making at the High Court level and at the Revenue level so that in future such anomalies do not arise.

110. To sum up, the Chief Justice of the Patna High Court is requested to convene a meeting of Administrative Judges and have a fresh look at the evaluation in the case of posting of Sri Paswan as Special Judge for C.B.I. (Fodder Scam Cases) at Patna, vide Minutes of Meeting dated 22-6-2005. At the same time, Union of India is directed to reconsider approaching the High Court against the decision of the Tribunal dated 2-7-2004 under section 260A of the Income Tax Act, 1961 in the light of what is stated above.

111. In the end it may be stated that true value of a decision lies in its propriety and not in the decision being right or wrong.

112. Writ Petition (Crl.) Nos.197-198 of 2004 are accordingly allowed to the extent indicated above.

Order accordingly.

———

Palitana Sugar Mills Pvt. Ltd.

v.

Smt. Vilasiniben Ramachandran

Contempt Petition (Civil) 136-137 of 2005 in C.A. No. 6798-6799 of 2004 with I.A. No. 21-30, I.A. Nos. 17-18 & I.A. No. 1 in I.A. Nos. 17-18 in C.A. No. 6798-6799 of 2004

Decided on: 20-3-2007

Coram: **Dr. AR. Lakshmanan, J.**

FACTS:

The Government Authorities of Bhavnagar District failed to comply with the order passed on 15-10-2004 by the Supreme Court in relation to Civil Appeal No. 6798 and 6799 of 2004. Hence this Contempt Petition.

ISSUE:

Contempt of Court.

HELD:

The Officials are guilty of willful and deliberate act of contempt of order dated 15-10-2004. However, taking a lenient view and taking into consideration of the future prospects of the officers, the Court is not imposing any punishment for their willful and contumacious violation of the order of this Court. They are severely warned that they shall not involve themselves or violate the order of the highest Court of the land and will not resort to the unacceptable new pleas by way of defence for the first time in the contempt proceedings. The inherent power will not only be available under section 151 CPC as available to this Court in such a case but it is bound to be exercised in that manner in the interest of justice and public interest. By this order four weeks time is granted to the respondents to comply with all the directions given in the judgment dated 15-10-2004. The petitioner is at liberty to move this Court if the directions are not complied with in its letter and spirit.

Dr. AR. Lakshmanan, J.—This Court, on 15-10-2004, by a detailed judgment and order passed in Civil Appeal No. 6798 and 6799 of 2004 issued, *inter alia,* the following directions:

> "73. In the result, we allow the appeals in part and direct the Collector, Bhavnagar to grant non-agricultural permission in respect of the land of about 76 acres 36 guntas comprised in Survey No. 469/1, Bhavnagar District after collecting the non-agricultural tax calculated at the rate of 5% per sq. m. applicable at the time when the application was made by the applicant *i.e.* 24-2-2003 which aggregate to Rs. 15,57,540. Dispute, if any, with regard to the tax calculated and the rate has to be agitated separately and collected later. The Commissioner of Bhavnagar Municipal Corporation is directed to consider the application for sanction within four weeks, the layout and building plans as per the current development control rules and pass order in accordance with law.
>
> 74. We also direct Respondents 1 and 2 to collect non-agricutural permission charges and conversion charges for the lands bearing Survey Nos. 470/1, 471/2, 471/3 and 472 situated at Village Wodera, Bhavnagar as prevalent in the year 1981."

2. The petitioners sent a representation to the Government along with a copy of the aforementioned judgment with a request to comply with the directions contained in the judgment. The petitioners, thereafter sent several reminders to the respondents to comply with the said judgment.

3. Notification was issued by the State Government wherein the lands of RS. Nos. 471/2 and 472 were notified as a water body in purported compliance with the High Court's order dated 2-8-2002. By the said order, the High Court had directed the State Government to notify the water bodies in the territory of the State that vest in the State and/or the Area Development Authorities or the Local Bodies including the Panchayat in the Official Gazette within 3 months from the date of this order and not a private land.

4. The Deputy Secretary of the Revenue Department wrote to the Collector, Bhavnagar District that the Government had accepted the said judgment of this Court except for the land of RS No. 472 and requested the Collector to take steps for the entire survey Nos. except for the above-mentioned survey No. 472 and to immediately inform the Government about the steps taken by him. This communication was sent on 16-2-2005. Although the direction from the Revenue Department was for accepting the judgment of this Court except for the land covered by survey No. 472, the Collector not only refused to follow the judgment for survey No. 472 but also for 80 acres of survey No. 471/2. On 28-6-2005, the above contempt petition was filed in this Court with the following prayer:—

(a) "initiate contempt proceedings against the respondents No. 1 to 10 herein for deliberately and willfully not complying with the specific directions of this Hon'ble Court contained in the judgment dated 15-10-2004 in Civil Appeal No. 6798-99 of 2004;

(b) direct the respondents to forthwith grant non-agricultural permission and other necessary building and development permission in respect of part of the land of R.S. No. 471/2 (admeasuring about 80 acres) and 472 (admeasuring about 50 acres) of Village Vadva, District Bhavnagar.

(c) Pass such other and suitable order/s as this Hon'ble Court may deem fit and necessary in the facts and circumstances of the case and in the interest of justice."

5. On 25-7-2005, this Court issued notice regarding non-compliance of directions contained in para 74 confining survey Nos. 471/2 and 472. After the notice was issued in the contempt petition, the State Government filed an application for directions in IA No. 17 and 18 of 2005 for certain directions. On 9-5-2006, this Court passed the following order:—

"The clarification sought for in these contempt petitions is by way of review petition. Let the entire matter be placed before the appropriate bench which delivered the judgment dated 15-10-2004.

The contemnors must be present on the next date of hearing".

6. This Court corrected the mistake in the order dated 9-5-2006 and passed the following order: "In our order dated 9-5-2006 in place of Contempt Petition the IAs shall be recorded".

7. A letter was written on 10-1-2007 to the Revenue Department by the Collector to take steps as the State Government has taken a decision to accept the judgment of this Court dated 15-10-2004 for land admeasuring 17 acres 4 guntas, 32 guntas and 1 acre 14 guntas upon which sundervas bungalow is located. However, to nullify the aforesaid acceptance of the judgment in respect of the land mentioned in survey Numbers above, permission for non-agricultural use has been given for the recreation use and not for the residential use thus depriving the petitioner of the right to construct residential building.

8. We heard Mr. Mukul Rohatgi, learned senior counsel for the petitioner in the contempt petition and Mr. L.N. Rao, learned senior counsel for the respondents in contempt petition and the petitioners in IA No. 17 and 18 of 2005.

9. At the time of hearing, our attention was drawn to the details of the earlier proceedings where the contention was that the land on survey Nos.

472 and 471/2 which form part of the lake/water body was taken by the State Government. Our attention was also drawn to the following documents:

> "1. Affidavit-in-reply dated 12-12-2001 filed by Shri Kantilal A Patel, former District Collector, Bhavnagar before this Hon'ble Court in IA Nos. 2-3 of 2001 in Civil Appeal No. 5556 of 2001.
>
> 2. Affidavit-in-rejoinder dated 21-3-2002 filed by Shri Natvarlal R Agravat, Legal Officer, Bhavnagar Municipal Corporation before this Hon'ble Court in Civil Appeal No. 5556 of 2001 filed by the Bhavnagar Municipal Corporation.
>
> 3. Affidavit-in-rejoinder dated 21-3-2002 filed by Shri Natvarlal R. Agravat, Legal Officer, Bhavnagar Municipal Corporation before this Hon'ble Court in Special Leave Petition No. 1561 of 2002 filed by the Bhavnagar Municipal Corporation.
>
> 4. Synopsis filed in Civil Appeal No. 5556 of 2001.
>
> 5. Chronology of events filed on behalf of Bhavnagar Municipal Corporation in the aforementioned Civil Appeal No. 5556 of 2001.
>
> 6. Civil Appeal No. 5556 of 2001 after elaborate arguments was dismissed as withdrawn by this Hon'ble Court *vide* order dated 14-11-2002.
>
> 7. Review Petition No. 33 of 2003 filed for the review of the judgment of this Hon'ble Court dated 5-12-2002 passed in SLP No. 1561-63 of 2002. The affidavit in support of this review petition was filed by Mr. Kantilal A Patel.
>
> 8. The Review Petition was dismissed by this Hon'ble Court vide order dated 6-2-2003."

10. Mr. Mukul Rohatgi invited our attention to the various findings and categories directions issued by this Court to the respondents State of Gujarat and its officers. It is well settled that the judgments of this Court are binding on all the authorities under article 142 of the Constitution and it is not open to any authority to ignore a binding judgment of this Court on the ground that the full facts had not been placed before this Court and/or the judgment of this Court in the earlier proceedings had only collaterally or incidentally decided the issues raised in the show-cause notices. Such an attempt is to belittle the issues and the orders of this Court. We are pained to say that the then Deputy Collector has scant respect for the orders passed by the Apex Court.

11. Our attention was also drawn to the letter dated 16-2-2005 by the Government of Gujarat to the Collector, Bhavnagar regarding the judgment of this Court dated 15-10-2004 and letter dated 11-5-2005 of the Collector, Bhavnagar in No. RO/KB-21/2005 and, in particular, to para 6 of the said communication which reads thus:

> "In connection with the judgment of the Hon'ble Apex Court dated 15-10-2004, the Revenue Department of the State Government *vide* letter dated 16-2-2005 at Reference No. 3 had accepted the judgment rendered by the Hon'ble Apex Court for all the lands except for the land of RS No. 472 of Mauje Vadva. Thus, directions have been given to this office to initiate

process for the land of all the survey numbers except for the area of S. No. 472 of Vadva. For initiating further process in connection with the letter dated 16-2-2005 of the Government, by the order at Reference No. 5 whereby the Scheme was sanctioned for construction of dwelling units for weaker sections of the society for total 34,47,918 sq.mtrs. out of which about 80 acres of land of Acres 550 and 31 gunthas of RSN 471/2 is being shown as "Water Body" in the sanctioned development plan of the Bhavnagar Area Development Authority and as the land of S. No. 472 is to be kept pending for the present, except this lands as well as the land for which earlier non-agricultural permission has been granted, considering the land of acres 699-03 gunthas (2829020.5 sq. mtrs) forming part of ULC Scheme to be Deemed NA (land termed to be non-agricultural land) pursuant to the judgment dated 15-10-2004 of the Hon'ble Apex Court, after assessment under the provisions of section 48 of the Bombay Land Revenue Code, 1879, it was intimated by this Office to the State Government by letter at Reference No. 4 that permission can be given."

12. Mr. Rohatgi, learned senior counsel further submitted that despite our clear and unambiguous direction the respondent No. 3 Deputy Secretary, Revenue Department of the State Government under specific instructions from respondent Nos. 1 and 2 Secretaries of the Revenue Department has *vide* letter dated 16-2-2005 conveyed to the Collector the stand of the Government not to accept the judgment dated 15-10-2004 in respect of the land admeasuring 50 acres situated in survey No. 472 and grounds which are wholly untenable. Pursuant thereto respondent No. 8 the Collector acting on the aforementioned instruction of respondent Nos. 1, 2 and 3 has also refused to grant such no objection in respect of survey No. 471/2 and 472. A perusal of the said correspondence would, in our view, show that the respondents have expressly stated that the Government has decided not to accept the judgment of this Court insofar as the aforementioned lands are concerned. It is needless to emphasize that judgments of this Court are binding on all authorities and the Government cannot arrogate to its powers to reject the judgment of this Court. As regards the land admeasuring 80 acres in survey Nos. 471/2 and 50 acres in 472 are concerned, the respondent-authorities are refusing to grant the NA permission on the self same issues, namely, that the said land is a government land. The said issues have already been finally concluded in favour of the petitioners by the various judgments of this Court in the earlier litigations.

In para 68 of the judgment, this Court has observed as under:—

"68. From the above discussion by us and of the record would clearly go to show that the following issues are covered by the earlier proceedings and finally decided by the Courts and reached its finality and which cannot be reopened again:

(1) The lands in Survey Nos. 469/1, 470/1, 471/2, 471/3 and 472 aggregating about 952 acres sold in favour of the appellants by the former ruler with the permission of the Collector and registered has become final and conclusive.

(2) The lands in question being pasture land (Bid land) and not being fit for cultivation was excluded from the purview of the Gujarat Agricultural Land Ceiling Act, 1960.

(3) The Right, Title Entry made in the revenue records in respect of the lands in question in the name of the appellant has become final and conclusive and, therefore, removal of the appellant from any of the Survey Numbers in question is not permissible.

(4) The declaration issued by the competent authority and Additional Collector under the ULC Act, in exercise of the power under section 21(1) of the ULC Act after verifying the title of the appellant in respect of the above survey numbers is final and conclusive.

(5) The writ petition filed by the Bhavnagar Municipality for quashing and setting aside the order dated 6-12-1979 granting exemption to the lands and sanctioning the scheme under section 21 of the ULC Act was valid and legal.

(6) It is not in dispute that the appellants have raised construction on the lands and the lands have been fully developed, save and except, the lands in Survey No. 469/1.

(7) The orders dated 9-11-1979 and 20-11-1979 whereby the Deputy Collector dropped the proceedings filed by the former Ruler under section 8 of the ALC Act for a declaration that the sale deed dated 31-3-1971 was not effected by him with a view to defeat the ALC Act was rejected by the Tribunal in Revision application by the State Government. In respect of the ALC proceedings, the said order was finally concluded since under the ALC Act no further appeal was preferred by the State Government.

(8) This also was not in dispute that pursuant to the cabinet decision of the Gujarat Government, the appellants withdraw all the pending proceedings and, thereafter notices were issued under rule 108(6) of the Bombay Land Revenue Code seeking to revise the right and title Entry No. 1950 principally contending that the sale deed dated 31-3-1971 was invalid. On the abovementioned grounds, the mutation entry was sought to be cancelled. The Deputy Collector, Bhavnagar held that the ownership of the land in question was of the appellant and a decision was taken that the revenue mutation No. 1950 as recorded in Village Form No. 6 was legal and valid which was also decided to withdraw the show cause notice dated 27-7-1991 and to drop all the proceedings commenced under the said notice.

(9) The Deputy Collector also confirmed the order of the City Mamlatdar dated 16-9-1962. The reservation of Survey No. 469/1 in favour of the Bhavnagar University had lapsed.

(10) The High Court, in its judgment, in SCA No. 1032 of 1996 quashed the notice dated 25-1-1996 of the Collector. The High Court observed that it is unfair for the Collector to raise various issues such as illegal

sale of bid land, breach of the Saurashtra Gharkhed Ordinance, ALC Act etc., which were closed and decided earlier.

(11) The issue of ULC Act and ALC Act was concluded by the judgment of the High Court in SCA No. 941 of 1980.

(12) No further action can be taken for disturbing the finality of the mutation entry in view of the judgment of the High Court rendered on 24-11-2000 in SCA No. 1032 of 1996 and, therefore, there is no question of disturbing the mutation entry on the strength of the contravention of the provisions of other enactments now.

(13) Civil appeal No. 5536 of 2001 preferred by the Municipal Corporation was dismissed as withdrawn. Thus the issue of ULC Act and ALC Act raised in SCA 941 of 1980 was finally concluded by the said judgment.

(14) in the judgment in *Bhavnagar University* v. *Palitana Sugar Mills Ltd.*, (supra), this Court decided the dispute between the Bhavnagar University and the appellant with reference to Gujarat Town Planning and Urban Development Act, 1976. The appeal filed by the Bhavnagar University was finally dismissed by this Court.

(15) Review petition No. 33 of 2003 was also dismissed by this Court."

13. It is thus clear and apparent that despite the clear observations of this Court in paragraphs above of the present judgment that no issue raised in prior litigations can be raised again and no attempt to challenge the right and title in respect of the land in question could be made against the petitioners, namely, the respondents have once again sought to raise the same issues with a view to flout the directions of this Court and deprive the petitioners of the legitimate rights accruing to them from the judgment of this Court. The aforesaid attitude persists notwithstanding that the judgment of this Court has been passed in contempt proceedings and this Court has expressly observed that any further lapse shall be viewed extremely seriously.

14. We have already elaborately dealt with the history of the present litigation between the parties which shows that despite the petitioners having succeeded before this Court in 4 different hotly contested litigations *vide* judgments dated 14-11-2002, 3-12-2002, 5-12-2002 and 6-2-2003, the respondents have in one way or the other not complied with the judgment or not given the petitioners the development and building permissions required to construct on the lands in question. In our opinion, the respondents have with impunity flouted our judgments dated 15-10-2004. Mr. L.N. Rao invited our attention to the reply filed by respondents in order to justify their action in the contempt petition raising new pleas and new contentions in regard to survey No. 472 and 47/1. This apart they also filed IA Nos. 17 and 18 for certain directions after the notice was issued by this Court in the contempt petition regarding non-compliance and directions. The learned senior counsel reiterated the submissions made in the two IAs. The respondents sought to file the above 2 IAs under the guise of filing the review petition. During the pendency of the contempt petition and the IAs, a letter was written by the Revenue Department to the Collector, Bhavnagar to take steps as the Government has taken a decision to accept the judgment of this Court dated 15-10-2004 for the land admeasuring 17 acres 4 guntas and 0.32 guntas and 1 acre 14 guntas upon which sundervas bungalow is located. The Collector was directed to comply with the said direction. However, in order to nullify the aforesaid acceptance of the judgment in respect of the land mentioned above, permission for non-agricultural use has been given for the recreation use and not for the residential use thus depriving the petitioner of the right to construct residential houses. The action of the respondents and the Collector in issuing permission for non-agricultural use for the recreation use is with an oblique motive to deprive the petitioner of the right to construct residential houses as already ordered in our judgment dated 15-10-2004. We, therefore, direct the Revenue Department and the Collector, Bhavnagar to forthwith issue permission to the petitioner for residential use with a right to construct residential houses for the above survey Nos. as mentioned in the letter dated 10-1-2007 of the Revenue Department to the Collector, Bhavnagar. In an answer to a query put by this Court to Mr. Mukul Rohatgi as to whether survey No. 471/2 was a water body, the learned senior counsel while disputing the statement of learned senior counsel for the State made a categorical statement that the said survey No. 471/2 is not a water body. The statement made by the learned senior counsel is placed on record. If it is not a water body, there cannot be any impediment on the part of the respondents' authorities in granting non-agricultural permission and other necessary building and development permission in respect of RS No. 471/2 admeasuring 80 acres and 472 admeasuring about 50 acres of village Vadva Dist. Bhavnagar. If 471/2 is the Water Body the respondents would be at liberty to decline Non-Agriculture permission.

15. We also direct the respondents to collect non-agricultural permission charges and conversion charges for the lands bearing survey Nos. 470/1, 471/2, 471/3 and 472 situated at village Wadera Bhavnagar as prevalent in the year 1981.

16. In our opinion, all the respondents had deliberately and with *mala fide* motive committed contempt of our order dated 15-10-2004. We have already explained their conduct and refusal to comply with our earlier orders. When they were advised to comply with the order by this Court during the pendency of the contempt proceedings, the act of the respondent in not complying is not only willful but also deliberate and contumacious. The respondents have not even tendered unqualified apology before this Court but filed an application in IA No. 17 and 18 of 2005.

17. We, therefore, hold them guilty of willful and deliberate act of contempt of our order dated 15-10-2004. However, taking a lenient view and taking into consideration of the future prospects of the officers, we are not imposing any punishment for their willful and contumacious violation of the order of this Court. They are severely warned that they shall not involve themselves or violate the order of the highest Court of the land and will not resort to the unacceptable new pleas by way of defence for the first time in the contempt proceedings. They shall not hereafter also take the plea of inventing an innovative defence that they did not realise the implications of the order passed by this Court when no such argument was ever advanced at the time of hearing before this Court and on earlier occasions. Courts have held in a catena of decisions that where in violation of an order of this Court, something has been done in disobedience, it will be the duty of this Court as a policy to set the wrong right and not to allow the perpetuation of the wrong doing. In our opinion, the inherent power will not only be available under section 151, CPC as available to us in such a case but it is bound to be exercised in that manner in the interest of justice and public interest. All the respondents are senior and experienced officers and must be presumed to know that under the constitutional scheme of this country orders of this Court have to be punctually obeyed and should not be trifled with. We have already found hereinabove that they have acted deliberately to subvert the orders of this Court. We, therefore, hold them guilty of contempt of Court and do hereby censure severely their conduct. Though a copy of this order could be sent which shall form part of the annual confidential record of service of each of the said officers, we refrain from doing so by taking a lenient view of the matter considering the future prospects of the officers. As already stated, the officers shall not indulge in any adventurous act and strictly obey the orders passed by the Courts of law. We by this order grant four weeks time to the respondents to comply with all our directions given in the judgment dated 15-10-2004. The petitioner is at liberty to move this Court if the directions are not complied with in its letter and spirit.

18. The contempt petition stands allowed and the IAs stand dismissed.

All Bengal Excise Licensees

v.

Raghabendra Singh

Appeal (Civil) 1246 of 2007 [Arising out of SLP (C) No. 15224 of 2006]

Decided on: 9-3-2007

Coram: **Dr. AR. Lakshmanan, J.**
A. Kabir, J.

FACTS:

The Calcutta High Court passed an interim order on 4-1-2005, to the effect that the respondent-authorities will be at liberty to process the applications in respect of grant of licenses for excise shops but no final selection in respect of such shops shall be made without obtaining specific leave of the Court. However, in deliberate and willful disregard of the order the respondent-authorities published advertisement in the newspapers for holding lottery for final selection of excise shops and the lottery has been held on 20-3-2005. A contempt petition filed before the High Court was dismissed. Hence this appeal before the Supreme Court by Special Leave.

ISSUE:

Contempt of Court.

HELD:

The respondents had deliberately and with *mala fide* motive have committed contempt of the High Court in conducting the lottery quite contrary to the order of injunction passed by the High Court on 4-1-2005 and its subsequent extensions. The High Court has miserably failed in not issuing direction to the contemnors to cancel the lottery held in violation of the solemn order passed by the High Court. The High Court committed a grave error of law by not holding that if there was a doubt about the implication of the order of the Court, the alleged contemnors should have approached the Court and have clarified their alleged confusion. However, taking a lenient view and taking into consideration of the future prospects of the respondent-officers, the Court is not imposing any punishment for their willful violation of the order of the High Court and accept the unqualified apology filed before the High Court. Respondents are severely warned that they shall not involve themselves or violate the order passed by any Court of law.

JUDGMENT

Dr. AR. Lakshmanan, J.—Leave granted.

2. The above appeal was filed by All Bengal Licensees Association, Kolkata against (1) Raghabendra Singh, Principal Secretary, Excise Department, Govt. of West Bengal (2) Tallen Kumar, Excise Commissioner, Excise Department, (3) Manoj Kumar Panth, District Magistrate and Collector, 24-Parganas (4) Parvez Siddique, Addl. District Magistrate, 24-Parganas as contesting respondents and (5) Pradyut Kumar Saha, General Secretary of All Bengal Excise Licensees Association, Kolkata as proforma respondent.

3. The above appeal is directed against the final judgment and order dated 29-8-2006 of the Calcutta High Court passed in CC No. 62 of 2005 arising out of Writ Petition No. 2248 of 2004 whereby a learned Single Judge of the said High Court has dismissed the application for contempt filed by the appellant herein. According to the appellant, the contesting respondents have deliberately and willfully violated and were in utter disregard of the solemn order dated 4-1-2005, 19-1-2005 and 20-1-2005 passed by Hon'ble Mr. Justice Pranab Kumar Chattopadhyay in Writ Petition No. 2248 of 2004 filed by *All Bengal Excise Licensees Assn.* v. *State of West Bengal,* The background facts are as under:—

4. By an order dated 4-1-2005, a learned Single Judge passed an interim order to the effect that the respondent-authorities will be at liberty to process the applications in respect of grant of licenses for excise shops but no final selection in respect of such shops shall be made without obtaining specific leave of the Court. The High Court made it clear that the respondent-authorities will not hold any lottery for the purpose of final selection of the excise shops in question without obtaining further orders from the High Court. The said order dated 4-1-2005 was passed after hearing and in the presence of the learned advocate for the respondents.

5. The said interim order dated 4-1-2005 was extended by the order dated 19-1-2005 until further orders by the High Court.

6. Thereafter, on 28-1-2005 a learned Single Judge gave direction for filing the affidavit and the said interim order was further extended until further orders and the said interim order is still continuing.

7. The said orders dated 4-1-2005, 19-1-2005 and 20-1-2005 were communicated by the appellant's advocate's letter dated 15-3-2005 enclosing therewith the Xerox copies of the signed copies of the said dictated order. In spite of full knowledge about the said order each of the respondents, in deliberate and wilful disregard of the orders, caused an advertisement to be published in the newspapers for holding lottery for final selection of excise shops to be held on 20-3-2005, 21-3-2005 and 22-3-2005.

8. Pursuant to the said advertisement, a lottery has been held on 20-3-2005 for the purpose of final selection of the excise shops. It was submitted by the appellants that from the act and conduct of the respondents, it is evident that each of them have no regard for the orders dated 4-1-2005, 19-1-2005 and 20-1-2005 passed by this Court and are deliberately violating the said orders passed by the High Court and are thus guilty of contempt of Court. With these allegations, the appellants filed CC No. 62 of 2005 in the High Court.

9. The appellant is an Association of Excise Licensees including the country spirit shop owners. Challenging the policy decisions for issuance of thousands of excise licenses for opening of new foreign liquor off shop and country spirit shops in the State of West Bengal in violation of the provisions of the Bengal Excise Act, 1909 and the rules framed thereunder, the appellant, amongst others, moved a writ petition being No. 1982 of 2004 in the High Court upon notice to the respondents. A copy of the writ petition was also filed and marked as annexures in this civil appeal. The High Court (Hon'ble Mr. Justice Pinaki Chander Ghosh), after hearing the advocates for the parties on 24-11-2004 passed an order, *inter alia* as follows:

> "that the respondent authorities will process the matter but will not finalise and issue the licence without the leave of the court.

The matter will appear on 9th December, 2004.

10. Thereafter, the above-mentioned matter appeared in the list on 09-12-2004 before the very same Judge. The learned Judge, after hearing the advocates for the parties, gave a direction to file affidavit and the matter was directed to appear 4 weeks after vacation and also further directed that the interim order already passed in the matter will continue.

11. Although there was no direction for making any further advertisement by the respondent-authorities inviting any application for obtaining excise licenses for the new excise shops proposed to be give on or about 20-12-2004, some of the members of the appellant came to know that an advertisement was published on 30-11-2004 in the Bengali Daily newspaper Janashakti by the Excise Department, Government of West Bengal, whereby applications had been invited for giving new licenses for excise including country spirit shops within the Districts of Coochbehar, Jalpaiguri, North 24 Parganas and Hooghly. The members also came to know that the Excise Authorities have issued a memo No. 23-5(XX)/2003-04 3268 (21E) dated 7-12-2004 and rest to the District Magistrates and Collectors that there has been a proposal for granting supplementary country spirit license to the existing tari shop owners. The appellants made representations before the Excise Authorities and contended that since the matter is sub-judice, the respondent authorities cannot publish the said advertisement on 30-11-2005 and cannot issue the said memo. However, the Excise Authorities have further decided to hold lottery on 5-1-2005 for allotment of excise shops including the country spirit and foreign liquor shops. Immediately after coming to know about the above-mentioned fact, the North 24 Parganas Excise Licenses Assn. have moved a writ petition on 30-12-2004 before the vacation Judge of the High Court. In the said writ petition, the appellant No.1 herein was made a party respondent. The vacation Judge did not pass any interim order on the said writ petition against the said order dated 30-12-2004. The North 24 Parganas Excise Licencees Assn. preferred an appeal on 30-12-2004 and the Division Bench of the High Court passed an interim order on 30-12-2004 to the effect that the processing in respect of grant of issuance of country spirit license will continue but finalization and selection will not be made till 3 weeks after the vacation. However, they made it clear that finalisation include holding of lottery. The said order was restricted to only in the case of District North 24 Parganas. It was submitted that the subject-matter of writ petition No. 2248 of 2004 is that during the pendency of earlier writ petition, the respondent-authorities cannot issue any advertisement for inviting applications for obtaining new excise license including the country spirit shops and foreign liquor shops and cannot hold any lottery and further they cannot give the effect to the proposal for giving supplementary excise licensees to the tari shops. It was submitted that in order to frustrate the order dated 24-11-2004, the respondent authorities have made an advertisement dated 30-11-2004 and thereby invited applications from intending candidates from obtaining new licenses in respect of 4 Districts and further making attempt to hold lottery in respect of applications already received. In spite of repeated requests, the respondents have pre-determined to hold the lottery on 5-1-2005 which amounts to finalization of the applications for granting of licenses and they are also trying to issue supplementary licenses to the existing shop owners.

On 04-1-2005, the Court passed the following order:—

> "Let this matter be listed before the regular bench one week after the Christmas vacation."

12. In the meantime, let there be an interim order only to the effect that the respondent authorities herein will be at liberty to process the applications in respect of grant of licence for excise shops but no final selection in respect of such shops shall be made without obtaining specific leave of this court.

13. I also make it clear that the respondent authorities will also not hold any lottery for the purpose of final selection of the aforesaid excise shops in question without obtaining further orders from this court. All parties are to act on a Xerox signed copy of this dictated order on the usual undertaking." Again, the interim order was directed to continue until further orders on 28-1-2005. As already stated, the counsel for the appellant communicated the said orders and served upon the respondents the Xerox copies of the signed copies of the order dated 4-1-2005, 19-1-2005 and 20-1-2005. Although the said interim order dated 4-1-2005 which has been extended from time to time and is still continuing the respondents in utter disregard caused publication of the advertisement of the newspapers for holding lottery for the purpose of final selection of excise shops in question. It is also pertinent to mention here that both the Division Bench of the High Court order dated 15-3-2005 in APOT No. 770/2004 vacated the interim order passed in the appeal preferred by the North 24 Parganas Excise Licensees Assn. but the interim order passed in the writ petition being No. 2248 of 2004 is relating to any proposed new excise licenses through out the State of West Bengal is still continuing. However, in pursuance to the advertisement, the respondent authorities on 20th March held lottery for final selection of the aforesaid excise shops and shall hold further lottery on 22nd and 23rd March, 2005. It was, therefore, submitted that each of the respondents deliberately and willfully and in utter disregard to the orders dated 04-1-2005 held lottery for final selection of excise shops. It is further submitted that the respondents are guilty of deliberate and willful violation of the 3 orders passed by this Court and committed contumacious act and in spite of full knowledge about the orders. It was further submitted that the respondents have scant respect for the orders passed on all the 3 days in January, 2005 and are deliberately ignoring the said orders and are thus guilty of contempt of court. According to the appellant, by the above-mentioned act and conduct of the contemnors/respondents the majesty and dignity of the High Court have been lowered down and, therefore, the respondents should be suitably dealt with and punished. It was also further submitted that having regard to the facts and circumstances of the case, the respondents should be restrained from holding any further lottery and/or from giving any effect and/or further effect of the lottery already held and/or from taking any further steps for issuance of any excise license to any person so that the majesty and dignity of the High Court is not lowered down. In the circumstances, they requested the High Court to issue rule *nisi* calling upon the respondents and each of them to show cause as to why the respondents and each of them should not be committed to prison or otherwise be suitably dealt with and/or punished for deliberate and willful violation and utter disregard of the solemn orders dated 04/19 and 20-1-2005 passed in writ petition No. 2248 of 2004.

14. In the contempt petition, rule was issued on 23-3-2005. The respondents filed an application praying for discharge of the rule issued in the contempt proceedings on 2-5-2005 North 24 Parganas Excise Licensees Assn. filed SLP (C) No. 10820 of 2005 against the order dated 15-3-2005 passed by the Division Bench of the High Court. The State of West Bengal filed an application for vacating the interim order dated 4-1-2005 passed in writ petition No. 2248 of 2004. On 26-7-2005, a learned Single Judge allowed the application and vacated the interim order but, however, directed the Government that they would be free to take steps in issuing license in terms of the policy but it will be mentioned in the license that it is subject to the result of the writ petition and further directed that all steps taken for issuing excise license would abide by the result of the writ petition.

15. Being aggrieved by the order of the learned Single Judge dated 26-7-2005, the appellant preferred an appeal being APOT No. 494 of 2005 on 10-8-2005. A Division Bench of the High Court dismissed the said appeal and confirmed the order of the single judge dated 26-7-2005. The Appellant's Assn. preferred SLP No. 17371 of 2005 against the said judgment. This Court on 29-8-2005 issued notice with an interim direction to the effect that no license be issued in terms of the circular dated 20-1-2004 and the matter was directed to be listed along with SLP No. 10820 of 2005. Both the SLPs were dismissed by this Court on 7-11-2005. In the contempt application filed by the appellants, the learned Advocate General appearing for the contemnors submitted that there is a violation of the order passed earlier on 4-1-2005 but the said violation is not willful as the contemnor wrongly understood the implications of the orders passed by the High Court on 4-1-2005 and extended subsequently on 19th and 20th January, 2005 and also by the Division Bench on 15-3-2005, 18-3-2005 in two other different proceedings. It was further submitted that in order to hold a person guilty of contempt of court two things have to be proved. Firstly, disobedience of the order passed by the court and secondly such disobedience must be willful. The Advocate-General submitted that in the instant case there is no willful violation and, therefore, the contempt application should be dismissed. Some rulings were relied on by the learned Advocate General in support of his aforesaid contention.

16. A learned Single Judge of the High Court was of the opinion that the contemnors did not understand the implications and consequences of a prohibitory order passed in an independent proceedings and by sheer mis-conception thought that there is no bar to issue excise license in view of the orders dated 15-3-2005 and 18-5-2005 and that failure to understand the implications and/ or consequences of the order passed by the High Court cannot be construed as an act of contempt.

17. In the light of the decisions cited, the High Court examined whether the alleged contemnors have committed any contempt of the High Court. While examining so, the High Court has observed as follows:—

> "Undisputedly this Bench on 4th January, 2005 passed an interim order restraining the alleged contemnors from holding any lottery for the purpose of final selection of the excise shops in question without obtaining further order from this court but the alleged contemnors published an advertisement in the daily newspaper for holding lottery for the purpose of final selection of excise shops in question. Therefore, there is no doubt that the alleged contemnors have disobeyed the specific direction passed earlier by this Bench."

18. The Division Bench of this Hon'ble court in two different proceedings passed two separate orders on 15th March, 2005 and 18th March, 2005 respectively whereby and whereunder the alleged contemnors herein were permitted to grant excise licenses. The alleged contemnors herein reasonably understood that the orders passed by the Division Bench will have overriding effect on the order passed by the learned Single Judge of this Hon'ble court and thus committed mistake by not realising the implication of the order passed by this Bench which remained operative at the relevant time.

19. If there is any doubt regarding interpretation and/or understanding of the orders passed by the courts of law, the alleged contemnors are entitled to have the benefit or advantage of such a doubt, as the act of contempt must be established beyond all reasonable doubt.

20. In the aforesaid circumstances, it cannot be said that the alleged contemnors herein willfully and deliberately violated the solemn order passed by this Bench on 4th January, 2005. Mere disobedience of an order is not sufficient to hold any one guilty under the Contempt of Courts Act unless such obedience is deliberate and willful.

The High Court also observed as under:

> "Although the alleged contemnors in their respective affidavits have tendered unqualified apology after categorically stating therein that they had no intention to willfully or deliberately violate the order passed earlier by this Bench but in view of the observations made hereinbefore, I am not inclined to go into the question of apology."

21. For the aforementioned reasons, the contempt petition was dismissed by the High Court. Aggrieved by the dismissal of the contempt petition, the appellant preferred the above appeal arising out of SLP No. 15224 of 2006. This Court on 18-9-2006 issued notice and in the meanwhile directed that no license shall be granted on the basis of the lottery and pursuant to the circular dated 20-1-2004.

22. We heard Mr. K.K. Venugopal, Mr. L.N. Rao, Mr. Pradip Ghosh, Mr. Joydip Gupta, learned senior counsel for the appellant and Mr. Gopal Subramanium, learned Addl. Solicitor General and Mr. Bhaskar P. Gupta, learned senior counsel for R1-R4 and Mr. Aman Vachher for R5 and Mr. P.N. Misra and Mr. M.N. Krishnamani, learned senior counsel in I.A. 3 and I.A. 4. We dismissed all applications for impleadments/intervention on 21-2-2007 and heard the arguments of the appellants on merits. Elaborate and lengthy submissions were made by the respective parties with reference to the entire pleadings and various orders passed by the High Court and of this Court and also other annexures and case laws. Learned senior counsel appeared for the appellant submitted that in view of the finding of the learned Judge "that there is no doubt that alleged contemnor have disobeyed the specific direction passed earlier by this Bench", the learned Judge of the High Court was not justified in holding that the alleged contemnor committed mistake by not realising the implication of the order passed by the High Court which remain operative at the relevant time and on that basis dismissing the application for contempt without making any order for restoration of the *status quo ante* to undo the mischief caused by such violation of the interim order. According to the learned senior counsel for the appellant, the impugned order is not sustainable in law and should not be allowed to operate as a precedent and the wrong perpetrated by the respondent/ contemnors in contumacious disregard of the orders of the High Court should not be permitted to hold. Likewise, the High Court also committed a grievous error of law in holding that the alleged contemnors did not understand the implication and consequences of a prohibitory order passed in an independent proceedings and by sheer mis-conception thought that there is no bar to issue excise licenses in view of the order dated 15-3-2005 and 18-3-2005 by two different Division Benches of the High Court. In support of their contention, they cited the following rulings:

(1) *Kapildeo Prasad Sah* v. *State of Bihar,* (1999) 7 SCC 569.

(2) *Tayabbhai M. Bagasarwalla* v. *Hind Rubber Industries Pvt. Ltd.,* (1997) 3 SCC 443.

(3) *Eastern Trust Company* v. *MaKenzie Mann & Co., Ltd.,* AIR 1915 PC 106.

(4) *Anil Ratan Sarkar* v. *Hirak Ghosh,* (2002) 4 SCC 21.

(5) *All India Regional Rural Bank Officers Federation* v. *Govt. of India,* (2002) 3 SCC 554.

(6) *Ravi S. Naik* v. *Union of India,* 1994 Supp (2) SCC 641.

(7) *Surjit Singh* v. *Harbans Singh,* (1995) 6 SCC 50.

(8) *T.M.A. Pai Foundation* v. *State of Karnataka,* (1995) 4 SCC 1.

(9) *Vidya Charan Shukla* v. *Tamil Nadu Olympic Assn.,* AIR 1991 Mad 323.

(10) *Century Flour Mills Ltd.* v. *S. Suppiah,* AIR 1975 Mad 270.

23. Mr. Gopal Subramanium and Mr. Bhaskar P. Gupta, appearing for the contesting respondent Nos. 1-4 reiterated the same contentions which have been urged before the High Court and since the learned single Judge clearly found that there was no willful and deliberate violation of the order of the learned Single Judge pursuing the same in the further appeal does not arise and inasmuch as it was held that there was no deliberate and willful violation as such, this Court may not issue direction of setting aside the lottery already held. It was also denied that lottery was held in breach of the interim orders passed as alleged or at all. On the contrary, the learned single Judge held that there was no willful and deliberate violation of the order. It was further submitted that the entire judgment of the single Judge is required to be read and not in bits and pieces and that it would appear from the judgment that the single Judge has unequivocally held that there was no deliberate and willful violation of the order and thus has rightly dismissed the contempt application.

24. We have carefully considered the rival submissions made by learned senior counsel appearing for the respective parties. It is not in dispute that an injunction order was passed on 4-1-2005 and on subsequent extension is still subsisting. Respondent Nos. 1-4 admittedly are highly qualified and highly placed government officials. Admittedly, by advocate's letter dated 15-3-2005, it was pointed out to them that the injunction order dated 4-1-2005 and its subsequent extensions are still subsisting. They have also acknowledged the receipt of the communication dated 15-3-2005. Under such circumstances, the High Court is not justified in holding that the highly qualified and well placed government officials did not understand the implication and/or consequence of prohibitory order in an independent proceedings and by sheer mis-conception though that there is no bar to issue excise licenses as was held by the learned Judge in the impugned order. This Court can only say it is rather unfortunate that such officers who are not capable of or not able to understand the implication of the prohibitory orders passed by the High Court should be allowed to hold such high offices. During the course of the hearing of the contempt application, the matter was adjourned by the High Court to enable the respondent to consider whether the contemnors was prepared to cancel the lottery held on 20, 21 and 22-3-2005 in violation of the Court's orders and on such adjourned date, the contemnors did not agree to cancel the lottery. Under such circumstances, the plea of mistake of understanding the order cannot at all be accepted. Likewise, the High Court also was not justified in not directing the contemnors to cancel the lottery held on 20, 21 and 22-3-2005 in violation of the solemn orders passed by the very same Judge and in view of the clear finding of the Court that they had acted in clear violation of the said interim order made by the High Court.

25. Even assuming that there was any scope for *bona fide* misunderstanding on the part of the respondents, once it was found that the respondent had disobeyed the specific order passed earlier by the Court, the High Court should have directed the contemnors to undo the wrong committed by them which was done in clear breach of the order of the Court by restoring the *status quo ante* by canceling the lottery wrongfully held by them. The learned Judge found that the respondent-contemnors had held the lottery in violation of the Court's order and the results of the said lottery should not be permitted to take effect and should be treated as unlawful and invalid for the purpose of grant of license. The learned Single Judge for the purpose of upholding the majesty of law and the sanctity of the solemn order of the court of law which cannot be violated by the executive authority either deliberately or unwittingly should have set aside the lottery held and should not have allowed the respondents to gain a wrongful advantage thereby. In our opinion, a party to the litigation cannot be allowed to take an unfair advantage by committing breach of an interim order and escape the consequences thereof. By pleading misunderstanding and thereafter retaining the said advantage gained in breach of the order of the Court and the wrong perpetrated by the respondent-contemnors in contumacious disregard of the order of the High Court should not be permitted to hold good. In our opinion, the impugned order passed by the High court is not sustainable in law and should not be allowed to operate as a precedent and the wrong perpetrated by the respondent-contemnors in utter disregard of the order of the High Court should not be permitted to hold good. The High Court has committed a grievous error of law in holding that failure to understand the implication and consequences of the order passed by the High Court by highly placed government officers cannot be construed as an act of contempt. The High Court has failed to understand that the highly educated and highly placed government officials have competent legal advisors and it was not open to them to allege and contend that the respondent-contemnors did not understand the implication of the order dated 4-1-2005. In our opinion, such officers are required to be dealt with effectively to uphold the dignity of the High Court and the efficiency of the system itself. The High Court committed a grave error of law by not taking into consideration the most important fact that in the course of the hearing of the contempt application the matter was adjourned in order to enable the contemnor to consider whether they were prepared to cancel the lottery held on 20, 21 and

22-3-2005 and on the adjourned date, the respondents did not agree to cancel the lottery. In such view of the matter, the significant stand being the plea of mistake of understanding cannot, in our opinion, prevail. The High Court in that view of the matter committed a grave mis-carriage of justice by not taking into consideration another most important fact that if actually the lottery was held by mistake or by misunderstanding of the orders, then the respondent would have immediately rectified it and would have cancelled the lottery but in the instant case, instead of canceling the lottery, the respondents have justified their conduct from which the determined declination of obeying the order is clearly proved. In other words, if there was a doubt about the implication of the order of the Court, the respondents should have approached the Court and should have clarified their alleged confusion. But in the instant case, the respondents have not only violated the order but when the contempt application was moved and opportunity was given by the Court to cancel the lottery they refused to cancel the said lottery from which it is proved that they deliberately held the lottery in clear violation of the order dated 4-1-2005 having regard to the admissions made on behalf of the contemnors that there is violation of the order dated 4-1-2005 and also having regard to the learned Single Judge's own finding that "there is no doubt that the alleged contemnor disobeyed the specific directions passed earlier by this Bench". The High Court should have directed the contemnor to cancel the lottery held on these 3 dates. The High Court also failed to consider the effect of the appellant's learned advocate's letter dated 15-3-2005 whereby it was clearly pointed out about the subsistence of the order dated 4-1-2005 and its subsequent extension. By the said letter, the appellant's advocate categorically pointed out further that in spite of the above if the lottery is held or further action is taken for issue of excise license, the appellant shall be compelled to take legal action.

26. In our opinion, the judgment and order passed by the High court are bad in law and is liable to be set aside.

LAW ON THE SUBJECT:

(1) *Kapildeo Prasad Sah* v. *State of Bihar,* (1999) 7 SCC 569.

"For holding the respondents to have committed contempt, civil contempt at that, it has to be shown that there has been willful disobedience of the judgment or order of the court. Power to punish for contempt is to be resorted to when there is clear violation of the court's order. Since notice of contempt and punishment for contempt is of far-reaching consequence, these powers should be invoked only when a clear case of willful disobedience of the court's order has been made out. Whether disobedience is willful in a particular case depends on the facts and circumstances of that case. Judicial orders are to be properly understood and complied with. Even negligence and carelessness can amount to disobedience particularly when the attention of the person is drawn to the court's orders and its implications. Disobedience of the court's order strikes at the very root of the rule of law on which Indian system of governance is based. Power to punish for contempt is for the maintenance of effective legal system. It is exercised to prevent perversion of the course of justice. Jurisdiction to punish for contempt exists to provide ultimate sanction against the person who refuses to comply with court's order or disregards the order continuously. No person can defy court's order. Wilful would exclude casual, accidental, *bona fide* or unintentional acts or genuine inability to comply with the terms of the order. A petitioner who complains breach of the court's order must allege deliberate or contumacious disobedience of the court's order."

(2) *Tayabbhai M. Bagasarwalla* v. *Hind Rubber Industries Pvt. Ltd.*, (1997) 3 SCC 443

"16. According to this section, if an objection is raised to the jurisdiction of the court at the hearing of an application for grant of, or for vacating, interim relief, the court should determine that issue in the first instance as a preliminary issue before granting or setting aside the relief already granted. An application raising objection to the jurisdiction to the court is directed to be heard with all expedition. Sub-rule (2), however, says that the command in sub-rule (1) does not preclude the court from granting such interim relief as it may consider necessary pending the decision on the question of jurisdiction. In our opinion, the provision merely states the obvious. It makes explicit what is implicit in law. Just because an objection to the jurisdiction is raised, the court does not become helpless forthwith - nor does it become incompetent to grant the interim relief. It can. At the same time, it should also decide the objection to jurisdiction at the earlier possible moment. This is the general principle and this is what section 9A reiterates. Take this very case. The plaintiff asked for temporary injunction. An ad-interim injunction was granted. Then the defendant came forward objecting to the grant of injunction and also raising an objection to the jurisdiction of the court. The court over-ruled the objection as to jurisdiction and made the interim injunction absolute. The defendants filed an appeal against the decision on the question of jurisdiction. While that appeal was pending, several other interim order were passed both by the Civil Court as well as by the High Court. Ultimately, no doubt, High Court has found that the Civil Court had no jurisdiction to entertain the suit but all this took about six years. Can it be said that orders passed by the Civil Court and the High Court during this period of six years were all non-est and that it is open to the defendants to flout them merrily, without fear of any consequence. Admittedly, this could not be done until the High Court's decision on the question of jurisdiction. The question is whether the said decision of the High Court means that no person can be punished for flouting or disobeying the interim/interlocutory orders while they were in force, *i.e.*, for violations and disobedience committed prior to the decision of the High Court on the question of jurisdiction Holding that by virtue of the said decision of the High Court (on the question of jurisdiction, no one can be punished thereafter for disobedience or violation of the interim orders committed prior to the said decision of the High Court, would indeed be subversive of rule of law and would seriously erode the dignity and the authority of the courts. We must repeat that this is not even a case where a suit was filed in wrong court knowingly or only with a view to snatch an interim order. As pointed out hereinabove, the suit was filed in the Civil Court *bonafide*. We are of the opinion that in such a case the defendants cannot escape the consequences of their disobedience and violation of the interim injunction committed by them prior to the High Court's decision on the question of jurisdiction."

(3) *Eastern Trust Company* v. *MaKenzie Mann & Co. Ltd.*, AIR 1915 PC 106.

"There is a well-established practice in England in certain cases where no petition of right will lie, under which the Crown can be sued by the Attorney-General, and a declaratory order obtained, as has been recently explained by the Court of Appeal in England in *Dyson* v. *Attorney-General*, 1911 (1) KB 410 and in *Burghes* v. *Attorney-General*, 1912 (1) Ch 173. It is the duty of the Crown and of every branch of the Executive to abide by and obey the law. If there is any difficulty in ascertaining it, the courts are open to the Crown to sue, and it is the duty of the Executive in cases of doubt to ascertain the law, in order to obey it, not to dis-regard it. The proper course in the present case would have been either to apply to the Court to determine the question of construction of the contract, and to pay accordingly, or to pay the whole amount over to the Receiver and to obtain from the Court an order on the Receiver to pay the sums properly payable for labour and supplies, as to the construction of which their Lordships agree with Supreme Court of *Nova Scotia*.

27. The duty of the Crown in such a case is well stated by Lord Abhinger Chief Barren in *Deare* v. *Attorney General*, 1835 (1) Y & C 197. After pointing out that the Crown always appears (in England) by the Attorney-General in a Court of Justice – especially in a Court of Equity – where the interest of the Crown is concerned, even perhaps in a bill for discovery, he goes on to say:

"It has been the practice, which I hope never will be discontinued, for the officers of the Crown to throw no difficulty in the way of any proceeding for the purpose of bringing matters before a court of Justice where any real point of difficulty that requires judicial decision has occurred."

(4) *Anil Ratan Sarkar* v. *Hirak Ghosh*, (2002) 4 SCC 21.

"20. Similar is the situation in the counter-affidavit filed presently in this matter as well: Is this fair ? The answer having regard to the factual backdrop cannot but be in the negative. It is neither fair nor reasonable on the part of a senior Civil Service Personnel to feign ignorance or plead understanding when the direction of this Court stands crystal clear in the judgment. Government employees ought to be treated on a par with another set of employees and this Court on an earlier occasion lent concurrence to the view of the learned Single Judge that the Circulars issued by the State Government cannot but be ascribed to be arbitrary: Government is not a machinery for oppression and ours being a welfare State as a matter of fact be opposed thereto. It is the people's welfare that the State is primarily concerned with and avoidance of compliance with a specific order of the Court cannot be termed to be a proper working of a State body in terms of the wishes and aspirations of the founding fathers of our Constitution. Classless, non-discriminate and egalitarian society are not meaningless jargons so that they only remain as the basic factors of our socialistic state on principles only and not to have any application in the realities of every-day life: one section of the employees would stand benefited but a similarly placed employee would not be so favoured why this attitude? Obviously there is no answer. Surprisingly, this attitude persists even after six rounds of litigation travelling from Calcutta to Delhi more than once the answer as appears in the counter-affidavit is an expression of sorrow by reason of the understanding cannot be countenanced in the facts presently under consideration. A plain reading of the order negates the understanding of the Respondent State and the conduct in no uncertain terms can be ascribed to be the manifestation of an intent to deprive one section of the employees being equally circumstanced come what may and this state of mind is clearly expressed in the counter-affidavit though however in temperate language. The question of *bona fide* understanding thus does not and cannot arise in the facts presently. Is it a believable state of affairs that the order of the learned Single Judge as early as the first writ petition, has not been properly understood by the senior most bureaucrat of the State Government: the same misunderstanding continues in terms of the appellate Court's order and the third in the line of order is that of the apex Court. The understanding again continues even after the second writ petition was filed before the learned Single Judge in the High Court and the similar understanding continues even after the so to say clarificatory order by this Court, as appears from the order dated 20th April, 2001. Even in the counter-affidavit, filed in Contempt Petition, the understanding still continues we are at a loss as to what is this understanding about: the defence of 'understanding' undoubtedly is an ingenious effort to avoid the rigours of an order of Court but cannot obliterate the action the attempted avoidance through the introduction of the so-called concept of lack of understanding cannot, however, be a permanent avoidance, though there may be temporary and short-lived gains. The order of this Court cannot possibly be interpreted as per the understanding of the Respondents, but as appears from the plain language used therein. Neither the order is capable of two several interpretations nor there is any ambiguity and the same does not require further clarity. The order is categorical and clear in its context and meaning. The Court's orders are to be observed in its observance, rather than in its breach."

(5) *All India Regional Rural Bank Officers Federation* v. *Govt. of India,* (2002) 3 SCC 554

"4. Mr. Mukul Rohtagi, the learned Additional Solicitor General, however tried to impress upon us the circumstances under which the notification had been issued, the same being severe financial crisis and the learned

Additional Solicitor General further urged that the monetary benefits of the employees of the banks will have to be so modulated so that the banks should be ultimately be closed down by merely paying the salary of the employees. Even though the financial position of the banks may not be disputed, but having regard to the directions issued by this Court, while disposing of the civil appeal and having regard to the circumstances under which such directions had been given, it would be difficult for us to sustain the plea of the Union Government that the Notification is in compliance with the judgment and directions of this Court. The financial capacity of the Government cannot be pleaded as a ground for non-implementation of the directions of the Court inasmuch as even in the matter of determination of the pay-scale of the employees of the Regional Rural Banks and maintenance of parity with their counterparts, serving under the sponsorer commercial banks, Justice Obul Reddi had not accepted the said plea and that award reached its finality. Since the financial capacity of the employer cannot be held to be a germane consideration for determination of the wage structure of the employees and the Parliament enacted the Act for bringing into existence these regional rural banks with the idea of helping the rural mass of the country, the employees of such rural banks cannot suffer on account of financial incapacity of the employer. We have no hesitation in coming to the conclusion that the issuance of notification dated 1-4-2001, by the Government of India cannot be held to be in compliance with the judgment and directions of this Court in S.M.G. Bank. But at the same time, we are of the opinion that the appropriate authority need not be punished under the provisions of the Contempt of Courts Act, even if the notification is in direct contravention of the judgment of this Court, as we do not find a case of deliberate violation. While, therefore, we do not propose to take any action against the alleged contemnors, we direct that the employees of the Regional Rural Banks should be paid their current salaries on the basis of determination made under the notification dated 11-4-2001, the new basic pay having arrived at, as on 1-4-2000 forthwith Paragraph (i) of the aforesaid notification dated 11-4-2001 should be immediately implemented and the employees should be paid accordingly. Paragraphs (ii) and (iii) of the notification are quashed and the Central Government is directed to issue a fresh notification for proper implementation of the Judgment of this Court. We make it clear that the period of moratorium with regard to the payment of arrears, since is going to be over on 31-3-2002, the arrear salary accruing to the employees be paid to them in three equal annual installments, the first being on 30th of April, 2002, the second on 30th of April, 2003 and the third on 30th April, 2004. This payment has to be made as aforesaid without being any way dependant upon any other considerations and there cannot be any distinction between the regional rural banks incurring loss and the regional rural banks, making profit. Further, the question of anticipated cash out-flow on account of increase in salary if exceeds 50% of the operating profit, then the current payment would be restricted only upto 50% is absolutely of no relevance, which was indicated in the impugned notification dated 11-4-2001. Having regard to the financial condition of the Government as well as these banks, the installment to be paid on 30-4-2002, pursuant to this order of ours, the same may be deposited in the employees' provident fund account. But all other installments will have to be paid in cash."

(6) *Ravi S. Naik* v. *Union of India*, 1994 Supp (2) SCC 641:

"40. We will first examine whether Bandekar and Chopdekar could be excluded from the group on the basis of order dated December 13, 1990 holding that they stood disqualified as members of the Goa Legislative Assembly. The said two members had filed Writ Petition No. 321 of 1990 in the Bombay High Court wherein they challenged the validity of the said order of disqualification and by order dated December 14, 1990 passed in the said writ petition the High Court had stayed the operation of the said order of disqualification dated December 13, 1990 passed by the Speaker. The effect of the stay of the operation of the order of disqualification dated December 13, 1990 was that with effect from December 14, 1990 the Declaration that Bandekar and Chopdekar were disqualified from being members of Goa Legislative Assembly under order dated December 13, 1991 was not operative and on December 24, 1990, the date of the alleged split, it could not be said that they were not members of Goa Legislative Assembly. One of the reasons given by the Speaker for not giving effect to the stay order passed by the High Court on December 14, 1990, was that the said order came after the order of disqualification was issued by him. We are unable to appreciate this reason. Since the said order was passed in a writ petition challenging the validity of the order dated December 13, 1990 passed by the Speaker it, obviously, had to come after the order of disqualification was issued by the Speaker. The other reason given by the Speaker was that Parliament had held that the Speaker's order cannot be a subject-matter of court proceedings and his decision is final as far as Tenth Schedule of the Constitution is concerned. The said reason is also unsustainable in law. As to whether the order of the Speaker could be a subject-matter of court proceedings and whether his decision was final were questions involving the interpretation of the provisions contained in Tenth Schedule to the Constitution. On the date of the passing of the stay order dated December 14, 1990, the said questions were pending consideration before this Court. In the absence of an authoritative pronouncement by this Court the stay order passed by the High Court could not be ignored by the Speaker on the view that his order could not be a subject-matter of court proceedings and his decision was final. It is settled law that an order, even though interim in nature, is binding till it is set aside by a competent could and it cannot be ignored on the ground that the Court which passed the order had no jurisdiction to pass the same. Moreover the stay order was passed by the High Court which is a Superior Court of Record and "in the case of a superior Court of Record, it is for the court to consider whether any matter falls within its jurisdiction or not. Unlike a court of limited jurisdiction, the superior Court is entitled to determine for itself questions about its own jurisdiction." [See: *Special Reference No. 1 of 1964*, (1965) 1 SCR 413 (499).]

42. In *Mulraj* v. *Murti Raghonathji Maharaj*, this Court has dealt with effect of a stay order passed by a court and has laid down:

"In effect therefore a stay order is more or less in the same position as an order of injunction with one difference. An order of injunction is generally issued to a party and it is forbidden from doing certain acts. It is well-settled that in such a case the party must have knowledge of the injunction order before it could be penalised for before disobeying it. Further it is equally well-settled that the injunction order not being addressed to the court, if the court proceeds in contravention of the injunction order, the proceedings are not a nullity. In the case of a stay order, as it is addressed to the court and prohibits it from proceeding further, as soon as the court has knowledge of the order it is bound to obey it and if it does not, it acts illegally, and all proceedings taken after the knowledge of the order would be a nullity. That in our opinion is the only difference between an order of injunction to a party and an order of stay to a court.

28. This would mean that the Speaker was bound by the stay order passed by the High Court on December 14, 1990 and any action taken by him in disregard of the said stay order was a nullity. In the instant case the Speaker, in passing the order dated February 15, 1991 relating to disqualification, treated Bandekar and Chopdekar as disqualified members. This action of the Speaker was in disregard of the stay order dated December 14, 1990 passed by the Bombay High Court."

(7) *Surjit Singh* v. *Harbans Singh*, (1995) 6 SCC 50.

"4. As said before, the assignment is by means of a registered deed. 'The assignment had taken place after the passing of the preliminary decree in which Pritam Singh has been allotted 1/3rd share. His right to property to that extent stood established. A decree relating to immovable property worth more than hundred rupees, if being assigned, was required to be registered, that has instantly been done. It is *per se* property, for it relates to the immovable property involved in the suit. It clearly and squarely fell within the ambit of the restraint order. In sum, it did not make any appreciable-difference whether property *per se* had been alienated or a decree pertaining to that property. In defiance of the restraint order, the alienation/assignment was made. If we were to let it go as such, it would defeat the ends of justice and the prevalent public policy. When the court intends a particular state of affairs to exist while it is in seizin of a *lis*, that state of affairs is not only required to be maintained, but it is presumed to exist till the Court orders otherwise. The Court, in these circumstances has the duty, as also the right, to treat the alienation/assignment as having not taken place at all for its purposes. Once that is so, Pritam singh and his assignees, respondents herein, cannot claim to be impleaded as parties on the basis of assignment. Therefore, the assignees-respondents could not have been impleaded by the trial court as parties to the suit, in disobedience of its orders. The principles of *lis pendens* are altogether on a different footing. We do not propose to examine their involvement presently. All what is emphasised is that the assignees in the present facts and circumstances had no cause to be impleaded as parties to the suit. On that basis, there was no cause for going into the question of interpretation of paragraphs 13 and 14 of the settlement deed. The path treated by the courts below was, in our view, out of their bounds. Unhesitatingly, we upset all the three orders of the courts below and reject the application of the assignees for impleadment under Order 22, rule 10, C.P.C.

(8) *Delhi Development Authority* v. *Skipper Construction Co. (P) Ltd.,* (1996) 4 SCC 622

"17. The principle that a contemnor ought not to be permitted to enjoy and/or keep the fruits of his contempt is well-settled. In *Mohd. Idris* v. *R.J. Babuji,* this Court held clearly that undergoing the punishment for contempt does not mean that the Court is not entitled to give appropriate directions for remedying and rectifying the things done in violation of its Orders. The petitioners therein had given an undertaking to the Bombay High Court. They acted in breach of it. A learned Single Judge held them guilty of contempt and imposed a sentence of one month's imprisonment. In addition thereto, the learned Single Judge made appropriate directions to remedy the breach of undertaking. It was contended before this Court that the learned Judge was not justified in giving the aforesaid directions in addition to punishing the petitioners for contempt of court. The argument was rejected holding that "the Single Judge was quite right in giving appropriate directions to close the breach (of undertaking)".

18. The above principle has been applied even in the case of violation of orders of injunction issued by Civil Courts. In *Clarke* v. *Chadbum,* (1985) 1 All ER 211, Sir Robert Megarry V-C observed:

I need not cite authority for the proposition that it is of high importance that orders of the court should be obeyed. Willful disobedience to an order of the court is punishable as a contempt of court, and I feel no doubt that such disobedience may properly be described as being illegal. If by such disobedience the persons enjoined claim that they have validly effected some charge in the rights and liabilities of others, one cannot see why it should be said that although they are liable to penalties for contempt of court for doing what they did, nevertheless those acts were validly done. Of course, if an act is done, it is not undone merely by pointing out that it was done in breach in law. If a meeting is held in breach of an injunction, it cannot be said that the meeting has not been held. But the legal consequences of what has been done in breach of the law may plainly be very much affected by the illegality. It seems to me on principle that those who defy a prohibition ought not to be able to claim that the fruits of their defiance are good, and not tainted by the illegality that produced them."

(9) *Vidya Charan Shukla* v. *Tamil Nadu Olympic Assn.,* AIR 1991 Mad 323 (FB)

"56-57. Adverting to the facts of this case, we knew that the main relief in the suit to declare that the notice dated 26-5-1990 issued by the first and second defendants on the basis of the requisition notices convening a Special General Meeting of the Association on 15-6-1990 is illegal, null and void cannot be said to have become infructuous merely because the Court instead of granting an injunction to hold the meeting on 15-6-1990, gave a direction to consider an agenda of no-confidence against the Executive Council and election of new President and members of the Council in a particular manner. It can still be found in the suit that the notice was illegal, null and void and as a consequence, the Court may suitably modulate the relief or permit the plaintiffs to amend the relief. Besides this the trial Court will have jurisdiction to consider the grant of a mandatory injunction even in a suit which stood disposed of if its decree is found to have been violated or frustrated. The trial Court being a Court of Record will have special jurisdiction/inherent power to pass such orders as are deemed necessary to meet the ends of justice since this power is saved for it under sections 4 and 151 of the Code of Civil Procedure and articles 215 and 225 of the Constitution. The instant suit which is still pending, shall give to the Court power to consider the desirability to grant a mandatory injunction, for the reason of its interim injunction having been violated, to remove the violation and until the suit is finally decided to preserve the property in dispute in *Status Quo*."

(10) *Century Flour Mills Ltd.* v. *S. Suppiah,* AIR 1975 Mad 270 (FB).

"9. In our opinion, the inherent powers of this court under section 151 C.P.C. are wide and are not subject to any limitation. Where in violation of a stay order or injunction against a party, something has been done in disobedience, it will be the duty of the court as a policy to set the wrong right and not allow the perpetuation of the wrong doing. In our view, the inherent power will not only be available in such a case, but it is bound to be exercised in that manner in the interests of justice. Even apart from section 151, we should observe that as a matter of judicial policy, the court should guard against itself being stultified in circumstances like this by holding that it is powerless to undo a wrong done in disobedience of the court's orders. But in this case it is not necessary to so to that extent as we hold that the power is available under section 151. C.P.C." *T.M.A. Pai Foundation* v. *State of Karnataka,* (1995) 4 SCC 1.

29. In this case, *suo motu* contempt proceedings was initiated by the Court against Secretary, Deputy Secretary and Under Secretary to Medical Education Department and few other officers of the State. Explanation was given by these officers admitting *bona fide* error made in interpreting this Court's order. This Court having regard to the sequence of events, extraordinary speed in processing the representation of the Association and conduct of the officers, held, explanation not acceptable. Since the order of this Court was explicit and clear but it was subverted on an *ex facie* faulty and deliberately distorted interpretation at the instance of the Association. Hence, this Court felt that to accept their unconditional apology would be travesty of justice and officers were thus held guilty of contempt of Court and their conduct censured by the Court. This Court also held that unconditional apology is not a complete answer to violations and infractions of the orders of this Court.

(12) *Satyabrata Biswas* v. *Kalyan Kumar Kisku,* (1994) 2 SCC 266. This Court held thus:

> 4. From the above it is seen that in relation to the properties an order of *status quo* as of today, that is, 15th September, 1988, had been passed by the court. It is complained that there is a violation of these three orders by the six respondents, Satyabrata Biswas, Rev. Bilash Chandra Das, Salil Biswas, Sushil Sharma, Rt. Rev. Dinesh Chandra Gorai and Rt. Rev. John E. Ghosh. The contempt was for: (1) putting a padlock to the main entrance of the premises on 3-7-1993; (2) disconnecting water supply, (3) obstructing sewerage line; and (4) preventing the appellants from getting the rooms repaired.

10. Under these circumstances the present civil appeal by special leave has come to be preferred. It is urged on behalf of the appellants that in view of *status quo* order dated 15th September, 1982 regarding the fixed property in possession of the Durgapur Diocese no tenancy or sub-tenancy rights could be created. It was also urged that the said Somani Builders became sub-tenant under an agreement dated 10th May, 1993. Such a sub-tenancy cannot be valid in view of the *status quo* order. It is somewhat strange that Somani Builders should made an oral application before the learned Single Judge. On the basis of the oral application, the order came to be passed in favour of the Somani Builders directing the Special Officer to remove the padlock. As to what was the nature of the prayer, that too by a person who was not a party to any one of these proceedings, is not known. Therefore, the removal of padlock on its instance, as directed by the learned Single Judge, was not warranted. As though to add insult to injury when the appellant was complaining about this order, the Division Bench goes one step further and directs possession be given to Somani Builders. This direction would amount to putting a premium on the illegality committed by the former alleged tenant A.K. Ghosh.

30. Apart from the fact whether A.K. Ghosh had a legal authority to sub-lease or not it was not open to him to grant a sub-lease in violation of the order. It is no use contending as Mr. Chidambaram, learned Counsel for the respondents does, that there was a bar to such a sub-lease under the terms of the *status quo* order. It has the effect of violating the preservation of status of the property. This will all the more be so when this is done without the leave of the court to disturb the state of things as they then stood. It would amount to violation of the order. The principle contained in the maxim: *'Actus Curiae Neminem Gravabit'* has no application at all to the facts of this case when in violation of *status quo* order a sub-tenancy has been created. Equally, the contention that even a trespasser cannot be evicted without recourse to law is without merit, because the state of affairs in relation to property as on 15-9-1988 is what the Court is concerned with. Such an order cannot be circumvented by parties with impunity and expect the court to confer its blessings. It does not matter that to the contempt proceedings Somani Builders was not a party. It cannot gain an advantage in derogation of the rights of the parties, who were litigating originally. If the right of sub-tenancy is recognised, how is *status quo* as of 15-9-1988 maintained? Hence, the grant of sub-lease is contrary to the order of *status quo*. Any act done in the teeth of the order of *status quo* is clearly illegal. All actions including the grant of sub-lease are clearly illegal.

31. In our opinion, the respondent Nos. 1-4 had deliberately and with *mala fide* motive have committed contempt of the High Court in conducting the lottery quite contrary to the order of injunction passed by the High Court on 4-1-2005 and its subsequent extensions. When the auction was held, the order passed by the High Court remain operative at the relevant time. The High Court has miserably failed in not issuing direction to the contemnors to cancel the lottery held on 20, 21 and 22-3-2005 in violation of the solemn order passed by the High Court. In view of the clear finding of the Court that the respondent had acted in clear violation of the order made by the High Court. It is settled law that a party to the litigation cannot be allowed to take an unfair advantage by committing breach of an interim order and escape the consequences thereof by pleading misunderstanding and thereafter retain the said advantage gained in breach of the order of the Court. Such violations should be put an end with an iron hand. We are unable to accept the argument advanced by learned Addl. Solicitor General that the respondents did not understand the implication and consequences of a prohibitory order passed by the High Court. We have already explained their conduct and the refusal to cancel the order when they were advised to do so by the High Court during the pendency of the contempt proceedings. The act of the respondent is not only willful but also deliberate and contumacious. The High Court committed a grave error of law by not holding that if there was a doubt about the implication of the order of the Court, the alleged contemnors should have approached the Court and have clarified their alleged confusion. Likewise, this Court while ordering notice in the present appeal @ SLP No. 15224 of 2006 have clearly directed on 18-9-2006 that no license shall be granted on the basis of the lottery and pursuant to the circular dated 20-1-2004. Even after the receipt of the order, the respondents have not cancelled the license, but allowed them to continue the business. The reason is obvious. The respondents though tendered unqualified apology before the High Court, the High Court was not inclined to go into the question of apology in view of the observations made by it in the order impugned in this civil appeal. Even before us no apology whatsoever was tendered by respondent Nos. 1-4. We, therefore, hold them guilty of willful and deliberate act of contempt. As it is evident that respondent Nos. 1-4 have no regard for the orders passed by this Court on 4, 19 and 20-1-2005 and have scant respect for the Court's orders and have deliberately and willfully and with utter disregard violated all the 3 orders and are thus guilty of contempt of Court. However, taking a lenient view and taking into consideration of the future prospects of the officers, respondent Nos. 1-4 we are not imposing any punishment for their willful violation of the order of the High Court and accept the unqualified apology filed before the High Court. Respondent Nos. 1-4 are severely warned that they shall not involve themselves or violate the order passed by any Court of law and will not resort to the unacceptable plea that the said highly placed and highly qualified government officials did not understand the implication and/or consequences of a prohibitory order passed by the Courts of law. They shall not hereafter also take the plea of inventing an innovative defence that they did not realise the implications of the order passed by the High Court which remained operative at the relevant time. In the instant case, the respondents have conducted the auction quite contrary to and in violation of an injunction order passed by the High Court. Courts have held in a catena of decisions that where in violation of a restraint order or an injunction order against a party, something has been done in disobedience, it will be the duty of the Court as a policy to set the wrong right and not allow the perpetuation of the wrong doing. In our opinion, the inherent power will not only be available under section 151 CPC as available to us in such a case but it is bound to be exercised in that manner in the interest of justice and public interest. As rightly observed by the Full Bench of the Madras High Court in AIR 1975 Mad 270, that as a matter of judicial policy the Court should guard against itself being stultified in circumstances like this by holding that it is powerless to undo a wrong done in disobedience of the Court's orders. We, therefore, cancel all the auctions held on 20, 21 and 22-3-2005 and direct the respondent Nos.1-4 not to allow the successful bidders to continue the business and shall stop them forthwith and submit a report to this Court of strict compliance. We make it clear that we are not expressing any opinion on the merits of the claim made by the appellant Association in the writ petition filed by them before the High Court which is pending. All the respondent Nos.1-4 are senior and experienced officers and must be presumed to know that under the constitutional scheme of this country orders of the High Court have to be obeyed implicitly and that orders of this Court for that matter any Court should not be trifled with. We have already found hereinabove that they have acted deliberately to subvert the orders of the High Court evidently. It is equally necessary to erase an impression which appears to be gaining ground that the mantra of unconditional apology is a complete answer to violations and infractions of the orders of the High Court or of this Court. We, therefore hold them guilty of contempt of Court and do hereby censure their conduct. Though a copy of this order could be sent which shall form part of the annual confidential record of service of each of the said officers, we refrain from doing so by taking a lenient view of the matter considering the future prospects of the officers. As already stated, the officers shall not indulge in any adventurous act and strictly obey the orders passed by the Courts of law. The civil appeal stands allowed. Though this is a fit case for awarding exemplary costs, again taking a lenient view, we say no costs.

State of Rajasthan

v.

Shambhoogiri

Appeal (Crl.) 955 of 2003
Decided on: 12-10-2004

Coram: **K. Balakrishnan, J.**
Dr. AR. Lakshmanan, J.

FACTS:

The respondent was convicted for corruption under section 161 I.P.C. and section 5(1)(d) and (2) of the Prevention of Corruption Act, 1947 and was sentenced by the Special Judge, Anti Corruption Cases, Udaipur to undergo two of years rigorous imprisonment and a fine of Rs. 250 on each count. Aggrieved against the conviction, the respondent preferred an appeal before the High Court which has set aside the conviction and sentence awarded by the Special Judge. Aggrieved against the same, the State of Rajasthan preferred an appeal before the Supreme Court.

ISSUE:

Corruption by police constable.

HELD:

Every citizen is competent and entitled to detect crimes and report and, if any, information regarding the commission of any crime is known to any person, such information can be passed on to the police or any other competent authority for taking appropriate action. If a crime is committed in the presence of any citizen, he can very well ascertain the truth of the fact and make all efforts to bring home the guilt of the accused. The Sub-Divisional Magistrate had only discharged his duties as a law abiding citizen and the High Court seriously erred in holding that the trial was vitiated owing to the investigation having been conducted by the SDM. The acquittal of the accused was improper and the judgment of the High Court is set aside as the High Court had not considered the criminal appeal filed by respondent on merits and the same is remitted to the High Court for proper consideration in accordance with law.

JUDGMENT

Dr. AR. Lakshmanan, J.—This appeal is directed against the judgment and order dated 16-1-2001 passed by the High Court of Rajasthan at Jodhpur in S.B. Criminal Appeal No. 198 of 1983 whereby the High Court allowed the appeal filed by the respondent herein. The said appeal before the High Court was directed against the order dated 3-5-1983 passed by the Special Judge, Anti Corruption Cases, Udaipur in Criminal Case No. 47 of 1978 convicting the respondent herein Shambhoogiri for the offence under section 161 I.P.C. and section 5(1)(d) and (2) of the Prevention of Corruption Act, 1947 (hereinafter referred to as "the PC Act") and sentencing him to undergo two years rigorous imprisonment and a fine of Rs. 250 on each count and in default of payment of fine to further undergo six months simple imprisonment. Both the sentences were ordered to run concurrently.

The case of the prosecution is as follows:

2. The respondent was working as Head Constable Police, Arnod, District Chittorgarh. One Fakir Chand PW-1 was the resident of the same local police station, where the respondent/accused was posted. There was some pending case against Fakir Chand PW-1 and his friends before the SDM, Pratapgarh, where he used to come in the Court of the SDM. The respondent arrested PW-1 under section 110 of the Cr. P.C. and demanded illegal gratification of Rs. 500 from him and further threatened him for lodging more complaints for not doing so. Therefore, PW-1 had to give Rs. 100 to the respondent. The respondent had to produce PW-1 before the SDM, Pratapgarh on 12-9-1977 and on the same day PW-1 had to give him Rs. 200 more. On that date, before appearance in the Court, PW-1 met PW-7 and told him about the accused/respondent, who advised PW-1 to give the entire details in written complaint with Rs. 200 currency notes. PW-1 did so. Thereafter, PW-7 had given the written complaint with Rs. 200 currency notes to the SDM, Pratapgarh. PW-6, who noted the numbers of the currency notes in his diary and after getting initials of the SDM, these notes were given to PW-1 and he was asked to give these currency notes to the respondent/accused. When the respondent demanded money from PW-1, the same was given in the presence of PW-5 and PW-7 to him. Thereafter, PW-5 informed the SDM PW-6 who called the accused in his chamber and asked him to produce Rs. 200 from his pocket. The accused is said to have produced that Rs. 200 before the SDM who verified the numbers of the currency notes from the entries noted in his diary, which was found the same. The SDM prepared a recovery Memo of those notes and thereafter sent the memo of recovery along with the notes to the Collector, Chittorgarh and also sent this information to the Superintendent of Police. Thereafter, the Superintendent of Police sent this information to the Anti-Corruption Department and the case was registered under section 161 I.P.C. and section 5(1)(d) and 5(2) of the PC Act. The Deputy S.P. Anti-Corruption Department collected the entire documents and after seeking permission filed the challan against the accused. On 11-9.1978, charges were framed against the accused in the Court of the Special Judge Anti-Corruption, Jaipur. The respondent denied the charges and claimed the trial. The case was committed in the Court of Special Judge, Anti-Corruption, Udaipur.

3. The prosecution examined eight witnesses in support of its case. The trial Court came to the conclusion that the respondent/accused being a public servant was guilty for the offence under section 161, I.P.C. and section 5(1) and 5(2) of the PC Act of having accepted Rs. 200 as bribe and convicted him *vide* judgment dated 3-5-1983 in Criminal Case No. 47 of 1978.

4. Aggrieved against the conviction, the respondent preferred an appeal before the High Court in which a question of law was raised on behalf of the respondent that as per section 5A of the PC Act the investigation has to be taken by a person not below the rank of Deputy Superintendent of Police or by Inspector of Police provided that there is a special authorization in that regard by the State Government generally or specially for a particular case. It was further argued on behalf of the respondent that the complaint was lodged before the SDM, Pratapgarh PW-6 who was not the competent person to investigate and that he did not have any such authorization generally or specifically to investigate the case of corruption.

5. The High Court, on 16-1-2001, has set aside the conviction and sentence awarded by the Special Judge on the ground that the prosecution based on investigation having been commenced at the instance of unauthorized person is without jurisdiction and faulty and, therefore, it cannot be sustained. Aggrieved against the same, the State of Rajasthan has come up on appeal before us. Leave was granted on 1-8-2003 by this Court.

6. Learned counsel for the appellant-State contended that the High Court seriously erred in holding that there was no compliance of section 5A of the PC Act. It was contended that the SDM who laid the trap and caught the accused red-handed was not conducting any investigation and the High Court wrongly assumed that the investigation by the SDM was without jurisdiction and the entire proceedings were vitiated by such illegality. The learned Counsel for the respondent, on the other hand, contended that section 5A of the PC Act authorises only specified person to conduct the investigation and action conducted by any authority other than the specified authority is illegal and the accused has been rightly acquitted by the High Court. Section 5A of the P.C. Act reads as follows:—

"5A. Investigation into cases under this Act.

(1) Notwithstanding anything contained in the Code of Criminal Procedure, 1898, no police officer below the rank,—

(a) in the case of the Delhi Special Police Establishment, of an Inspector of Police;

(b) in the presidency-towns of Calcutta and Madras, of an Assistant Commissioner of Police;

(c) in the presidency-town of Bombay, of a Superintendent of Police; and

(d) elsewhere, of a Deputy Superintendent of Police,

shall investigate any offence punishable under section 161, section 165 or section 165A of the Indian Penal Code or under section 5 of this Act without the order of a Presidency Magistrate or a Magistrate of the first class, as the case may be, or make any arrest therefor without a warrant:

Provided that if a police officer not below the rank of an Inspector of Police is authorized by the State Government in this behalf by general or special order, he may also investigate any such offence without the order of a Presidency Magistratre or a Magistrate of the first class, as the case may be, or make arrest therefore, without a warrant:

Provided further that an offence referred to in clause (e) of sub-section (1) of section 5 shall not be investigate without the order of a police officer not below the rank of a Superintendent of Police."

7. The above provision shows that only the authorities specified in sub-clause (a) to (d) of clause 5A alone are authorised to conduct the investigation and no Police Officer below the rank of those categories of officers are not competent to conduct investigation unless there is an order of a Presidency Magistrate or a Magistrate of the first class, as the case may be, and the State can authorize any officer for the purpose of investigation of such crimes under the PC Act but not below the rank of any Inspector of Police.

8. In the instant case, the High Court took the view that SDM conducted the investigation of the case and that he was not competent to do so. This view of the High Court is incorrect. The SDM got an information from PW 1 that the accused had been demanding illegal gratification. The SDM wanted to ascertain whether this allegation is true or not. He asked PW-1 to give a written complaint with Rs. 200 currency notes. The SDM noted the numbers of the currency notes in his diary and these notes were given to PW-1 who, in turn, gave these currency notes to the accused as illegal gratification. The SDM called the accused who was working under him and asked him to produce 200 rupees given by PW-1. The accused produced the notes before the SDM and the numbers of the currency notes were verified with the entries noted earlier by him in the diary. SDM himself prepared a recovery memo and sent it to the Superintendent of Police with a complaint alleging that the accused received bribery. He also sent a note to his superior officer. Here, the SDM was not doing any investigation. The High Court was of the view that he laid a trap and recovered the notes and thus conducted an investigation of the crime. The investigation of the crime would start only after the complaint is given by the SDM to the Superintendent of Police (Anti-Corruption) and investigation as such is defined under the Code of Criminal Procedure under section 2(h) of the Act which is to the following effect:—

> "Investigation" includes all the proceedings under this Code for the collection of evidence conducted by a police officer or by any person (other than a Magistrate) who is authorised by a Magistrate in this behalf."

9. Every citizen is competent and entitled to detect crimes and report and, if any, information regarding the commission of any crime is known to any person, such information can be passed on to the police or any other competent authority for taking appropriate action, for example, under the Food Adulteration Act, an ordinary citizen is competent to collect samples and send to public analysis and based on the report of the public analyst, the complaint can be filed before the appropriate authority. The collection of the samples and the analysis by the public analyst do not amount to investigation. If a crime is committed in the presence of any citizen, he can very well ascertain the truth of the fact and make all efforts to bring home the guilt of the accused. The Sub-Divisional Magistrate had only discharged his duties as a law abiding citizen and the allegation that SDM had conducted investigation of the case is incorrect and the High Court seriously erred in holding that the trial was vitiated owing to the investigation having been conducted by the SDM. The acquittal of the accused was improper and we set aside the Judgment of the High Court as the High Court had not considered the criminal appeal filed by respondent on merits and the same is remitted to the High Court for proper consideration in accordance with law.

10. In the result, the appeal is remitted to the High Court for disposal in accordance with law. The appeal would stand disposed of accordingly.

Suresh

v.

Mahadevappa Shivappa Danannava

Appeal (Crl.) 308 of 2005 [arising out of Special Leave Petition (Criminal) No. 3306 of 2004]
Decided on: 16-2-2005

Coram: **A. Bhan, J.**
Dr. AR. Lakshmanan, J.

FACTS:

The accused persons committed offences under sections 196, 209, 386, 403, 406 and 420 of I.P.C.. The Complaint was filed after 11 years from the date of the offence. The Addl. Chief Metropolitan Magistrate directed to register the case as PCR and refer the same to the sub-inspector for investigation and submit a report as per section 156(3) of Cr. P.C. Aggrieved by the order the appellant accused preferred a criminal revision under section 401 of Cr. P.C. praying the High Court to set aside the said order. The said revision was dismissed by the High Court. Aggrieved thereby, the appellant preferred an appeal to the Supreme Court by Special Leave Petition.

ISSUE:

Inordinate delay in filing of complaint.

HELD:

The impugned order of the High Court and that of the Magistrate are set aside. The complaint is liable to be dismissed on the question of inordinate latches on the part of the complainant himself. Accordingly, the appeal stands allowed.

JUDGMENT

Dr. AR. Lakshmanan, J.—Leave granted.

2. The present appeal was filed against the final judgment and order dated 17-2-2004 passed by the High Court of Karnataka at Bangalore in Criminal Revision Petition No. 932/2000 dismissing the said petition filed by the appellant-herein (accused No. 1).

3. The short facts leading to the filing of the above appeal are narrated herein below:

> Respondent No. 1 is the complainant. According to the complaint, the appellant herein had executed an agreement to sell dated 25-12-1988 in respect of the house premises bearing No. 120, K.H.B. Colony, Agrahara Dasarahalli, Bangalore in favour of the wife of the complainant Renukamma and as per the said agreement a sum of Rs. 1,25,000 was paid as advance out of the total consideration of Rs. 2,50,000 and the remaining amount was to be paid at the time of registration of sale deed. It is stated in the complaint that the second accused being the father of the first accused, the appellant herein was a member of the Karnataka Housing Board, who negotiated the transaction among the parties and in spite of several requests and demands made by the complainant it did not yield any fruits and that the first accused had sold the said property in favour of the wife of the fourth accused. It was further stated that the complainant approached all the accused persons several times for possession of the said premises and was ready to pay the balance sale consideration, but all the accused persons failed to discharge the obligations of the contract. Certain other averments have also been made in the complaint in regard to the receipt of Rs.5 lacs from one Uma Belagavi and Nadigar for vacating the said premises on filing civil cases with which we are not presently concerned in this appeal. A legal notice dated 11-7-1996 was also issued by the complainant calling upon the appellant herein to execute the sale deed in respect of the premises in question. The appellant herein on 18-7-1996 replied to the said legal notice. He denied the very existence of the alleged agreement to sell. He also denied that he had ever received Rs. 1,25,000 as consideration amount.

4. According to the complainant, all the accused persons committed offences attracting penal provisions of I.P.C. under sections 196, 209, 386, 403, 406 and 420. The complainant requested the Chief Metropolitan Magistrate, Bangalore to take cognizance of the offence against the accused persons and punish them in accordance with law in the interest of justice and equity. This complaint was numbered as PCR No. 453/1999 dated 17-5-1999.

5. The appellant denied the execution of such an agreement or received any advance from the complainant or his wife.

6. The IV-Addl. Chief Metropolitan Magistrate directed the office to register the case as PCR and refer the same to the sub-inspector Kamakshi Palya P.S. for investigation and submit a report as per section 156(3) of Cr. P.C. by 27-8-1999. This order was passed by the Magistrate on 17-5-1999 (Annexure-P2). On 4-8-2000 the IV-Addl. Chief Metropolitan Magistrate passed the following order:

"ORDER

Perused the record. Cognizance of the offence alleged against the accused is taken under section 190(i)(b) of Cr. P.C. Office to register the case in CC register and issue SS to accused by 30-9-2000.

Sd/- 4-8-2000"

7. Aggrieved by the order dated 4-8-2000 passed by the IV-Addl. CMM, the appellant accused preferred a criminal revision under section 401 Cr. P.C. praying the High Court to set aside the said order. The said revision was dismissed by the High Court by the impugned order dated 17-2-2004.

8. We have perused the entire pleadings and the order passed by the High Court in revision and heard the counsel appearing for the appellant. Though notice was served on the first respondent, no one has entered appearance on his behalf. Mr. Sanjay R. Hegde, learned counsel for the respondent filed vakalatnama on behalf of the State but has not filed any counter-affidavit on behalf of respondent No. 2 State of Karnataka.

9. It is pertinent to notice that the alleged agreement to sell was executed on 25-12-1988. A legal notice was issued to the appellant herein on 11-7-1996 calling upon the appellant to execute the sale deed in respect of the premises in question. Thus the complaint was submitted after 7½ years of splendid silence from the date of the alleged agreement to sell *i.e.* 25-12-1988. It is further to be noticed that the appellant herein responded to the legal notice dated 11-7-1996 by his reply dated 18-7-1996 through his lawyer specifically denying the alleged agreement and the payment of Rs. 1,25,000 as advance. Nothing was heard thereafter and the complainant after keeping quiet for nearly 3 years filed private complaint under section 200, Cr. P.C. before the IV Addl. CMM, Bangalore on 17-5-1999. The learned Magistrate on the same date directed his office to register the case as PCR and referred the same to the local police for investigation and to submit a report as per section 156(3), Cr. P.C. A charge-sheet was filed on 4-8-2000 by the police against the appellant/accused No.1 only for offence under section 420, I.P.C. The learned Magistrate took cognizance of the alleged offence under section 190(1)(b), Cr. P.C. and issued summons to the accused/appellant herein. Aggrieved by the aforesaid process order dated 4-8-2000 passed by the Magistrate, the appellant accused preferred the above criminal revision which was dismissed by the High Court for the reasons stated therein.

10. We have also perused the Annexures P1-P3 which are copies of the pleadings/documents which form part of the records of the case in the High Court against whose order leave to appeal was sought for in this appeal. We have carefully perused the order passed by the High Court. The High Court, in our opinion, has passed the order in a mechanical way without applying its mind. A perusal of the complaint would show that the entire dispute raised by the complainant is based on the alleged agreement to sell dated 25-12-1988 nearly 11 years prior to the filing of the private complaint on 17-5-1999. The existence of any such agreement or any advance taken has been specifically denied by the appellant by way of his reply dated 6-7-1996 in response to the legal notice dated 11-7-1996 sent by the complainant through his lawyer. For nearly 3 years from the date of reply, the complainant kept quiet before filing his complaint on 17-5-1999 before the Magistrate. It is stated that even as per the police report, no offence is made out against accused Nos. 2-4. Despite this, the Magistrate issued process against accused Nos. 2-4 as well which clearly shows the non-application of mind by the Magistrate. A perusal of the complaint would only reveal that the allegations as contained in the complaint are of civil nature and do not *prima facie* disclose commission of alleged criminal offence under section 420, I.P.C. The Magistrate, in our opinion, has not considered the report filed by the police under section 156(3), Cr. P.C. judicially. Irrespective of the opinion of the police, the Magistrate may or may not take cognizance under section 190(1) of Cr. P.C. In the instant case, as could be seen from the records, that the police has given a clean chit to accused Nos. 2-4. In our opinion, the Magistrate ought not to have taken cognizance of the alleged offence against the accused No. 1, the appellant herein and that the complaint has been made to harass the accused No. 1 to come to terms by resorting to criminal process.

11. As already noticed, the complaint was filed on 17-5-1999 after a lapse of 11 years and, therefore, the very private complaint filed by the respondent No. 1 is not at all maintainable at this distance of time. It is the specific case of accused No.1 that he has not executed any agreement to sell or received any advance payment. In our view, the complaint does not disclose the ingredients of section 415 of Cr. P.C. and, therefore, we have no hesitation to set aside the order passed by the Magistrate taking cognizance of the offence alleged. It is also not clearly proved that to hold a person guilty of cheating, it is necessary to show that he had a fraudulent or dishonest intention at the time of making the promise. The order of the Magistrate and of the High Court requiring the accused No. 1 appellant herein to face trial would not be in the interest of justice. On the other hand, in our considered opinion, this is a fit case for setting aside the order of the Magistrate as confirmed by the High Court of issuance of process and the proceedings itself.

12. We, therefore, set aside the impugned order of the High Court and of the Magistrate. The complaint is liable to be dismissed on the question of inordinate latches on the part of the complainant himself. Viewed from any angle, we do not find any good reasons to maintain the order passed by the learned single Judge of the High Court confirming the orders of the Magistrate. Accordingly, this appeal stands allowed and the judgment and order dated 17-2-2004 in Criminal Revision Petition No. 932/2000 of the High Court of Karnataka at Bangalore is set aside.

Safiya

v.

Government of Kerala

AIR 2003 SC 3562: 2003 (2) ALD Cri 323: 2003 Cr LJ 3736

Coram: **M. Shah, J.**

Dr. AR. Lakshmanan, J.

FACTS:

The husband of the appellant was found in possession of Indian and foreign currencies and gold biscuits during a search conducted by the Superintendent, Central Excise and Customs and was detained under section 3(i)(iv) of the COFEPOSA Act, 1974. Safiya, the wife of the detenu, filed a writ petition before the High Court of Kerala challenging the detention of her husband which was dismissed. Aggrieved thereby, the appellant filed an appeal before the Supreme Court.

ISSUE:

Detention under COFEPOSA Act, 1974.

HELD:

A careful perusal of the records placed before this Court would show that there are enough materials to show the involvement of the detenu in the smuggling activities. The liberty of a citizen is undoubtedly very important. It is our duty to ensure that there is strict compliance with the provisions of law. In our view, strict compliance of the provisions of law has been made. The Court, in our opinion, cannot be lose sight of the fact that those who commit economic offences do harm to the national interest and economy. The instant appeal filed by the wife of the detenu is totally devoid of any merit or substance and as such is rejected. The appeal shall stand dismissed.

JUDGMENT

Dr. AR. Lakshmanan, J.—Leave granted.

2. This appeal is directed against the final judgment and order dated 11-2-2003 passed by the High Court of Kerala of O.P. No. 29561 of 2002 filed by the appellant herein, who is the wife of the detenu - T.P. Moideen Koya who is under preventive detention under the COFEPOSA Act *vide* order of detention dated 21-2-2001.

3. The case of the prosecution in brief is that on 18-8-2001 a search was conducted by the Superintendent, Central Excise and Customs on the residence of one Kunjumon. In the search Indian and Foreign currencies and Gold biscuits were found. During the course of investigation, the statement of Mohd. Mustaffa, driver and employee of the said Kunjumon and P. Mohammed, the cousin of Kunjumon were recorded. According to the prosecution, the detenu is involved in dealing in smuggled goods and, therefore, report was made to the detaining authority for detaining the detenu under section 3(i)(iv) of the COFEPOSA Act, 1974. The detenu was detained in execution of the order of detention on 4-9-2002 and detained in Central Jail, Thiruvananthapuram. The detenu submitted his representation to be Detaining Authority and the Central Government and the same were rejected.

4. Safiya, the wife of the detenu, filed a writ petition before the High Court of Kerala challenging the detention of her husband T.P. Moideen Koya (the detenu) on the grounds that the order of detention of the detenu is primarily based upon the statement recorded from Mohammed Mustaffa, an employee of Kunjumon and that an order of detention was passed against the said Mohammed Mustaffa and he was detained by an order of detention dated 17-10-2001 passed by the detaining authority. The said case was placed before the Advisory Board and the Advisory Board submitted in its opinion that there is no ground for detaining the said Mohammed Mustaffa. In accordance with the report of the Advisory Board, the detaining Authority, the State of Kerala, by its order dated 15-1-2002 revoked the detention against the said Mohammed Mustaffa. It is the case of the appellant that since facts relating to the said Mohammed Mustaffa is similar and arising out of the same set of circumstances and the order of detention having been held to be improper by the Advisory Board and subsequently having been revoked by the State Government, the said facts and materials ought to have been placed before the detaining Authority by the sponsoring Authority and the same ought to have been considered before passing the order of detention against the detenu herein. The appellant also raised the contention that there has been inordinate delay in considering and disposing of the representation of the appellant. It was also contended that there is no material to justify the involvement of the detenu and, therefore, the order of detention is based on no material.

5. The High Court dismissed the writ petition holding that the delay in disposing of the representation was reasonable. The High Court passed a detailed judgment considering all the contentions raised by the counsel for the appellant before it including the rulings cited before it. Aggrieved by the said judgment, the present appeal has been filed before this Court.

6. We have perused the pleadings and the other Annexures filed along with this appeal and also the counter-affidavits filed by the State Government of Kerala and the Government of India both in the High Court and also in this Court. We heard Mr. B. Kumar, learned senior counsel for the appellant and Mr. R.N. Trivedi, learned Additional Solicitor General for the Union of India and Mr. T.L. Viswanatha Iyer, learned senior counsel for the State of Kerala.

7. Mr. B. Kumar after inviting our attention to the pleadings raised the following three contentions:—

1. Non-placing of the opinion of the Advisory Board which has opined that there is no sufficient case for detention of the detenu Mohammed Mustaffa involved in the same occurrence which opinion was rendered even in December, 2001, long before the passing of the order of detention

in the instant case on 22-1-2002 amounts to non-placing of relevant and important document such that the subjective satisfaction stands vitiated.

2. There is inordinate delay in considering the representation of the detenu.

3. Several documents on which the grounds of detention are substantially based are only in Malayalam and no translation thereof into English has been provided and, therefore, the consideration of the representation without taking into the consideration of these vital material is no consideration in the eyes of law as in all probabilities the person who dealt with the representation and took a decision thereof on behalf of the second respondent could not be knowing Malayalam. Mr. Kumar also submitted that in the facts disclosed in the grounds of detention it would be a case of no material against the detenu and sweeping allegations of violations of the Customs Act and dealing in smuggled goods to a huge figure has been arrived at totally unsupported by any material. Therefore, he would submit that the detention order is vitiated since the conclusion is not supported by any material annexed to the grounds of detention.

8. Learned Additional Solicitor General appearing for the Union of India submitted that the appeal is devoid of any merit or substance and deserves to be rejected outright by this Court and that the delay, if any, on the part of the Central Government has been properly explained in para 3 of its counter-affidavit filed in this Court. He, therefore, submitted that the time of six days taken by the competent authority was not a negligence or callous in action on the part of the Central Government and since there has been no undue or unexplained delay in disposing of the representation of the detenu, the appeal is liable to be rejected by this Court.

9. Mr. T.L. Viswanatha Iyer appearing for the Government of Kerala drew our attention to the relevant paragraphs in the counter-affidavit and submitted that the appellant has no case on merits and, therefore, is liable to be dismissed.

10. In regard to contention No. 1, the answering respondent submitted that the case against the detenu was not built upon the statement of Mohammed Mustaffa alone. The records clearly show that Mohammed Mustaffa was dealing in gold biscuits and distributing tube money as instructed by Kunjumon and that the business between Kunjumon and the detenu was not done through Mohammed Mustaffa. In our opinion, the revocation of the detention order issued against Mohammed Mustaffa has no relevance as far as the detenu T.P. Moideen Koya is concerned. The detenu was personally heard by the Advisory Board. After hearing the detenu and perusing the records, the Advisory Board opined that there were sufficient grounds for the detention of the detenu. Under the circumstances, we are of the opinion that the non-placing of the order revoking the detention order of Mohammed Mustaffa before the Advisory Board does not vitiate the detention order issued against the detenu. The detention order was issued after perusing the relevant and material documents and after arriving at subjective satisfaction of the authorities. We are, therefore, of the view that the High Court has rejected the said contention, rightly so in our opinion.

11. In regard to contention No. 2 delay in consideration of representation, the Central Government has clearly and explicitly explained the reasons for the delay insofar as they relate to the Central Government. It is seen from the records produced that a copy of the representation dated 26-9-2002 in Malayalam language of the detenu, sent by the Superintendent, Central Prison, Thiruvananthapuram dated 26-9-2002 was received in the COFEPOSA unit of the Ministry of Finance, Department of Revenue, Central Economic Intelligence Bureau, New Delhi. Parawise comments and the English translation of the representation were called from the Sponsoring Authority on the same day *i.e.*, 30-9-2002. The comments on the representation along with English translation, sent by the Sponsoring Authority *vide* their letter dated 04-10-2002 were received in the COFEPOSA unit on 07-10-2002 (in between 05-10-2002 and 06-10-2002 were holidays, being Saturday and Sunday). The case filed along with relevant material was submitted to the Under Secretary, COFEPOSA on 7-10-2002. The Under Secretary processed the case and put up to the Joint Secretary on the same day *i.e.* 7-10-2002. The Joint Secretary submitted the file to the Secretary Ministry of Finance, Department of Revenue on 7-10-2002 itself. The Secretary Ministry of Finance, Department of Revenue, considered the said representation on behalf of the Central Government and rejected the same on 17-10-2002 (in between 12th and 13th October, 2002 were holidays being Saturday and Sunday and 14th and 15th October, 2002 were holidays being Mahanavemi and Dussehra festivals. The file was received back from the office of the Secretary, Revenue on 18-10-2002. Memorandum of rejection of representation was issued to the detenu herein through the concerned Jail Authority at Thiruvananthapuram on 18-10-2002 and the same was received by the detenu through the concerned Jail Authority on 21-10-2002. The dates and other details given above in the counter-affidavit by the Central Government would only show that there has been no undue or explained delay in disposing of the representation of the detenu herein. The said contention is, therefore, rejected.

12. Regarding the third contention, we are of the opinion that the same has no merits. In this regard, it is submitted by the respondents that the Detaining Authority of the Government of Kerala had forwarded to the Central Government the report under section 3(2) of the COFEPOSA Act, which consisted of Detention Order, the ground of detention and relied upon documents including the English translation of the documents which were in Malayalam language. Thus, the English translation of the Malayalam representation of the detenu and the English translation of the documents relied upon were available before the second respondent at the time of consideration of the representation of the detenu was also available. Therefore, the allegation of the petitioner that English translation of the documents which were in Malayalam language has not been supplied to the second respondent is baseless.

13. A careful perusal of the records placed before this Court would show that there are enough materials to show the involvement of the detenu in the smuggling activities. The State Government (Detaining Authority) have considered all the aspects and perused the relevant material documents before issuing the detention order. Such detention order was issued based on the subjective satisfaction as to the necessity of detaining the detenu by invoking the provisions of the COFEPOSA Act. The detenu, therefore, in our opinion, is not entitled to challenge the subjective satisfaction arrived at by the detaining Authority in these proceedings.

14. Learned senior counsel for the appellant, contended that there is non-application of mind on the part of the detaining Authority. This contention has no merits. It is argued that the detention order was issued against the detenu with a view to prevent him from dealing in smuggled goods otherwise than by engaging in transporting or concealing or keeping smuggled goods. A perusal of the representation submitted by detenu dated 26-9-2002 shows that he has understood the grounds of detention properly and has made an effective and meaningful representation for revoking the detention order. The translated version of the ground of detention has also been furnished to detenu. While serving the grounds of detention on the detenu on 12-9-2002, he has made an endorsement to the effect that he has read and understood the grounds of detention and he has no complaint in this regard. We are not required to decide whether subjective satisfaction of the Authority is justified or not, yet a perusal of the records would reveal that the detaining Authority has considered all the relevant aspects borne out from the aforesaid records before issuing the detention order and after arriving at the subjective satisfaction as to the necessity of detaining him by invoking the provisions of the COFEPOSA Act. The seized documents show that the detenu in this case had dealt with 290 smuggled gold biscuits valued at Rs. 1.5 crores with Kunjumon and had carried out transactions worth Rs. 18 crores during the period 1-8-2001 to 15-8-2001. Mr. Bapu who was involved in the contribution of tube money stated that the detenu is an accomplice of Kunjumon and he had telephoned him at his residence on the No. 370444 appearing in his note book.

15. It is also seen from the counter-affidavit filed by the Government of Kerala in this Court (para 2.11) that about 9,300 smuggled gold biscuits were transported by Kunjumon as per the documents seized from his residence and out of this the detenu T.P. Moideen Koya had transacted about 290 gold biscuits valued approximately Rs. 1.5 crores. Out of 40 crores of Hawala transactions made by Kunjumon, the detenu Moideen Koya had transacted about Rs. 18 crores. This, according to the respondent, is a very vital evidence establishing their smuggling activities.

16. As already seen, the case against the detenu is not built upon the statement of Mohammed Mustaffa alone. The said Mustaffa was also dealing in gold biscuits and distributing tube money as instructed by Kunjumon.

17. Since we are disposing of the appeal on factual basis and on the basis of the records placed before us, we are not referring to the judgments cited by the learned counsel for both the sides.

18. The liberty of a citizen is undoubtedly very important. It is our duty to ensure that there is strict compliance with the provisions of law. In our view, strict compliance of the provisions of law has been made. The Court, in our opinion, cannot be lose sight of the fact that those who commit economic offences do harm to the national interest and economy. Thus, the High Court, while examining the case, has taken a cumulative view of the situation and had seen all the relevant facts.

19. On a consideration of the totality of the circumstances, the High Court came to the conclusion that the detenu has violated the provisions of law and his activities are not in the larger national interest and that the Court should be slow to come to the aid of the detenu. We agree with the conclusion arrived at by the High Court.

20. The instant appeal filed by the wife of the detenu is totally devoid of any merit or substance and as such we have no hesitation in rejecting the same. The appeal shall stand dismissed.

State Rep. By Inspector of Police

v.

N.M.T. Joy Immaculate

Appeal (Crl.) 575-576 of 2004 [Arising out of S.L.P.(Crl.) Nos. 3143-3144 of 2002]
AIR 2004 SC 2282: 2004 AIR SCW 2828
Decided on: 5-5-2004

Coram: **G.P. Mathur, J.**
Dr. AR. Lakshmanan, J.

FACTS:

One Joy Immaculate was interrogated by police in connection with the murder of one Rizwan Sait. She filed a criminal revision petition before the High Court praying that the order to take her in custody for interrogation passed by Metropolitan Magistrate be set aside.

The High Court gave a direction to the State Government to issue circulars to all the police stations instructing the police officials that the woman accused/witness should not be summoned or required to attend at any police station under section 160, Cr. P.C. but they must be enquired only by women police or in the presence of a women police, at the places where they reside.

ISSUE:

Summoning woman accused/witness under section 160 of Cr. P.C.

HELD:

There is absolutely no occasion for the High Court to record any finding regarding the conduct of the investigation or the records on which the prosecution places reliance, in a revision petition preferred against an order granting police remand and that too solely on the basis of the affidavits filed by the rival parties.

The High Court has virtually scuttled the trial even before it has commenced and that too by a process wholly unknown to law.

The High Court has committed a serious error in giving such a direction contrary to the statutory provisions under section 160 of the Cr. P.C. which is applicable only to the witnesses and not to the accused. The impugned order is set aside to prevent the abuse of the process of court or otherwise to secure the ends of justice. It is a principle of cardinal importance in the administration of justice that the proper freedom and independence of Judges and Magistrates must be maintained and they must be allowed to perform their functions freely and fearlessly and without undue interference by anybody. At the same time, it is equally necessary that in expressing their opinions, Judges and Magistrates must be guided by considerations of justice, fair play and restraint. It is not infrequent that sweeping generalization defeat the very purpose for which they are made.

JUDGMENT

G.P. Mathur, J.—1. Leave granted.

2. These appeals have been preferred by the State of Tamil Nadu against the judgment and order dated 11-4-2002 of a learned single Judge of the High Court of Madras by which the criminal revision-petition preferred by the respondent-N.M.T. Joy Immaculate was allowed and the revision was disposed of with certain directions.

3. A written FIR was lodged at P.S. P1-Puliyanthope on 9-10-2001 by one Jaffar Sait alleging that his brother Rizwan Sait was missing since around 9.00 a.m. on 7-10-2001 and on the basis of same a case was registered. On 15-10-2001 Haroon Sait (brother of Rizwan Sait) filed a Habeas Corpus Petition in the High Court of Madras being H.C.P. No. 1458 of 2001, wherein besides the State and Inspector of Police, P.S. P1-Puliyanthope, R. Sathish, Miss Joy Immaculate and Miss Nithya were arrayed as respondent Nos. 3 to 5 and a prayer was made that a writ of habeas corpus be issued directing the respondents to produce his brother Rizwan Sait, who is illegally detained by respondents Nos. 3 to 5 and to set him at liberty. It was averred in the writ petition that Rizwan Sait lends money on interest to various businessmen including the shopping business complex of Spencers Plaza, Chennai. Respondents No. 3 to 5 and their friends, namely, Vijay and Ranjit had taken money from Rizwan Sait. Miss Joy Immaculate had conducted a fashion show at Music Academy and in that connection she had borrowed more than Rs. 50,000 and her sister Miss Nithya, who was running a business in the name and style of Fashion World at Spencers Plaza, had also borrowed a sum of Rs. 65,000. Joy Immaculate and her sister Nithya did not repay the interest and when Rizwan Sait went to the latter's shop, R. Sathish undertook to clear off their dues. At about 9.00 a.m. on 7-10-2001 R. Sathish came to the writ petitioner's house and thereafter his brother Rizwan Sait left along with him in a Maruti car. While leaving, he had said that he was going to Chittur (A.P.) and would return back in the night. However, as Rizwan Sait did not come back till the morning of 8-10-2001, they started looking for him and went to the shop of Nithya and asked her to give the address of R. Sathish, which she refused to do. However, in the morning of 9-10-2001, R. Sathish himself came to their house and said that their programme of going to Chittur was cancelled and accordingly Rizwan Sait had returned back to his house on the morning of 7-10-2001 itself. A photocopy of a cheque for a sum of Rs. 1,50,000 dated 2-9-2001 issued by Miss Nithya was found in the cupboard of Rizwan Sait. In the Habeas Corpus Petition Haroon Sait raised a suspicion that respondent Nos. 3 and 5 have done some foul play with his brother who had advanced money to them.

4. An unidentified dead body was found at Kanagavallipuram and on the report of Village Administrative Officer a case was registered with the concerned police station. After autopsy in the Government Hospital, Tiruvellore, the dead body was buried. One Deva alias Dev Raj was arrested by Inspector of P1-Puliyanthope Police Station. He confessed to the police about the commission of crime and showed the place where Rizwan Sait was murdered. It was thereafter ascertained that the unidentified dead body found on 10-10-2001 at Tiruvellore Taluka was that of Rizwan Sait. Thereafter, the case registered on 9-10-2001 at P.S. P1-Puliyanthope was altered to sections 363, 302, I.P.C. Dev Raj was remanded to judicial custody on 23-10-2001. Joy Immaculate surrendered in the Court of Judicial Magistrate, Alandhur, Chennai on 24-10-2001 and was remanded to judicial custody and R. Sathish surrendered before XXIII Metropolitian Magistrate, Saidpet, Chennai on 25-10-2001. The Investigating Officer made an application before the concerned Magistrate on 31-10-2001 for giving Sathish on police remand. This application was allowed and the learned Metropolitan Magistrate *vide* his order dated 1-11-2001 granted police remand of accused-Sathish for 3 days *i.e.* from 1-11-2001 to 3-11-2001. It is alleged that he made some sort of a confession to the police and on the basis of the statement made by him, some incriminating articles were recovered. Thereafter, the Investigating Officer moved an application before the concerned Magistrate for grant of police remand of Joy Immaculate, which was opposed by her. The learned Vth Metropolitan Magistrate, Egmore, Chennai passed a detailed order on 6-11-2001, whereunder she was given in police custody for one day and was to be produced in Court by 4.00 p.m. on 7-11-2001. It was directed that she would be detained in All Women Police Station and would be interrogated at the office of the Asstt. Commissioner of Police, in the presence of the women Inspector of Police. It was further directed that during the period of police custody, the accused should not be harassed physically or psychologically and should be produced before the Court, in the same condition.

5. According to the prosecution, Joy Immaculate made some confessional statements before the Investigating Officer and on her pointing out in the wrist watch and shirt of the deceased and also the nylon rope used the commission of murder were recovered. Thereafter, on 7-11-2001 she was produced before the Vth Metropolitan Magistrate who remanded her to judicial custody. Two weeks thereafter, Joy Immaculate filed a criminal revision petition under section 397, Cr. P.C. being Crl. R. C. No. 1569 of 2001, wherein it was prayed that the order dated 6-11-2001 passed by Vth Metropolitan Magistrate granting police custody be set aside as the same is against the principles laid down in section

167, Cr. P. C. and that the Court may pass such other and further orders as it may deem fit and proper. In the revision petition, accused Joy Immaculate filed an affidavit making serious allegations against the police personnel to the effect that she was interrogated and detained at the police station on 18th and then from 20th to 24th October, 2001 and also referred to certain telegrams which were sent to the Chief Justice of the High Court in this connection. Affidavits in reply were filed by the concerned police personnel. The High Court by the impugned order, which is the subject matter of challenge in the present appeals disposed of the revision petition by issuing several directions and directions No. (a), (b), (c), (d), (g) and (h) are being reproduced below:

(a) The order granting police custody in respect of the petitioner passed by the learned Magistrate is ex facie illegal. Consequently, it is held that the said order is *non est* and has to be erased from the records.

(b) In view of the fact that the order granting custody has become *non est*, the consequent so-called confession and alleged recovery has no evidentiary value.

(c) The investigation conducted by P1 and P4 Police with reference to the petitioner is not *bona fide* and false records have been created to implicate the petitioner, thereby caused serious injustice to the petitioner.

(d) The petitioner had been wrongfully and illegally detained in P4 Police Station for four days and she was harassed and tortured by the Police personnel.

(g) The Commissioner of Police is also directed to take immediate departmental action against the P1 Inspector of Police, P4 Inspector of Police and other Police Personnel who were responsible for the illegal detention and other obscene acts committed on the petitioner at P4 Police Station.

(h) The Home Secretary to the Government of Tamil Nadu is directed to pay a compensation of Rs. 1,00,000 to the petitioner, the victim for her illegal detention in the P4 Police Station by the police personnel who committed the acts of molestation, obscene violation and teasing on the petitioner, within one month from the date of receipt of this order.

The prayer made by the accused for transfer of investigation to C.B. C I.D. or C.B.I. was declined and the Commissioner of Police was directed to constitute a special team of investigating agency headed by an Assistant Commissioner of Police to continue the investigation of the case. A direction was also issued to the State Government to issue circulars to all the police stations that woman accused/witness should not be brought to the police station and they must be inquired only by the woman police at the place where they reside.

6. We have heard Shri Altaf Ahmad, Additional Solicitor General appearing for the Appellant State of Tamil Nadu and also learned counsel appearing for respondent (accused Joy Immaculate) and have examined the record. In our opinion, the High Court seems to have been carried away by sentiments and has displayed a complete ignorance of the relevant provisions of law, especially that of Code of Criminal Procedure and the Evidence Act.

7. The learned Vth Metropolitan Magistrate by his order dated 6-11-2001 had granted police remand for one day of the accused Joy Immaculate in exercise of powers conferred by section 167 Cr. P. C. She was given in police custody on the same day and was produced before the learned Metropolitan Magistrate on 7-11-2001 and thereafter she was sent to judicial custody. The order had exhausted itself as the police custody was actually given. However, the accused challenged the aforesaid order by filing a criminal revision petition under section 397, Cr. P. C. after two weeks on 21-11-2001.

8. The first question which needs examination is whether the revision petition was maintainable. Sub-section (2) of section 397, Cr. P. C. lays down that the power of revision conferred by the sub-section (1) shall not be exercised in relation to any interlocutory order passed in any appeal, enquiry, trial or other proceedings. The expression "interlocutory order" has not been defined in the Code. It will, therefore, be useful to refer to its meaning as given in some of the dictionaries:

The New Lexicon Webster's Dictionary	Pronounced and arising during legal procedure, not final.
Webster's Third New International Dictionary	Not final or definitive; made or done during the progress of an action.
Wharton's Law Lexicon	An interlocutory order or judgment is one made or given during the progress of action, but which does not finally dispose of the rights of the parties e.g., an order appointing a receiver or granting an injunction, and a motion for such an order is termed an interlocutory motion.
Black's Law Dictionary	Provisional; temporary; not final. Something intervening between the commencement and the end of a suit which decides some point or matter, but is not a final decision of the whole controversy.

9. Ordinarily and generally, the expression interlocutory order has been understood and taken to mean as a converse of the term 'final order'. In Volume 26 of *Halsbury's Laws of England* (4th Edn.) it has been stated as under in para 504:

> "............. a judgment or order may be final for one purpose and interlocutory for another, or final as to part and interlocutory as to part. It is impossible to lay down principles about what is final and what is interlocutory. It is better to look at the nature of the application and not at the nature of the order eventually made. In general, orders in the nature of summary judgment where there has been no trial of the issues are interlocutory."

In para 505 it is said that in general a judgment or order which determines the principal matter in question is termed "final".

In para 506 it is stated as under:

> "An order which does not deal with the final rights of the parties, but either (1) is made before judgment, and gives no final decision on the matters in dispute, but is merely on a matter of procedure, or (2) is made after judgment, and merely directs how the declarations of right already given in the final judgment are to be worked out, is termed "interlocutory". An interlocutory order, even though not conclusive of the main dispute, may be conclusive as to the subordinate matter with which it deals."

10. In *S. Kuppuswami Rao* v. *King*, AIR 1949 FC 1, the following principle laid down in *Salaman* v. *Warner*, (1891) 1 QB 734, was quoted with approval:

> "If their decision, whichever way it is given, will, if it stands, finally dispose of the matter in dispute. I think that for the purposes of these rules it is final. On the other hand, if their decision, if given in one way, will finally dispose of the matter in dispute, but, if given in the other, will allow the action to go on, then I think it is not final, but interlocutory".

The test laid down therein was that if the objection of the accused succeeded, the proceeding could have ended but not vice versa. The order can be said to be a final order only if, in either event, the action will be determined.

11. However, in *Madhu Limaye* v. *State of Maharashtra*, AIR 1978 SC 47, such an interpretation and the universal application of the principle that what is not a final order must be an interlocutory order was not accepted as this will render the revisional power conferred by section 397(1) nugatory. After taking into consideration the scheme of the Code of Criminal Procedure and the object of conferring a power of revision on the Court of Sessions and the High Court, it was observed as follows:

> "In such a situation, it appears to us that the real intention of the Legislature was not to equate the expression "interlocutory order" as invariably be converse of the words 'final order'. There may be an order passed during the course of a proceeding which may not be final in the sense noticed in *Kuppuswami's* case, AIR 1949 FC 1 (*supra*), but yet it may not be an interlocutory order - pure or simple. Some kinds of order may fall in between the two. By a rule of harmonious construction, we think that the bar in sub-section (2) of section 397 is not meant to be attracted to such kinds of intermediate order."

12. Same question has recently been considered in *K.K. Patel* v. *State of Gujarat*, (2000) 6 SCC 195. In this case a criminal complaint was filed against the Superintendent of Police and Deputy Superintendent of Police alleging commission of several offences under the Indian Penal Code and also under section 147G of the Bombay Police Act. The Metropolitan Magistrate took cognizance of the offence and issued process to the accused, who on appearance filed a petition for discharge on the ground that no sanction as contemplated by section 197, Cr. P.C. had been obtained. The Metropolitan Magistrate dismissed the petition against which a revision was filed before the Sessions Judge, who allowed the same on the objection raised by the accused based upon section 197, Cr. P.C. and also section 161(1) Bombay Police Act, which creates a bar of limitation of one year. The revision preferred by the complainant against the order of discharge was allowed by the High Court on the ground that the order passed by the Metropolitan Magistrate rejecting the prayer of the accused to discharge them was an interlocutory order. In the appeal preferred by the accused, this Court after referring to *Amar Nath* v. *State of Haryana*, (1977) 4 SCC 137; *Madhu Limaye* v. *State of Maharashtra*, AIR 1978 SC 47 and *V.C. Shukla* v. *State*, AIR 1980 SC 962 held that in deciding whether an order challenged is an interlocutory or not, as for section 397(2) of the Code, the sole test is not whether such order was passed during the interim stage. The feasible test is whether by upholding the objections raised by a party, it would result in culminating the proceedings. If so, any order passed on such objections would not be merely interlocutory in nature as envisaged in section 397(2) of the Code. It was further held that as in the facts of the case, if the objections raised by accused were upheld, the entire prosecution proceedings would have been terminated, the order was not an interlocutory order and consequently it was revisable.

13. Section 167, Cr. P.C. empowers a Judicial Magistrate to authorise the detention of an accused in the custody of police. Section 209, Cr. P.C. confers power upon a Magistrate to remand an accused to custody until the case has been committed to the Court of Sessions and also until the conclusion of the trial. Section 309, Cr. P.C. confers power upon a Court to remand an accused to custody after taking cognizance of an offence or during commencement of trial when it finds it necessary to adjourn the enquiry or trial. The order of remand has no bearing on the proceedings of the trial itself nor it can have any effect on the ultimate decision of the case. If an order of remand is found to be illegal, it cannot result in acquittal of the accused or in termination of proceedings. A remand order cannot affect the progress of the trial or its decision in any manner. Therefore, applying the test laid down in *Madhu Limaye's* case (*supra*), it cannot be categorised even as an "intermediate order". The order is, therefore, a pure and simple interlocutory order and in view of the bar created by sub-section (2) of section 397 Cr. P.C. a revision against the said order is not maintainable. The High Court, therefore, erred in entertaining the revision against the order dated 6-11-2001 of the Metropolitan Magistrate granting police custody of the accused Joy Immaculate for one day.

14. The High Court after holding that the order granting police custody is ex facie illegal has further held that the so-called confession and alleged recovery has no evidentiary value. It has also been held that the investigation conducted by P-1 and P-4 Police with reference to the accused is not bona fide and false records have been created to implicate the accused. The question then arises whether the High Court was right in making the aforesaid observations, even if it is assumed that the order dated 6-11-2001 granting police custody was illegal (though we have held above that the aforesaid order being a purely interlocutory order, no revision lay against the same and the high Court committed manifest error of law in entertaining the revision and setting aside the said order). The admissibility or otherwise of a piece of evidence has to be judged having regard to the provisions of the Evidence Act. The Evidence Act or the Code of Criminal Procedure or for that matter any other law in India does not exclude relevant evidence on the ground that it was obtained under an illegal search and seizure. Challenge to a search and seizure made under the Criminal Procedure Code on the ground of violation of fundamental rights under Article 20(3) of the Constitution was examined in *M.P. Sharma* v. *Satish Chander*, AIR 1954 SC 300 by a Bench of 8 Judges of this Court. The challenge was repelled and it was held as under:

> "A power of search and seizure is in any system of jurisprudence an over-riding power of the State for the protection of social security and that power is necessarily regulated by law. When the Constitution makers have thought fit not to subject such regulation to constitutional limitations by recognition of a fundamental right to privacy, analogous to the American Fourth Amendment, we have no justification to import it, into a totally different fundamental right, by some process of strained construction. Nor is it legitimate to assume that the constitutional protection under article 20(3) would be defeated by the statutory provisions for searches."

15. The law of evidence in our country is modelled on the rules of evidence which prevailed in English Law. In *Kuruma* v. *The Queen*, 1955 AC 197 an accused was found in unlawful possession of some ammunition in a search conducted by two police officers who were not authorised under the law to carry out the search. The question was whether the evidence with regard to the unlawful possession of ammunition could be excluded on the ground that the evidence had been obtained on an unlawful search. The Privy Council stated the principle as under:

> "The test to be applied, both in civil and in criminal cases, in considering whether evidence is admissible is whether it is relevant to the matters in issue. If it is, it is admissible and the Court is not concerned with how it was obtained."

This question has been examined threadbare by a Constitution Bench in *Pooran Mal* v. *Director of Inspection*, (1974) 1 SCC 345 and the principle enunciated therein is as under:

> "If the Evidence Act, 1872 permits relevancy as the only test of admissibility of evidence, and, secondly, that Act or any other similar law in force does not exclude relevant evidence on the ground that it was obtained under an illegal search or seizure, it will be wrong to invoke the supposed spirit of our Constitution for excluding such evidence. Nor is it open to us to strain the language of the Constitution, because some American Judges of the American Supreme Court have spelt out certain constitutional protections from the provisions of the American Constitution. So, neither by invoking the spirit of our Constitution nor by a strained construction of any of the fundamental rights can we spell out the exclusion of evidence obtained on an illegal search.

So far as India is concerned its law of evidence is modelled on the rules of evidence which prevailed in English Law, and Courts in India and in England have consistently refused to exclude relevant evidence merely on the ground that it is obtained by illegal search or seizure. Where the test of admissibility of evidence lies in relevancy, unless there is an express or necessarily implied prohibition in the Constitution or other law evidence obtained as a result of illegal search or seizure is not liable to be shut out."

This being the law, the direction (b) given by the High Court that the confession and alleged recovery has no evidentiary value is clearly illegal and has to be set aside. The effect of the confession and also the recovery of the incriminating article at the pointing out of the accused has to be examined strictly in accordance with the provisions of the Evidence Act.

16. The High Court has also recorded a finding that the investigation conducted by P-1 and P-4 Police with regard to accused Joy Immaculate is not *bona fide* and false records have been created to implicate her causing her serious injustice and further that she was detained in the police station for four days and was harassed and tortured by the police personnel. It is needless to mention that the High Court was hearing a criminal revision petition filed under section 397, Cr. P.C. against an order passed by a Metropolitan Magistrate granting police custody of the accused. The scope of the revision, even if it is assumed to be maintainable, was a limited one, *viz.,* whether the order granting police remand was legally correct or not having regard to the material placed before the learned Magistrate. The High Court at that stage could not have gone into the merits of the prosecution case as if hearing an appeal against an order of conviction or acquittal as the trial of the accused is yet to begin. The only material available before the High Court was the affidavit filed by the accused, copies of telegrams and the reply affidavits filed by the concerned police officials. The affidavit of the accused has been accepted as a gospel truth and very disparaging and strong remarks have been made against the investigating officers and the investigation done by them. Though we do not want to express any opinion, one way or the other, but at the same time one should not lose sight of the fact that a person who has been accused by the prosecution for having entered into a conspiracy to commit murder, can go to any extent in making wild allegations against the concerned police authorities. The High Court lost sight of the fact that much before the accused Joy Immaculate claims to have been interrogated in the police station (20th October, 2001 and subsequently) and the police came into picture, the brother of the deceased had filed a Habeas Corpus Petition in the High Court on 15-10-2001, wherein she and her sister Miss Nithya had been arrayed as respondents and serious allegations had been made against them and in para 12 it was specifically alleged that these two sisters along with Sathish had illegally detained Rizwan Sait (deceased).The alleged ill-treatment meted out to her subsequently by the police cannot have the effect of wiping out the crime committed earlier *viz.* entering into a conspiracy and thereafter murder of Rizwan Sait on 9th October. The High Court seems to have been very much swayed by the fact that she was a student and was studying in M.A. and like all normal students must be totally devoted to studies. But the statements of witnesses under section 161, Cr. P.C. show that the mother and sister Nithya of accused Joy Immaculate were also carrying on business, that both the sisters borrowed money from Rizwan Sait and that the interest amount had not been timely paid due to which some altercation took place on 4th October when Rizwan Sait used some filthy language against her that if by a particular date the amount was not paid she should come and sleep with him. However, these are all factual aspects of the case which have to be examined by the trial Court at the appropriate stage after parties have adduced evidence.

17. Chapter XVIII of the Code of Criminal Procedure contains detailed and exhaustive provisions of the trial of an accused before the Court of Sessions. It provides for framing of charge (section 228), taking of evidence as may be produced in support of the prosecution (section 231) and an opportunity to the accused to enter upon his defence and to adduce evidence in support thereof (section 233). Section 313, Cr. P.C. enjoins that circumstances appearing in evidence against the accused by put to him to enable him to explain the same. The accused Joy Immaculate would get full and complete opportunity to defend herself in the trial. It is for the trial Court to weigh the evidence adduced by the prosecution and then record a finding on its basis whether the investigation has been fair or not or whether any records have been fabricated. If any party feels aggrieved by the finding recorded and ultimate order passed by the learned Sessions Judge deciding the case it will have a right of appeal before the High Court. There is absolutely no occasion for the High Court to record any finding, regarding the conduct of the investigation or the records on which the prosecution places reliance, in a revision preferred against an order granting police remand and that too solely on the basis of the affidavits filed by the rival parties. The High Court has virtually scuttled the trial even before it has commenced and that too by a process wholly unknown to law.

18. The High Court has also awarded Rs. 1 lakh as compensation to the accused on the ground that she was illegally detained in the police station and the police personnel committed acts of molestation, obscene violation etc. It is noteworthy that after investigation, police has submitted charge sheet against accused Joy Immaculate. Her application for bail was rejected by the learned Sessions Judge and thereafter by the High Court on 18-1-2002 prior to the decision of the revision. There is absolutely no justification for awarding compensation to a person who is facing prosecution for a serious offence like murder even before the trial has commenced. This direction, therefore, deserves to be set aside.

19. In view of the discussion made, the appeals are allowed and the impugned judgment and order of the High Court dated 11-4-2002 is set aside. If the amount of compensation of Rs. 1 lakh has already been paid to the accused Joy Immaculate, she is directed to refund the same within two months, failing which it may be recovered from her as arrears of land revenue.

20. It is made clear that any observation made in this order is only for the limited purpose of deciding the present appeals and shall not be construed as an expression of opinion on the merits of the case. The learned Sessions Judge trying the case shall decide the same strictly on the basis of the evidence adduced by the parties and in accordance with law without being influenced in any manner with any observation made in this order or in that of the High Court.

21. Dr. AR. LAKSHMANAN, J.:—I have had the privilege of perusing the judgment proposed by my learned brother Hon'ble Mr. Justice G. P. Mathur. I respectfully agree with the opinion expressed by him. However, I would like to add the following few lines.

22. Section 160 of the Code of Criminal Procedure deals with police officer's power to require attendance of witnesses. This section aims at securing the attendance of persons who would supply the necessary information in respect of the commission of an offence and would be examined as witnesses in the inquiry or trial therefor. This section applies only to the cases of persons who appear to be acquainted with the circumstances of the case, *i.e.* the witnesses or possible witnesses only. An order under this section cannot be made requiring the attendance of an accused person with a view to his answering the charge made against him. The intention of the legislature seems to have been only to provide a facility for obtaining evidence and not for procuring the attendance of the accused, who may be arrested at any time, if necessary. In other words, this section has reference to the persons to be examined as witnesses in the trial or inquiry to be held after the completion of the investigation. As an accused cannot be examined as a witness either for or against himself, he cannot be included in the class of persons referred to in the section. But the police officers are fully authorised to require the personal attendance of the suspects during the investigation.

23. In the instant case, the High Court, by an impugned order has given a direction to the State Government to issue circulars to all the police stations instructing the police officials that the woman accused/witness should not be summoned or required to attend at any police station under section 160, Cr.P.C. but they must be enquired only by women police or in the presence of a women police, at the places where they reside. The High Court has issued a further direction to the Government to ensure that this instruction is strictly followed by the police in future.

24. In our opinion, the High Court has committed a serious error in giving such a direction contrary to the statutory provisions under section 160 of the Cr.P.C. which is applicable only to the witnesses and not the accused. The High Court has also committed a grave error in giving a finding as to the confession and recovery of a nylon rope alleged to have been used in the commission of murder, thereby stifling/foreclosing the investigation into an offence of murder even before a final report in the case as contemplated under section 173(2) of the Cr.P.C. is filed.

25. The High Court in the present case, while dealing with the revision has not only set aside the order granting police custody, but has held that the consequent confession and the alleged recovery have no evidentiary value in the case. In other words, what has got to be decided in a full-fledged trial, the High Court merely on the pleadings of the parties has given a finding that the order granting police custody and the consequent confession and the alleged recovery had no evidentiary value whatsoever in the case. The learned single Judge has also given a finding that records were created to implicate the respondent Joy Immaculate in the case. Needless to state that any further investigation in the case permitted by the learned Judge would be an exercise in futility in the context of such finding which could be given only during the course of a full-fledged trial. The High Court, while disposing of the criminal revision, has given several findings/directions in para 40 of the judgment/order. In our opinion, the learned Judge has miserably erred in allowing the criminal revision petition against the order of the lower Court in criminal M.P. No. 5171/2001, as the order passed by the lower Court was acted upon, *i.e.* one day police custody was granted, the accused was taken into custody and surrendered back, and thus the petition to set aside that order has become infructuous. Further, the learned Judge has erred in directing the State Government to issue a circular to all the police stations instructing the police officials that the woman accused/witness should not be brought to the police station and that they must be enquired only by women police or in the presence of women police at the places where they reside. The learned Judge has failed to note that the aforementioned findings is contrary to the statutory provisions contained in section 160 of the Cr. P.C. in fact, the learned Judge has erred in expanding the scope of section 160 Cr. P.C. to the accused as well, which might lead to hardship to an investigating agency. If the directions of the learned single Judge is accepted, no purposeful investigation into any serious offence involving women accused could be conducted successfully.

26. Above all, the learned Judge has committed a grave error in awarding a compensation of Rs. 1 lakh on the ground that the police personnel committed acts of obscene violation, teasing the respondent herein. The learned Judge has relied upon only on the basis of the affidavit filed in the case for coming to the conclusion and also on the basis of the assumption that the respondent was not involved in the incident which will foreclose the further enquiry ordered by the learned Judge in the matter. There is no justification for awarding compensation to a person who is facing prosecution for a serious offence like murder even before the trial has started.

27. The learned Judge has also directed to take immediate departmental action against P-1 Inspector of Police and P-4 Inspector of Police and other Police Personnel who were responsible for the detention and other alleged acts committed on the respondent at P-4 police station. This direction, in our opinion, is not warranted in view of the fact of our allowing the criminal appeal and setting aside the judgment of the learned single Judge. The said direction issued by the learned Judge is set aside.

28. We, therefore, set aside the order in the criminal revision to prevent abuse of process of Court or otherwise to secure the ends of justice. It is a principle of cardinal importance in the administration of justice that the proper freedom and independence of Judges and Magistrates must be maintained and they must be allowed to perform their functions freely and fearlessly and without undue interference by anybody. At the same time, it is equally necessary that in expressing their opinions, Judges and Magistrates must be guided by considerations of justice, fair play and restraint. It is not infrequent that sweeping generalization defeat the very purpose for which they are made. It has been recognised that judicial pronouncements must be judicial in nature, and should not normally depart from sobriety, moderation and reserve, as observed by this Court in *The*

State of Uttar Pradesh v. *Moh. Naim*, AIR 1964 SC 703. It is also very apt to quote para 13 of the judgment in *A.M. Mathur* v. *Pramod Kumar Gupta*, AIR 1990 SC 1737 which reads thus: (Para 13)

> "Judicial restraint and discipline are as necessary to the orderly administration of justice as they are to the effectiveness of the army. The duty of restraint, this humility of function should be a constant theme of our Judges. This quality in decision making is as much necessary for Judges to command respect as to protect the independence of the judiciary. Judicial restraint in this regard might better be called judicial respect, that is, respect by the judiciary. Respect to those who come before the Court as well to other coordinate branches of the State, the Executive and Legislature. There must be mutual respect. When these qualities fail or when litigants and public believe that the judge has failed in these qualities, it will be neither good for the judge nor for the judicial process."

29. This Court, in a number of other decisions, has also observed that the Courts should not make unjustifiable observations and directions beyond the scope and ambit of the *lis* pending before it and that such a direction and observation issued will only hamper the free-flow of justice and cause lot of inconvenience to the litigants who come before the Court for redressal of their genuine grievances.

30. It is also apt to quote hereinbelow the observations made by this Court in *Kashi Nath Roy* v. *State of Bihar*, (1996) 4 SCC 539 wherein this Court held that granting of bail on the ground of an infirmity in evidence in the criminal trial was not a glaring mistake or impropriety so as to attract adverse remarks and suggestion for initiation of action against the Judge-subordinate from the High Court Judge. While stating the proper course to be adopted in such a case, this Court held as follows:

> "The Courts exercising bail jurisdiction normally do and should refrain from indulging in elaborate reasoning in their orders in justification of grant or non-grant of bail. For, in that manner, the principle of "presumption of innocence of an accused" gets jeopardized; and the structural principle of "not guilty till proved guilty" gets destroyed, even though all sane elements have always understood that such views are tentative and not final, so as to affect the merit of the matter. Here, the appellant has been caught and exposed to a certain adverse comment and action solely because in reasoning he had disclosed his mind while granting bail. This may have been avoidable on his part, but in terms not such a glaring mistake or impropriety so as to visit the remarks that the High Court has chosen to pass on him as well as to initiate action against him as proposed.

Whenever any such intolerable error is detected by or pointed out to a superior Court, it is functionally required to correct that error and may, here and there, in an appropriate case, and in a manner befitting, maintaining the dignity of the Court and independence of judiciary, convey its message in its judgment to the officer concerned through a process of reasoning, essentially persuasive, reasonable, mellow but clear, and result-orienting, but rarely as a rebuke. The premise that a Judge committed a mistake or an error beyond the limits of tolerance, is no ground to inflict condemnation on the Judge-Subordinate, unless there existed something else and for exceptional grounds."

31. I respectfully agree with all other directions and the observations made by brother G.P. Mathur, J. in allowing the criminal appeal and setting aside the impugned judgment of the High Court dated 11-4-2002.

Appeal allowed.

State of Rajasthan

v.

Teg Bahadur

Appeal (Crl) No. 639 of 1998

Decided on: 29-9-2004

Coram: **K.G. Balakrishnan, J.**
Dr. A.R. Lakshmanan, J.

FACTS:

The respondent was accused of committing dowry death of his wife Suman. The Sessions Judge, after trial convicted the accused under section 498A, 304B and 201 of IPC and sentenced him to 8 years of rigorous imprisonment. Aggrieved thereby, the respondent preferred appeal against the judgment of the Sessions Judge to the High Court. The High Court held that the evidence adduced by the prosecution is not reliable and on the basis of such weak and unreliable evidence, the guilt of the accused cannot be proved successfully. Aggrieved against the final judgment and order passed by the High Court, the State of Rajasthan has preferred an appeal before the Supreme Court.

ISSUE:

Evidence in cases of dowry death.

HELD:

Different witnesses have given different statements regarding demand of dowry. There is no corroboration about the statement of father of the deceased by the mother of the deceased. Under these circumstances, we are of the opinion that there is lack of evidence to prove the demand of dowry and that the evidence led by the prosecution bristle with discrepancies and contradictions. On the basis of the evidence, it could not be treated to have been proved that actually the accused had made demand of dowry and that was made soon before the death and due to this, the deceased was harassed.

The prosecution relied upon the recovery of ear-rigns, hair clip, pieces of bangles belonging to the deceased from the well upon the disclosure statement made by police. These are articles of common use and can be found out in any house. That apart, no family member of the deceased has identified these articles or claimed that the same belonged to the deceased and/or she was wearing the same at the time of occurrence. Further, in this case one of the main ingredients of the offence of demand of dowry being absent, the High Court is right in acquitting the accused for the offence under section 304B of the Indian Penal Code. The appeal therefore fails and is dismissed.

JUDGMENT

Dr. AR. Lakshmanan, J.—1. This appeal is directed against the final judgment and order dated 14-3-1997 passed by the High Court of Rajasthan at Jaipur in S.B. Criminal Appeal No. 487 of 1996 whereby the High Court allowing the appeal held that the evidence adduced by the prosecution is not reliable and on the basis of such weak and unreliable evidence, the guilt of the respondents-accused cannot be proved successfully.

The short facts giving rise to the appeal are as follows:

> On 5-5-1993, the deceased Suman aged 18 years was married to the respondent-accused Teg Bahadur in accordance with Hindu rites and ceremonies. After the Gauna ceremony was completed, deceased Suman was sent back to her maternal house by her in-laws and she complained to her parents that she had been sent back because she had not brought enough dowry with her. She also told them that she had been threatened not to return if she was unable to bring a Television, Cooler and money. However, after lot of discussions and negotiations with her in-laws, Suman was taken back by her in-laws. But the demand for dowry still persisted and within five months that Suman stayed in her maternal house, she was sent back to her matrimonial house three/four times and threatened to bring new dowry items every time. According to the prosecution, she was harassed, tormented and tortured by her in-laws, husband and other relatives and physically abused for bringing insufficient dowry in her marriage.
>
> On 9-9-1994, at about 10.30 p.m. death of the deceased Suman took place in mysterious circumstances in the intervening night without assigning any logical or cogent reasons for her demise. Even before sunrise, the cremation ceremony was performed in a hasty manner without the parents of the deceased Suman being duly informed about the death of their daughter.
>
> On 11-9-1994, the information about the death of their daughter Suman was received by the father of the deceased - Om Prakash PW-13 from their relative Chunilal PW-8, who was residing in Garhwalon Ki Dhani. Upon receiving this information, Om Prakash and Ganpat Ram left for the house of Ghanshyam *i.e.* grandfather of the respondent-accused, who told them that their daughter Suman died due to Haiza. But upon asking the neighbours they gathered altogether different information that their daughter had been killed mercilessly, being thrown in the well. An F.I.R. was lodged on 13-9-1994 by the father of the deceased – Om Prakash who was accompanied by a number of villagers. On the basis of the written

report, F.I.R. was lodged and a case was registered under sections 498A, 302 and 202 I.P.C. The Investigation Officer PW-24 reached the place of incident and prepared the site plan of the well Ex.P-1 in the presence of witnesses – Radheyshyam and Lichman Ram. Rameshwar was made to go down the well from which one gold ear-ring, glass/lak bangle pieces and a metal clip was recovered and sealed then and there. The mud on the motor installed in the well was also taken along with the mud which was stuck on the sides of the well was also scraped and sealed and marked as Ex.P-4. Thereafter, the site plan of the place of incident was prepared and samples of plain earth and suspicious mud from the residential house of the respondent-accused were taken and sealed. In the presence of the witnesses, the remains of ashes and bones belonging to the deceased Suman were collected from the cremation place and sealed them there. During investigation, the statements of various witnesses were recorded under section 161 Cr.P.C. Upon completion of investigation, charge sheet was filed against the respondents-accused Teg Bahadur, Ghanshyam and Smt. Singari under sections 304B, 498A and 201 I.P.C. in the Court of Addl. Chief Judicial Magistrate, Navalgarh. On committal for trial, it was numbered as Sessions Case No. 7 of 1995.

2. The prosecution examined as many as 24 witnesses to prove their case. No witness was examined by the Defence side. Out of 24 witnesses, 8 of them have turned hostile. Relying upon the facts and circumstances and the evidence adduced on record, the learned Sessions Judge, Jhunjhunu held the respondents-accused guilty under sections 498A, 304B, 201 I.P.C. and were sentenced to 8 years of rigorous imprisonment. However, no sentence was passed separately for the offence committed by them under section 498A.

3. Aggrieved against the judgment and order passed by the learned Sessions Judge, the respondents-accused filed S.B. Criminal Appeal No. 487 of 1996 in the High Court of Rajasthan at Jaipur. Final judgment and order was passed by the High Court while allowing the appeal filed by the respondents herein. The High Court held that the evidence adduced by the prosecution is not reliable and on the basis of such weak and unreliable evidence, the guilt of the accused cannot be proved successfully.

4. Aggrieved against the final judgment and order passed by the High Court, the State of Rajasthan has filed the above appeal in this Court.

5. We heard Ms. Madhurima Tatia, learned counsel for the appellant and Mr. M.L. Lahoty, learned counsel for the respondent. We have perused the records and also of the judgments of both the Sessions Court and of the High Court and heard lengthy arguments advanced by the counsel appearing on either side.

6. Ms. Madhurima Tatia, learned counsel appearing for the appellant submitted that the High Court has erred in acquitting the respondents-accused even when the facts and circumstances which were proved beyond reasonable doubt and the evidence adduced on record clearly proves the guilt of all the respondents-accused that in all probabilities the respondents-accused had caused the death of the 18 year old deceased Suman. She further submitted that the High Court is not correct in not appreciating the testimonies of PW-13 – Om

Prakash and PW-4 - Ram Kishan who have clearly stated in their statements the entire chronology of events, which led to the death of the deceased. According to the learned counsel for the appellant, such clear and lucid statement of facts, which were proved beyond reasonable doubt should not have been overlooked and ignored by the High Court even when their testimonies clearly corroborate the evidence adduced by the prosecution and has successfully proved the guilt of the accused. The counsel for the appellant contended that all the ingredients of offence under section 304B were made out and it was urged that there was sufficient evidence to hold that before the death of Suman there was demand for dowry by the appellant and there was consequential harassment on his part. Counsel also urged that the presumption under section 113B of the Evidence Act should have been drawn and the High Court seriously erred in acquitting the accused without properly appreciating the evidence.

7. In view of these submissions, the learned counsel for the appellant submitted that the High Court has erred in acquitting the accused even when the chain of circumstances was complete which clearly point out towards the guilt of the respondents-accused. Winding up her arguments, the learned counsel submitted that the cremation of the body of the deceased Suman was cremated in the hasty manner without even informing the parents of the deceased. Learned counsel for the appellant prayed that the appeal against the final judgment of the High Court be set aside and the judgment of the Sessions Court be restored.

8. *Per contra,* Mr. M.L. Lahoty, learned counsel for the respondents-accused submitted that the information regarding the death of Suman was given to her family members who were present at the time of cremation and though many neighbours were examined, none of them supported the case of the prosecution. He further submitted that the alleged recovery of one golden ear-ring, pieces of bangles and hair clip has not been proved as those of the deceased-Suman. With regard to the demand of dowry, the important witness is the mother of deceased, Smt. Hira Bai, PW-22 but she also has not supported the case of the prosecution. Learned counsel for the accused took us through the evidence of the witnesses and submitted that the death of Suman was not for the reasons, as alleged by the prosecution and, therefore, the High Court has rightly allowed the appeal filed by the accused-respondents herein.

9. In the instant case, the prosecution has examined as many as 24 witnesses. In these, the father of the deceased, Suman, PW-13, Om Prakash, grand-father of PW-5, Ganpat and mother of the deceased, Smt. Hira Bai, PW-22, PW-2, Lachhman and PW- 3, Radhey Shyam were examined. PW-6, PW-7, PW-14, PW-15 and PW-16 were declared hostile. The accused Teg Bahadur, in his statement under section 313 of the Criminal Procedure Code, stated that his marriage with Suman was solemnised without dowry and even after marriage, there was no demand for dowry and that they were living happily together and that a false case has been lodged against him. The accused-Ghanshyam, stated in his statement that Teg Bahadur is his grand son whose marriage was solemnised without dowry and there was no demand of dowry. It is also in the evidence that at the time of death of Suman, as spoken to by PW-18, Chunnilal, that Suman's father, mother, grand-father came to the funeral ceremony of Suman at Ghanshyam's house at Meelo Ki Dhani. The said witness has also stated that there was no dispute of dowry.

10. The learned Sessions Judge, on the basis of the evidence produced, held that Suman died on 9/10 September, 1994 in unnatural circumstances and that she had died due to fall in well and that the death of Suman took place within seven years from the date of marriage and, therefore, under section 113B of the Evidence Act, presumption could be made against the accused person and that prior to cremation, the parents of the Suman and other members of the family were not informed and that the cremation was done in undue haste. Learned Sessions Judge, in our opinion, is not correct in holding so. The finding of the learned Sessions Judge is contrary to the evidence led in this case.

11. This apart, there is also discrepancy in regard to the statement of reports in the police station. It is seen that two reports were submitted by Om Prakash, one report is Ex. P-10 and other report has not been produced. Likewise, PW-12, Mukhram, has stated in his statement that report was given in the police station on 13th which was written by Bhagwan Singh, whereas Om Prakash himself has stated that Bhagwan Singh has written the report. Therefore, it is seen that Ex.P-10 is not the first report and the other report filed prior to Ex.P-10 was removed and afterwards second report was filed.

12. In brief, for proving the offence under section 304B of the Indian Penal Code, the prosecution has to prove the following things:

(a) The death of the married woman was within seven years of the marriage.

(b) A little prior to death, her husband or relative on the point of demand of dowry subjected cruelty to her or harassed her.

13. In the present case, it is proved that Suman was married on 5-5-1993 and she died on 10-9-1994. Thus Suman's death took place within seven years of her marriage.

14. In regard to the cause of death, there are two versions. According to the prosecution, the death was due to falling in well whereas according to the accused, Suman died due to Plague. However, the facts stated by Om Prakash, PW-13, in FIR, Ex.P-10, are otherwise. From the evidence, it is not known whether Suman died during the day time or in the night. PW-8, Ramlal, has stated in his statement that the wife of Teg Bahadur had died due to vomiting and loose motions and no voice of beating was heard. Therefore, this witness was declared hostile. Likewise, Radheyshyam and Ramlal, as mentioned in the First Information Report, told Om Prakash that in the night in the house of Ghanshyam they heard the cries of woman weeping and this fact has not been proved. PW-2, Lachhman, was declared hostile since he has not supported the case of the prosecution. He, in his statement, has stated that the father of Teg Bahadur has taken the thick rope and also stated that the air of Motor of well is to be taken out. Out of the women mentioned in the First Information Report, the statements of PW-6, Manbhari, PW-7, Smt. Mani, PW-14, Smt. Manohari, PW-15, Smt. Parmeshwari, PW-16, Smt. Barji and PW-19, Suman was available. All these witnesses have been declared hostile because they have not supported the prosecution case and the facts mentioned in Ex.P-10 that when they got bath to Suman before cremation, no injuries were seen. Likewise, there is no evidence in regard to the recovery from the well of Suman's ear-rings, pieces of bangles and hair clip and that these articles found at the well at the time of search were of Suman. There was no evidence to that effect. The Investigating Officer, in our view, has not given any attention to this and had not investigated regarding this. As already noticed, Om Prakash, PW-13, Ganpat, Ramkishan and Shri Ram had stated that they have no information about the death and that no information was given to the family members of Suman and that they have denied to have participated in the cremation. Whereas the other persons of the village, whose statements the prosecution has produced, had stated the presence of the parents of Suman at the time of cremation, as to be seen from the statements of Manbhari, Smt. Mani, Ram Lal, Kushal Singh, Smt. Manohari, Smt. Parmeshwari, Smt. Barji, Smt. Suman and Chunnilal. PW-18, Chunnilal had also accepted, in cross-examination, that on his telling, Om Prakash, father of Suman, and the mother of Suman had come for cremation of Suman in the house of Ghanshyam in Milon Ki Dadhi. As already noticed, for proving an offence under section 304B of the Indian Penal Code, it is necessary that the prosecution should prove this that a little prior to death on the issue of demand of dowry, her husband or the relatives of her husband have subjected cruelty with her.

15. Our attention was drawn to section 113B of the Evidence Act and section 304B of the Indian Penal Code by the learned counsel appearing for the accused. A conjoint reading of section 113B of the Indian Evidence Act and section 304B of the Indian Penal Code shows that there must be material to show that soon before her death the victim was subjected to cruelty or harassment. The prosecution has to rule out the possibility of a natural or accidental death so as to bring it within the purview of "death occurring otherwise than in normal circumstances." For the above proposition, learned counsel appearing for the accused, cited the judgment of this Court in the case of *Hira Lal* v. *State (Govt. of NCT), Delhi,* (2003) 8 SCC 80. In that case this Court observed thus:

> "The expression "soon before" is very relevant where section 113B of the Evidence Act and section 304B IPC are pressed into service. The prosecution is obliged to show that soon before the occurrence there was cruelty or harassment and only in that case presumption operates. Evidence in that regard has to be led by the prosecution. "Soon before" is a relative term and it would depend upon the circumstances of each case and no straitjacket formula can be laid down as to what would constitute a period of soon before the occurrence. It would be hazardous to indicate any fixed period, and that brings in the importance of a proximity test both for the proof of an offence of dowry death as well as for raising a presumption under section 113B of the Evidence Act. The expression "soon before her death" used in the substantive section 304B, IPC and section 113B of the Evidence Act is present with the idea of proximity test. No definite period has been indicated and the expression "soon before" is not defined. A reference to the expression "soon before" used in section 114 Illustration (a) of the Evidence Act is relevant. It lays down that a Court may presume that a

man who is in the possession of goods "soon after the theft, is either the thief or has received the goods knowing them to be stolen, unless he can account for their possession". The determination of the period which can come within the term "soon before" is left to be determined by the Courts, depending upon facts and circumstances of each case. Suffice, however, to indicate that the expression "soon before" would normally imply that the interval should not be much between the cruelty or harassment concerned and the death in question. There must be existence of a proximate and live link between the effect of cruelty based on dowry demand and the death concerned. If the alleged incident of cruelty is remote in time and has become stale enough not to disturb the mental equilibrium of the woman concerned, it would be of no consequence."

16. With regard to the dowry, there are different versions. PW-1, Sanwarmal stated that he had not heard anything about the dowry with the wife of Teg Bahadur. PW-2, Lachhman stated that he does not know this that from Suman, her in-laws have asked for dowry or not. PW-4, Ram Kishan stated, in cross examination, that at the time of marriage, the accused persons have not raised any objection regarding dowry. The statement of this witness is contrary to the statement of Om Prakash. According to Ram Kishan, when Suman came back for the first time from her in- laws then she complained regarding dowry whereas Om Prakash and Hira Bai had not stated so. PW-5, Ganpat, uncle of Om Prakash, in his statement, stated that at the time of marriage on the issue of dowry Teg Bahadur and Ghanshyam raised the dispute. PW-9, Shriram, stated that no dowry was demanded at the time of marriage but afterwards dowry was demanded. PW-10, Kushal Singh, stated that at the time of marriage on the point of dowry displeasure was shown.

17. On the careful scrutiny of the statements of the aforesaid witnesses, it is seen that witnesses have given different statements regarding demand of dowry. According to him, with respect to dowry, dispute was raised at the time of marriage. According to Om Prakash, when Suman returned to her parents' house, she complained about demand of dowry by the in-laws. There is no corroboration about the statement of Om Prakash by the statement of his wife Smt. Hira Bai. Under these circumstances, we are of the opinion, that there is lack of evidence to prove the demand of dowry and that the evidence led by the prosecution bristle with discrepancies and contradictions. On the basis of the evidence, it could not be treated to have been proved that actually the accused had made a demand of dowry and that was made soon before the death and due to this, the deceased was harassed.

18. In the instant case, the witnesses having given the statements about the facts within their special knowledge, under section 161 of the Criminal Procedure Code recorded during investigation, have resiled from correctness of the versions in the statements. They have not given any reason as to why the investigating officer could record statements contrary to what they had disclosed. It is equally settled law that the evidence of a hostile witness would not be totally rejected if spoken in favour of the prosecution or the accused, but it can be subjected to close scrutiny and that portion of the evidence which is consistent with the case of the prosecution or defence may be accepted.

19. The prosecution relied upon the recovery of ear-rings, hair clip, pieces of bangles belonging to the deceased from the well upon the disclosure statement made by police. It may stated that these are articles of common use and can be found out in any house. That apart, no family member of the deceased has identified these articles or claimed that the same belonged to the deceased and/or she was wearing the same at the time of occurrence.

20. In the instant case, one of the main ingredients of the offence of demand of dowry being absent, the High Court is right in acquitting the accused for the offence under section 304B of the Indian Penal Code.

21. A reading of the judgment of the trial Court clearly shows that the Sessions Judge proceeded as if the prosecution is available against the accused merely because an allegation of death within seven years of marriage was made without even the prosecution having proved the required preliminary fact. Having so shifted the onus, the Court then proceeded to hold that the accused had not discharged the said onus and hence convicted the accused primarily based on the presumption under section 113B of the Evidence Act. The approach by the Sessions Court is not correct.

22. In this view of the matter, we are of the opinion that the prosecution has failed to prove the circumstances alleged against the accused persons. The High Court, in our opinion, has not committed any error in interfering with the conviction of the accused passed by the Sessions Court.

The appeal, therefore, fails and stands dismissed.

•••